COMPUTER SECURITY: INTRUSION, DETECTION AND PREVENTION

Computer Security: Intrusion, Detection and Prevention

Ronald D. Hopkins

and

Wesley P. Tokere

Editors

Nova Science Publishers, Inc.
New York

LIBRARY OF CONGRESS CATALOGING-IN-PUBLICATION DATA
Computer security : intrusion, detection, and prevention / editors, Ronald D. Hopkins and Wesley P. Tokere.
   p. cm.
 Includes index.
 ISBN 978-1-60692-781-6 (hardcover)
 1. Computer security. 2. Computers--Access control. 3. Computer networks--Security measures. I. Hopkins, Ronald D., 1961- II. Tokere, Wesley P.
 QA76.9.A25C6492 2009
 005.8--dc22
                2009001829

Published by Nova Science Publishers, Inc. ✛ New York

CONTENTS

Preface   vii

Chapter 1   Self-Organising Maps in Computer Security   1
             Jan Feyereisl and Uwe Aickelin

Chapter 2   Network Management Focused on Client Computer   31
             Kazuya Odagiri and Naohiro Ishii

Chapter 3   Trends, Problems and Misconceptions in Testing Network   51
             Intrusion Detection Systems' Effectiveness
             Agustin Orfila, Juan M. E. Tapiador and Arturo Ribagorda

Chapter 4   Reconfigurable Hardware in Modern Security Systems   63
             Issam Damaj, Youssef Iraqi and Safaa Kasbah

Chapter 5   Performance for Cryptography: A Hardware Approach   91
             Athanasios P. Kakarountas and Haralambos Michail

Chapter 6   Fast Face Detector and Recognition for Biometrical Security   107
             Systems
             Jose M. Chaves-González, Miguel A. Vega-Rodríguez,
             Juan A. Gómez-Pulido and Juan M. Sánchez-Pérez

Chapter 7   Morpheus: A Word-Oriented Stream Cipher   125
             Nikos Komninos

Chapter 8   Preserving Data Authenticity in Wireless Sensor Networks: 139
             Attacks and Countermeasures
             Fan Ye, Hao Yang, Starsky H.Y. Wong, Songwu Lu, Zhen Liu,
             Lixia Zhang and Mani Srivastava

Chapter 9   Long-Term Security for Signed Documents: Services,   159
             Protocols, and Data Structures
             Thomas Kunz, Susanne Okunick and Ursula Viebeg

Short Communication

Access Control in Healthcare Information Systems – Context   **175**
Aware Attribute Based Approach
Snezana Sucurovic and Dejan Simic

Index   **193**

PREFACE

The objective of computer security varies and can include protection of information from theft or corruption, or the preservation of availability, as defined in the security policy. Computer security imposes requirements on computers that are different from most system requirements because they often take the form of constraints on what computers are not supposed to do. This makes computer security particularly challenging because it is hard enough just to make computer programs do everything they are designed to do correctly. Furthermore, negative requirements are deceptively complicated to satisfy and require exhaustive testing to verify, which is impractical for most computer programs. Computer security provides a technical strategy to convert negative requirements to positive enforceable rules. This new book presents the lastest research from around the globe in this ever-changing field.

Chapter 1 - Some argue that biologically inspired algorithms are the future of solving difficult problems in computer science. Others strongly believe that the future lies in the exploration of mathematical foundations of problems at hand. The field of computer security tends to accept the latter view as a more appropriate approach due to its more workable validation and verification possibilities. The lack of rigorous scientific practices prevalent in biologically inspired security research does not aid in presenting bio-inspired security approaches as a viable way of dealing with complex security problems. This chapter introduces a biologically inspired algorithm, called the Self-Organising Map (SOM), that was developed by Teuvo Kohonen in 1981. Since the algorithm's inception it has been scrutinised by the scientific community and analysed in more than 4000 research papers, many of which dealt with various computer security issues, from anomaly detection, analysis of executables all the way to wireless network monitoring. In this chapter a review of security related SOM research undertaken in the past is presented and analysed. The algorithm's biological analogies are detailed and the author's views on the future possibilities of this successful bio-inspired approach are given. The SOM algorithm's close relation to a number of vital functions of the human brain and the emergence of multi-core computer architectures are the two main reasons behind our assumption that the future of the SOM algorithm and its variations is promising, notably in the field of computer security.

Chapter 2 - Recently, P2P system is attracting great attention as one of the next generation network services. While the conventional Client-Server system is a network service putting an important role to the network server, the P2P system is realized on the P2P Network where client computers communicate each other directly. The P2P system is suitable to the current network situation where users are handling large-capacity contents such as moving or streaming data. However, the P2P network is not generally developed yet. Actually, the current network is managed through network infrastructure and network server mainly, and is not sufficient to manage client computers for P2P system. A DACS (Destination Addressing Control System) Scheme has been developed by authors, which is a method to manage the whole network through the management of the client computer. The authors propose here that DACS Scheme is compatible with P2P system putting an important role to the client computer. The development of the P2P system is described by the developed results of DACS Scheme. They explain the motivation for the research of the DACS Scheme, its basic principle and security function of the DACS scheme. Then, the authors explain the new user support realized by DACS Scheme as an example for showing the effectiveness of this scheme.

Chapter 3 - Network Intrusion Detection Systems (NIDS) are hardware or software systems that are used to identify and respond to intrusions in computer networks. An intrusion is a deliberate or accidental unauthorized access to or activity against any of the elements of the network. Evaluation of how effective different intrusion detection technologies are becomes mandatory, in order to know which is the one that better fits in a particular scenario. Nevertheless this is not an easy task. This chapter reviews the main problems regarding testing effectiveness: the absence of standard test methodologies and metrics, the drawbacks of current datasets, the different requirements for testing different technologies, etc. These conditions made evaluation difficult not only for the industry but also for researchers. Scientific proposals are often na\"ively compared. The authors focus on providing evidence of this situation by means of supporting examples. Some guidelines for the future are finally proposed.

Chapter 4 - The rapid progress and advancement in electronic chips technology provides a variety of new implementation options for system engineers. The choice varies between the flexible programs running on a general purpose processor (GPP) and the fixed hardware implementation using an application specific integrated circuit (ASIC). Many other implementation options present, for instance, a system with a RISC processor and a DSP core. Other options include graphics processors and microcontrollers. Specialist processors certainly improve performance over general-purpose ones, but this comes as a quid pro quo for flexibility. Combining the flexibility of GPPs and the high performance of ASICs leads to the introduction of reconfigurable computing (RC) as a new implementation option with a balance between versatility and speed.

Field Programmable Gate Arrays (FPGAs), nowadays are important components of RC-systems, have shown a dramatic increase in their density over the last few years. For example, companies like Xilinx and Altera have enabled the production of FPGAs with several millions of gates, such as, the Virtex-2 Pro and the Stratix-2 FPGAs. Considerable research efforts have been made to develop a variety of RC-systems. Research prototypes with fine-grain granularity include Splash, DECPeRLe-1, DPGA and Garp. Examples of systems with coarse-grain granularity are RaPiD, MorphoSys, and RAW. Many other systems were also developed, for instance, rDPA, MATRIX, REMARC, DISC, Spyder and PRISM.

The focus of this chapter is on introducing the use of reconfigurable computers in modern security applications. The chapter investigates the main reasons behind the adoption of RC-systems in security. Furthermore, a technical survey of various implementations of security algorithms under RC-systems is included laying common grounds for comparisons. In addition, this chapter mainly presents case studies from cryptography implemented under RC-systems.

Chapter 5 - Cryptography can be considered as a special application of coding schemes. High speed execution of Encoding and Decoding processes is crucial in the majority of the so-called security schemes. In fact, the characteristics of a cryptographic algorithm in terms of throughput are usually the most important requirement to adopt the algorithm in a security scheme. As the need for higher security increases, the market urges for strong cryptographic protocols that will offer the desired degree of privacy. However, most of the algorithms now and forthcoming are complex and do not seem to be efficient for performance-oriented purposes. In this chapter, an algorithmic approach for designing high-speed cryptographic primitives is presented. Setting as target the high throughput, a complete methodology for developing various types of cryptographic primitives, focusing on hardware (without however excluding software, or a combination of them) is offered. The application of the proposed design approach also highlights the effect of designing for supercomputing on a critical application, such as cryptography. Parallelism and code transformation are few of the techniques that will be used for achieving the desired target, the implementation of the ever best proposed cryptographic primitives in terms of speed and throughput.

Chapter 6 - This chapter explains the process which involves building a simple but fast face recognition system using computer vision and image processing techniques. Face recognition is included in biometrical identification methods, which are based on the study and evaluation of biometrical features, such as fingerprints, iris, voice, handprint, DNA... or as the authors are concerned in this chapter, human face. There are a huge amount of applications which use face recognition, but the more common ones are related to authentication, surveillance, criminal detection and, in general, security systems. The authors have developed a face recognition using a feature-based method. In general, a generic face recognition system is divided into three stages. In the first one, the detection of the face from a simple image is done. The second step consists in the segmentation of the facial principal components and the feature extraction from the face regions. Finally, in the third stage the recognition or verification of the human face is done. Among the different techniques of face recognition, the authors explain in this chapter a geometrical technique. The recognition using this technique is very fast, because it is based on the extraction of local features of the human face to do the recognition –which is a very fast feature extraction method. To perform the most robust geometrical face recognition, the authors use 31 different facial features. These features are calculated from the different geometrical regions located in the segmentation stage (eyebrows, eyes, pupils, nose, tip of the nose, mouth and the four sides of the face –the forehead, the chin and the left and right sides) using an improvement of K-means clustering algorithm. Therefore, the input to the system is a single photograph of the face of the person who wants to be authenticated by the system; whereas the output of the system will depend on the application that the authors give to the system. In identification problems, the system will give back the determined identity from a database of known individuals, but in verification problems, the system will confirm or reject the claimed identity of the input face. To summarize, in this chapter the authors overview the different techniques of face recognition and they study in depth the steps and basis to build a fast and functional face recognition based on geometrical features. Finally, in the future work section the authors point out the way to improve the face recognition to build a more robust security system.

Chapter 7 - One of the most important information security objectives is confidentiality, which is usually achieved by encryption schemes or encryption algorithms. Even though there are plenty of encryption algorithms in the literature where some of them have become standards, encryption comes along with the application implemented. In this paper, an efficient word-oriented stream cipher, also referred to as Morpheus, for both hardware and software devices, is proposed. Morpheus was created to protect multimedia context for applications such as Games-On-Demand or IPTV, where data are usually streamed over different kinds of networks. Morpheus behaves very well in all known statistical tests and is resilient to known attacks for both synchronous and self-synchronous encryption modes.

Chapter 8 - Preserving data authenticity in a hostile environment, where the sensor nodes may be compromised, is a critical security issue for wireless sensor networks. In such networks, once a real event is detected, nearby sensors generate data reports which are subsequently forwarded to the data collection point. However, the subverted sensors, which have access to the stored secret keys, can launch attacks to compromise data authenticity. They can act as sources for forged reports and inject an unlimited number of bogus reports that fabricate false events "happening" at arbitrary locations in the field. Such false reports may exhaust network energy and bandwidth resources, trigger false alarms and undesired reactions. In this chapter, the authors explain such attacks and critically examine more than a dozen state-of-the-art countermeasures proposed in the past several years. The authors look into both passive and proactive approaches for the defense mechanisms. For the passive defenses, they describe the basic en-route filtering framework and examine the cons and pros of both uniform and route-specific key sharing schemes. For the active defenses, the authors examine the merits and constraints of the group re-keying scheme and the log-based traceback scheme. Finally, they identify future research directions for comprehensive protection of data authenticity in sensor networks.

Chapter 9 - Long-term retention of electronically signed documents brings with certain problems: Signed documents may loose their probative value over the years and changing of data formats breaks the original signature. In this paper, the authors analyze the state of the art to resolve these problems and describe requirements, existing and partially field-tested concepts, data structures and specifications of service protocols. Solutions for the aging problem are already in an advanced state, whereas in the area of secure transformation merely first requirements and solution concepts may be presented. Since many organizations, and, in particular, SMEs and individuals are confronted by the challenge how to technically and organizationally implement existing concepts the authors describe services caring about the long-term and law-abiding preservation of electronic documents. In this way, users of a web service are not forced to deal with the complex process of securing their documents over long periods of time.

Short Communication - Role based access control has been in use for years. However, when the Internet based distributed large scale information systems come in use a need for context aware access control becomes evident. This approach has been implemented using attributes of subject of access control, resource of access control environment and the action used while the resource is accessed. Implementing this approach doesn't exclude RBAC. A role becomes a subject's attribute. EXtensible Access Control Markup Language is standardized language for writing access control policies, access control requests and access control responses using attributes. XACML can provide decentralized administration and credentials distribution. In the 2002 version of CEN ENV 13 606 attributes have been attached to EHCR components, and in such a system context aware or Attribute Based Access Control and XACML have been easy to implement. In 2008 CEN ENV 13 606 has been revised and becomes ISO 13 606 while access control in a healthcare information system has been standardized in ISO 22 600. This paper presents writing XACML policies in the case when attributes are in hierarchical structure and examines performances.

In: Computer Security: Intrusion, Detection and Prevention   ISBN 978-1-60692-781-6
Editors: R. D. Hopkins and W. P. Tokere   © 2009 Nova Science Publishers, Inc.

Chapter 1

SELF-ORGANISING MAPS IN COMPUTER SECURITY

Jan Feyereisl* and Uwe Aickelin
The University of Nottingham
Nottingham, UK

Abstract

Some argue that biologically inspired algorithms are the future of solving difficult problems in computer science. Others strongly believe that the future lies in the exploration of mathematical foundations of problems at hand. The field of computer security tends to accept the latter view as a more appropriate approach due to its more workable validation and verification possibilities. The lack of rigorous scientific practices prevalent in biologically inspired security research does not aid in presenting bio-inspired security approaches as a viable way of dealing with complex security problems. This chapter introduces a biologically inspired algorithm, called the Self-Organising Map (SOM), that was developed by Teuvo Kohonen in 1981. Since the algorithm's inception it has been scrutinised by the scientific community and analysed in more than 4000 research papers, many of which dealt with various computer security issues, from anomaly detection, analysis of executables all the way to wireless network monitoring. In this chapter a review of security related SOM research undertaken in the past is presented and analysed. The algorithm's biological analogies are detailed and the author's view on the future possibilities of this successful bio-inspired approach are given. The SOM algorithm's close relation to a number of vital functions of the human brain and the emergence of multi-core computer architectures are the two main reasons behind our assumption that the future of the SOM algorithm and its variations is promising, notably in the field of computer security.

1. Introduction

"Nothing in security really works!" A recurring theme during a panel discussion on biologically inspired security that summarises current state of the security field [99]. The security community frequently argues that approaches stemming from the biological realm are a

---

*E-mail address: jqf@cs.nott.ac.uk

frequent source of poor science or research that is not applicable to the real world. Nevertheless the fact that the community itself has trouble finding answers to many prevailing problems is testament to the need of the security field to look beyond traditional means of solving problems.

The issue of security has been pursuing every species on our planet since life began. The survival of any species is based on its ability to ensure its own security. Over the millennia different species have evolved and learned numerous techniques to increase the level of security that pertained to their survival. Man evolved gestures, better physical stamina, invented fences, weapons, law and many other tools and techniques that enabled him to keep up with the world around him. In the last fifty years however, the explosive nature of the digital age opened up new challenges that have never been dealt with before. The creation of complex systems that have been develop by us, in many cases for purposes other than security, are now increasingly being misused exactly for that purpose. To exploit the insecure nature of these devices and their possible gain to the malicious users.

The digital security field, as we know it today, has started with the creation of cryptographic protocols that have been used to transfer military secrets during the second world war. Since then computers have become increasingly part of everyday life and security focus has shifted from specialised applications to more mainstream, business oriented protection of assets and data. In the last decade this focus has also broadened into the area of personal computing where the lack of knowledge of digital systems by their users provides easy target for attackers.

Numerous different techniques have been devised over the years for the purpose of detecting and stopping intruders, identifying malicious users, categorising malicious behaviour and dealing with all types of illegal or rogue activities in the digital realm. These range from user-centric approaches, such as educating the users about possible threats that can be encountered within the digital world, to techno-centric ones where mathematical, engineering and other technological methods are employed to tackle the various security issues.

In this chapter we will focus on the introduction of an approach that has stemmed from a biological inspiration, yet is based on strong mathematical foundations, that gave it a number of properties suitable for various security purposes. This algorithm, developed by Teuvo Kohonen in 1981, is called the Self-Organising Map (SOM) [55]. It has found a wide audience across many disciplines of computer science, including security. We will describe its functionality, its advantages as well as disadvantages, the algorithm's variations and present work that has been undertaken in order to exploit the algorithm's capabilities in the computer security field. A discussion of the algorithm's possible future, with references to state of the art hardware as the underlying mechanism to push the algorithm's capabilities in real-world applications, will conclude the chapter.

2.   The SOM Algorithm

The Self-Organising Map algorithm was developed more than two decades ago [55], yet its success in various fields of science, over the years, surpasses many other neural inspired algorithms to date. The algorithm's strengths lie in a number of important scientific domains. Namely visualisation, clustering, data processing, reduction and classification. In more specific terms SOM is an unsupervised learning algorithm that is based on the competitive learning mechanism with self-organising properties. Besides its clustering properties, SOM can also be classed as a method for multidimensional scaling and projection.

2.1. SOM as a Biological Inspiration

Various properties of the brain were used as an inspiration for a large set of algorithms and computational theories known as neural networks [38]. Such algorithms have shown to be successful, however a vital aspect of biological neural networks was omitted in the algorithm's development. This was the notion of self-organisation and spatial organisation of information within the brain. In 1981 Kohonen proposed a method which takes into account these two biological properties and presented them in his SOM algorithm [55].

The SOM algorithm generates, usually, two dimensional maps representing a scaled version of n-dimensional data used as the input to the algorithm. These maps can be thought of as "neural networks" in the same sense as SOM's traditional rivals, artificial neural networks (ANNs). This is due to the algorithm's inspiration from the way that mammalian brains are structured and operate in a data reducing and self-organised fashion. Traditional ANNs originated from the functionality and interoperability of neurons within the brain. The SOM algorithm on the other hand was inspired by the existence of many kinds of "maps" within the brain that represent spatially organised responses. An example from the biological domain is the somatotopic map within the human brain, containing a representation of the body and its adjacent and topographically almost identical motor map responsible for the mediation of muscle activity [58].

This spatial arrangement is vital for the correct functioning of the central nervous system [47]. This is because similar types of information (usually sensory information) are held in close spatial proximity to each other in order for successful information fusion to take place as well as to minimise the distance when neurons with similar tasks communicate. For example sensory information of the leg lies next to sensory information of the sole.

The fact that similarities in the input signals are converted into spatial relationships among the responding neurons provides the brain with an abstraction ability that suppresses trivial detail and only maps most important properties and features along the dimensions of the brain's map [91].

2.2. Algorithmic Detail

As the SOM algorithm represents the above described functionality, it contains numerous methods that achieve properties similar to the biological system. The algorithm comprises of competitive learning, self-organisation, multidimensional scaling, global and local ordering of the generated map and its adaptation.

There are two high-level stages of the algorithm that ensure a successful creation of a map. The first stage is the *global ordering* stage in which we start with a map of predefined size with neurons of random nature and using competitive learning and a method of self-organisation, the algorithm produces a rough estimation of the topography of the map based on the input data. Once a desired number of input data is used for such estimation, the algorithm proceeds to the *fine-tuning* stage, where the effect of the input data on the to-pography of the map is monotonically decreasing with time, while individual neurons and their close topological neighbours are sensitised and thus fine tuned to the present input.

The original algorithm developed by Kohonen comprises of initialisation followed by three vital steps which are repeated until a condition is met:

- *Choice of stimulus*

- *Response*

- *Adaptation*

Each of these steps are described in detail in the following sections.

2.2.1. Initialisation

A number of parameters have to be chosen before the algorithm is to begin execution. These include the size of the map, its shape, the distance measure used for comparing how similar nodes are, to each other and to the input feature vectors, as well as the kernel function used for the training of the map. Kohonen suggested recommended values for these parameters [58], nevertheless suitable parameters can also be obtained experimentally in order to tailor the algorithm's functionality to a given problem. Once these parameters are chosen, a map is created of the predefined size, populated with nodes, each of which is assigned a vector of random values, w_i, where i denotes node to which vector w belongs.

2.2.2. Stimulus Selection

The next step in the SOM algorithm is the selection of the stimulus that is to be used for the generation of the map. This is done by randomly selecting a subset of input feature vectors from a training data set and presenting each input feature vector, x, to the map, one item per epoch. An epoch represents one complete computation of the three vital steps of the algorithm.

2.2.3. Response

At this stage the algorithm takes the presented input x and compares it against every node i within the map by means of a distance measure between x and each nodes' weight vector w_i. For example this can be the Euclidean distance measure shown in Equation 1, where $||.||$ is the Euclidean norm and w_i is the weight vector of node i. This way a winning node can be determined by finding a node within the map with the smallest Euclidean distance from the presented vector x, here signified by c.

$$c = argmin\{||x - w_i||\} \qquad (1)$$

2.2.4. Adaptation

Adaptation is the step where the winning node is adjusted to be slightly more similar to the input x. This is achieved by using a kernel function, such as the Gaussian function (h_{ci}) as seen in Equation 2 as part of a learning process.

$$h_{ci}(t) = \alpha(t).exp\left(-\frac{||r_c - r_i||^2}{2\sigma^2(t)}\right) \tag{2}$$

In the above function $\alpha(t)$ denotes a "learning-rate factor" and $\sigma(t)$ denotes the width of the neighbourhood affected by the Gaussian function. Both of these parameters decrease monotonically over time (t). During the first 1,000 steps, $\alpha(t)$ should have reasonably high values (e.g. close to 1). This is called the *global ordering* stage and is responsible for proper ordering of w_i. For the remaining steps, $\alpha(t)$ should attain reasonably small values (≥ 0.2), as this is the *fine-tuning* stage where only fine adjustments to the map are performed. Both r_c and r_i are location vectors of the winner node (denoted by subscript c) and i respectively, containing information about a node's location within the map.

$$w_i(t + 1) = w_i(t) + h_{ci}(t)[x(t) - w_i(t)] \tag{3}$$

The learning function itself is shown in Equation 3. Here the Gaussian kernel function h_{ci} is responsible for the adjustment of all nodes according to the input feature vector x and each node's distance from the winning node. This whole adaptation step is the vital part of the SOM algorithm that is responsible for the algorithm's self-organisational properties.

2.2.5. Repetition

Stimulus selection, Response and Adaptation are repeated a desired number of times or until a map of sufficient quality is generated. Kohonen [57] states that the number of steps should be at least 500 times the number of map units. Another possible mechanism for the termination of the algorithm is the calculation of the quantisation error. This is the mean of $||x - w_c||$ over the training data. Once the overall quantisation error falls below a certain threshold, the execution of the algorithm can stop as an acceptable lower dimensional representation of the input data has been generated.

2.3. Variations of the SOM Algorithm

Kohonen's original incremental SOM algorithm was the first in a series of algorithms based on the idea of maps created by the process of self-organisation for the purpose of visualisation, clustering and dimensionality reduction. Kohonen proposed a number of improvements to his original algorithm, such as the "Batch SOM" [58] as well as the "Dot-Product SOM" [58] and most recently a SOM which identifies a linear mixture of model vectors instead of winner nodes [59]. Kusumoto [63] proposed a more efficient SOM algorithm called $0(log_2M)$, which introduced a new method of self-organisation based on a sub-division technique which inherently deals with information propagation to neighbourhood nodes within the generated map. Due to the unique structured approach of self-organisation, the search for the "winner" neurons can be performed using a binary search, which greatly enhances the performance of the algorithm [64]. Berglund and Sitte [6] proposed a *Parameterless* SOM, where the problem of selection of suitable learning rate and annealing scheme is solved, however at the cost of introduction of some errors with the topology preservation of the generated map.

The above mentioned approaches are mainly improvements in terms of optimisation and data representation. Other algorithms which attempt to extend or alter Kohonen's original idea in a more significant manner were proposed by a number of other researchers. These include the *Hierarchical* SOM [49], which contains an additional layer of maps, linked to and generated from nodes within the original map, where the node's activation level exceeds a predefined threshold or other approaches that attempt automatic determination of the map's size, based on the properties of the original algorithm. These include the *Growing Grid* SOM [28] and *Growing Neural Gas* [27] algorithms. Such algorithms start with a minimal size of the map (usually 2x2 nodes), which over the duration of execution incrementally grows as and when required by the input data. These algorithms present some advantages in comparison with the original SOM, for example improved data representation as well as memory and speed optimisations, however they also bring some drawbacks, such as issues with visualisation.

2.4. SOM in Computational Intelligence

From a computational intelligence point of view, the strengths of the SOM algorithm lie particularly in three areas. First of all due to the fact that the SOM algorithm generates a lower dimensional feature map, the algorithm is suitable for *visualising* multi-dimensional and complex data in a way that enables better understanding of such data. Secondly the self-organisational properties and topological preservation provide a way for data to be organised in *clusters*. This also aids in visualising the relationship between the observed data as well as the possibility to use this knowledge for many computational intelligence problems, such as anomaly/novelty detection or general exploratory data analysis within data mining. Ultsch and Siemon devised a technique, called the *Unified Distance Matrix* (U-Matrix), to meaningfully represent a feature map generated by a SOM algorithm [100]. This technique is now the de facto standard for visualising SOM feature maps. The SOM algorithm on its own is first and foremost regarded as a visualisation and clustering algorithm, nevertheless with additional steps added at the post-processing stage, the algorithm can also be used as a *classification* tool. Kohonen however suggests to use the *Learning Vector Quantisation* (LVQ) algorithm, which is more suited for this task [56].

The use of the SOM algorithm generally falls into one of the three above mentioned categories. In the next section we will refer to this categorisation in order to distinguish the use of the algorithm within the security field.

3. Self-Organising Map and Security

The SOM algorithm has been applied to many different areas of computer security in the past. There are over a hundred research papers written on this topic, where the SOM algorithm is used to solve or aid another technique in dealing with a security problem. In the rest of this chapter we will describe existing research, evaluate the algorithm's impact on the field and provide pointers for future research within this area.

This section is structure based on existing security problem areas. We start with the description of the most researched area, software security, followed by the application of the algorithm in the more tactile area of security, hardware security. Other security problems also tackled using SOM, such as forensics and cryptography follow. The section ends with the description of application of the SOM algorithm within the more exotic, or difficult to classify, areas of security, such as home security.

3.1. Software Security

SOM algorithms have been first applied to computer security applications almost ten years after the algorithm's inception [26]. The majority of existing research however is limited to anomaly detection, particularly network based intrusion detection. Some work has been done on host based anomaly detection using Kohonen's algorithm, however such work is still rare, which is surprising, due to the algorithm's suitability to handle multidimensional, thus multi-signal data. On numerous occasions SOM algorithms have been used as a pre-processor to other computational intelligence tools, such as Hidden Markov Models (HMM) [15] [14] [52] or Radial Basis Function (RBF) Networks [42]. Comparisons of SOM algorithm with other anomaly detection approaches have been performed on numerous occasions in the past. Notably a comparison with HMM [104], Artificial Immune Systems (AIS) [32] [33], traditional neural networks [93] [66] [46] [65] [8] as well as Adaptive Resonance Theory (ART) [2].

Besides anomaly and intrusion detection, the SOM algorithm has been applied to binary code analysis for the purpose of virus, payload and buffer overflow detection as well as attack and vulnerability characterisation and classification. Alert filtering and correlation are also areas that benefit from the capabilities of the SOM algorithm. There are many other software security areas that Kohonen's algorithm has been applied to. These are described in detail in the following section.

3.1.1. Intrusion and Anomaly Detection

The field of intrusion and anomaly detection (IDS) has been one of the most actively researched areas of security for many years. There are a number of different types of intrusion detection systems, depending on their functionality and approach with which they deal with intrusions and anomalies. There are two high level categorisations of such systems. The first category group being signature and anomaly based systems. These two categories of systems differ in the way that they hold knowledge about possible intrusions. *Signature* based systems contain a database of generated signatures which are used to recognise existing malicious entities. *Anomaly* based systems on the other hand hold a baseline of normal behaviour of a system, which is used to recognise if a system's behaviour somehow deviates from this baseline. For a more detailed definition of such systems, please refer to [31]. A general overview of novelty detection using neural networks including SOM can be found in [73].

Anomaly Based Systems   The majority of systems described in the following sections are anomaly based. This is mainly due to the fact that the SOM algorithm enables the creation of a baseline suitable for such types of systems.

Signature Based Systems   There are only a few systems that can be thought of as signature based in the traditional sense. All of these systems are hybrid systems, which combine both anomaly as well as signature based techniques in order to achieve the best possible detection capabilities. An example of such a system was developed by Powers and He [85]. In their work the SOM algorithm is used to generate higher level description of attack types which are subsequently used to classify anomalous connections detected by an anomaly detector. Another example is work by Depren et al. [18], who use SOM as an anomaly detector in combination with a decision tree algorithm called J.48 used as a misuse detector. In their work it is shown that the combined system has a better detection performance than the algorithms individually on their own.

The second category group distinguishes systems based on what type of information they monitor. These systems can be categorised into *network* and *host* based detection systems.

Network Based Systems   As mentioned earlier, the majority of research done using the SOM algorithm has been based on network intrusion detection. In general such work is based on the observation of various features of network packets and their impact on the detection of malicious network traffic or behaviour. In this section we will provide an overview of some network based IDS systems that have used SOM.

The majority of IDS-based work has been tested on a number of seminal datasets developed by the DARPA Intrusion Detection Evaluation Program in 1998, 1999 and 2000. The 1998 dataset has been used for the challenge of the Fifth International Conference on Knowledge Discovery and Data Mining (KDD'99). The following research work related to the SOM algorithm has been tested using this dataset [68, 50, 49, 48, 92, 103, 76, 110, 43, 67, 70, 83, 46, 18, 33, 42, 93, 81]. Besides network data the 1999 dataset contains a small set of system data, namely file system data, however this is not always used in experiments. This dataset has been used in the following work [111, 112, 9, 33, 52, 98]. The 2000 dataset has thus far not been employed in the context of SOM research. These datasets have been heavily criticised in the past [75], nevertheless they are still the only available datasets that can be used to some extent for the purpose of comparison of various security research.

Besides these datasets, a number of research work has been tested either on synthetic or real world datasets created by authors themselves [2, 8, 48]. For example Kayacik and Zincir-Heywood [48] state that their framework for creating synthetic data for security testing purposes can generate data that is more similar to real-world data than the KDD'99 dataset. They use SOM in order to compare the two datasets and determine which dataset is more suitable for real-world security testing.

Some work has also been tested on real-life scenarios as part of an existing network. An example of such system is a seminal paper on the use of SOM algorithms for intrusion detection by Ramadas et al. [89]. Their work employs the original SOM algorithm as a network based anomaly detection module for a larger IDS. Besides being able to monitor all types of network traffic including SMTP protocol, the authors state that the SOM algorithm is particularly suitable for the detection of buffer overflow attacks. However, as with the majority of anomaly detection systems, the algorithm struggles to recognise attacks which resemble normal behaviour in addition to boundary case behaviour, giving rise to false positives. Another example is the work of Rhodes [90], who monitors requests to Domain Name Service (DNS) ports in order to also detect buffer overflows. In this work only TCP traffic is observed.

Other interesting network based research using Kohonen's algorithm includes the work of Amini et al. [2], who developed a real-time system for the monitoring of TCP/UDP and ICMP packets. In their work SOMs are combined with Adaptive Resonance Theory (ART) networks, which were found to be better than SOM. Amini's work includes time as one of the input attributes, which is said to be vital for denial of service (DoS) detection.

Bivens et al. [8] also test their system against DoS as well as distributed denial of service (DDoS) attacks and portscans. In their work SOM is used as a clustering method for multilayer perceptrons (MLP). By using SOM, it is possible to scale down a dynamic number of inputs into a preset lower dimensional representation. Jirapummin et al. [46] use SOM for the detection of SYN flooding and port scanning attacks. In their work SOM is used as a first layer into an *resilient propagation* neural network (RPN).

Other researchers also attempt to detect DoS attacks. For example Mitrokotsa and Douligeris [77] use an improved version of Kohonen's SOM algorithm called *Emergent SOM* (ESOM) where the created feature map is not limited to a small number of nodes. The advantage of using ESOM is the automatic creation of higher level structures that cannot be created using the original SOM algorithm. On the other hand the fact that the size of the created feature map is usually large, means that the computational overhead is too large for real world scenarios. Li et al. [67] use another extended version of the SOM algorithm, however in this case to detect DDoS attacks. Their findings show that their extended SOM algorithm surpasses Kohonen's original algorithm in DDoS detection.

Host Based Systems   Host based intrusion detection systems do not appear in such abundance as network based systems, nevertheless this area of intrusion detection is becoming more active in the last few years. In host based intrusion detection, attributes other than only network features are observed in order to detect intrusions. These can include system specific signals, such as file usage, memory usage and other host based indicators.

For example Wang et al. [104] use the University of New Mexico live FTP dataset, which contains system call information about running processes on a system, as well as their own system call based dataset from a university network. In their work they compare the SOM algorithm with a HMM method. Their conclusion is that focusing on the transition property of events, used within HMM, can yield better results than focusing on the frequency property of events, used for their SOM. Nevertheless their work uses data which does not contain many dimensions.

On the other hand the work of Wang et al. [102] attempts to perform host based intrusion detection using system data with many dimensions. In their work three layers of system signals are used, system layer, process layer and network layer. A feature map is generated for each layer, thus a total of 21 different host and network based signals are used as input into the SOM algorithm. Wang and colleagues conclude that their work shows promising results, nevertheless a sensitivity analysis has to be performed in order to select the most suitable parameters.

Hoglund et al. [40] use SOM in order to monitor user behaviour in a real-life UNIX environment. A total of 16 different host based features are chosen as input into the SOM algorithm. Their results are encouraging however they state that the system is susceptible to false positives as well as the possibility of the system to gradually adapt to attacks if deviations are not dealt with immediately.

Cho [14] uses various host based features, such as system calls, file access and process information in order to perform intrusion detection using a hybrid system, which employs SOM, HMM and fuzzy logic. In this system, SOM determines the optimal measure of audit data and performs a data reduction function in order to be able to feed the audit data into a HMM model. Cho's conclusion is that the combination of soft- and hard-computing techniques can be successfully combined for the purpose of intrusion detection.

Lichodzijewski et al. [69] develop a hierarchical SOM based intrusion detection system that focuses on monitoring host "session information". The authors state that this method has a significant advantage over traditional system audit trail approaches in terms of smaller computational overhead. Another important remark in this work is the finding that an implicit method for representing time, which has no knowledge of time of day, is able to provide a much clearer identification of abnormal behaviour in comparison to a method which has explicit knowledge of time. "Session activity" is also used by Khanna and Liu [52] who use other host based indicators such as system calls, CPU, network and process activity as well.

Hybrid Approaches   Besides Kohonen's algorithm, many approaches to intrusion detection exist. A number of researchers attempted to extract the best features of two or more approaches to intrusion detection and combine them in order to increase their performance. For example Albarayak et al. [1] proposed a unique way of combining a number of existing SOM approaches together in a node based IDS. Their thesis is of automatically determining the most suitable SOM algorithm incarnation for each node within their system. Such a decision can be achieved using heuristic rules that determine the most suitable SOM algorithm based on the nodes' environment.

Miller and Inoue [76] on the other hand suggest using multiple intelligent agents, each of which contains a SOM on its own. Such agents combine a signature and anomaly based detection technique in order to achieve a collaborative IDS, which is able to improve its detection capabilities with the use of reinforcement learning.

A number of researchers combine SOM with other neural network approaches. For example Jirapummin et al. [46] use SOM as a first layer into a *resilient propagation* neural network. Sarasamma and Zhu [93] use a *feedforward* neural network in order to create a *hyper-ellipsoidal* SOM which generates clusters of maximum intra-cluster and minimum inter-cluster similarity in order to enhance the algorithm's classification ability. Kumar and Devaraj [61] combine SOM with a *back propagation* neural network (BPN) for the purpose of visualising and classifying intrusions. Lee and Heinbuch [65] use SOM as part of a *hierarchical* neural network approach where SOM is used as an anomaly classifier. The authors state that their approach is 100% successful in detecting specific attacks without *a priori* information about the attacks.

Horeis [42] combines SOM with RBF networks. His results show that the combination of the two approaches provides better results than RBF itself at the expense of larger computational overhead. Horeis describes human expert integration within his system, which provides for fine-grained tuning of the system based on expert knowledge. Pan and Li [83] also combine SOM with RBF in order to determine the optimal network architecture of the RBF network for the purpose of novel attack detection.

Carrascal et al. [12] combine the SOM algorithm with Kohonen's classification, LVQ, algorithm. In their work SOM is used for traffic modelling, while LVQ is used for final network packet classification.

Support Vector Machines have also been used in the past. Both Khan et al. [51] and Shon and Moon [97] use SVMs for the purpose of anomaly detection along with SOM. Khan et al. [51] use SVM for classification, while employing dynamically growing self-organising tree for clustering, for the purpose of finding boundary data points between classes that are most suitable for the training of SVM. This approach is said to improve the speed of the SVM training process. Shon and Khan [97] on the other hand use SOM as part of an enhanced SVM for the purpose of packet profiling and normal profile generation. Their enhanced SVM system is compared to existing signature based systems and have shown comparable results, however with the advantage that no *a priori* knowledge of attacks is given to the enhanced SVM system, unlike the signature based systems.

Hidden Markov Models have been used on numerous occasions [15, 52, 14]. Choy and Cho [15] use SOM as a data reduction tool for raw audit data which is subsequently used for normal behaviour modelling of users using HMM. In this work it has been shown that modelling of individual users surpasses modelling of groups of users in terms of performance as well as detection ability. In the work of Khanna and Liu [52] a supervised SOM is again used as a data reduction tool for creating more suitable input for HMM. Their HMM method is used to predict an attack that exists in the form of a hidden state. Cho [14] uses a combination of SOM, HMM and fuzzy logic, where SOM acts again as a data reduction tool necessary for the functionality of HMM.

Other hybrid approaches include a combination of SOM with a *decision tree algorithm* (DTA) [18], AIS approaches such as the one developed by Powers and Hu [85] and Gonzales et al. [34] as well as a combination with *Bayesian belief networks* [21], *principal component analysis* (PCA) [4] or *genetic algorithms* (GA) [72].

Depren's [18] work employs a DTA called J.48 in order to create a hybrid anomaly and misuse detection system. Powers and Hu [85] developed a system with similar intentions, however in this case the authors combine the SOM algorithm with an AIS algorithm called Negative Selection. Another AIS based approach was developed by Gonzales et al. [34]. In their work the SOM algorithm is also combined with the Negative Selection algorithm, but rather than used only as a classification tool it is also used for the visualisation of self/non-self feature space. This visualisation enables the understanding of the space that contains normal as well as both known and unknown abnormal. Faour et al. [21] use a combination of SOM and Bayesian belief networks in order to automatically filter intrusion detection alarms. Bai et al. [4] introduce PCA as a method for feature selection, while a multi-layered SOM is used to enhance clustering of a single SOM for the purpose of anomaly detection. The authors state that PCA reduces computational complexity and in combination with SOM provides suitable functionality as a classifier for intrusion detection.

Ma [72] suggests the use of a GA to create a genetic SOM. In this model the GA is used to train the synaptic weights of the SOM. Ma's results show that this method can be used as a clustering method, however at present time only on small-scale datasets. Another issue with this system being the necessity of *a priory* knowledge of cluster count.

From the available research it is apparent that hybrid approaches generally superseed the performance of systems based on only one method. The SOM algorithm, whether used as a clustering, visualisation or classification tool, does bring advantages to other intrusion detection methods in terms of better performance, easier understanding of the problem or better detection capabilities.

Hierarchical Approaches   A number of papers discuss the advantages of using multiple or hierarchical SOM networks in contrast to a single network SOM. These include the work of Sarasamma et al. [94], Lichodzijewski et al. [68, 69] and Kayacik et al. [49, 50] who all use various versions of the *Hierarchical* SOM or employ multiple SOM networks for the purpose of intrusion detection. Kayacik et al. [49] state that the best performance is achieved using a 2-layer SOM and that their results are by far the best of any unsupervised learning based IDS to date.

As mentioned earlier Albarayak et al. [1] propose a method for combining different SOM approaches based on their suitability for a particular problem. In their model different SOM algorithms are implemented at different layers.

Rhodes et al. [90] develop a system which combines three Kohonen maps, each of them for a separate protocol. The authors argu that it would be unreasonable for a single Kohonen map to usefully characterise information from all three protocols. Their results show encouragement for their method, however they state that even a single map is able to detect anomalous features of a buffer overflow attack. Their claims are however not statistically proven.

A similar approach was taken by Wang et al. [102]. In their work the authors also create three SOM maps, each of which represents one of the following layers, system, process and network. Their results are also said to be encouraging, nevertheless a more thorough sensitivity analysis has to be performed first in order to tune the system to an acceptable level.

Khan and colleagues [51] use a hierarchical approach based on a dynamically growing self-organising tree in order to perform clustering for the purpose of finding most suitable support vectors for an SVM algorithm.

Comparison with Other Approaches   Some researchers attempted to compare and contrast SOM based approaches with other established IDS techniques. Gonzalez and Dasgupta [32] for example compare SOM against an AIS algorithm. Their Real-Valued Negative Selection algorithm is based on the original Negative Selection algorithm proposed by Forrest et al. [25] with the difference of using a new representation. The original Negative Selection algorithm has been applied to intrusion detection problems in the past and has received some criticism regarding its "scaling problems" [54]. Gonzalez and Dasgupta argue that their new representation is the key to avoiding the scaling issues of the original algorithm. Their results show that for their particular problem the SOM algorithm and their own algorithm are comparable overall. Another comparison of SOM to a novel AIS based approach is performed by Greensmith et al. [35]. Their comparison is of Kohonen's original SOM versus an algorithm based on a cell of the human immune system called the dendritic cell. Their results have shown that the Dendritic Call algorithm performed statistically significantly better than SOM in a port scanning scenario.

Lei and Ghorbani [66] compare SOM to an *improved competitive learning* network (ICLN) which is based on a single-layer neural network. The authors state that the ICLN approach is comparable to results obtained by a SOM, however at a dramatically smaller computational overhead.

Wang et al. [104] compare Kohonen's original SOM algorithm with HMM. Their findings are that HMM is better than SOM for one type of dataset (Sendmail), while for another (Live FTP) both approaches have comparable results. Nevertheless the HMM approach requires a considerable amount of time in comparison to the SOM approach, making the SOM more suitable for real-world applications.

Amini et al. [2] compare SOM with two types of ART algorithms. The results of their work show that their ART algorithms perform better, both in terms of speed as well as detection accuracy. Durgin and Zhang [20] also perform comparison of SOM and ART methods for intrusion detection. Their version of the ART algorithm incorporates fuzzy logic and is said to be significantly more sensitive than the tested SOM approach.

Sarasamma and Zhu [93] compare their hyperellipsoidal SOM against a number of other intrusion detection approaches, including ART, RBF, MLP, ESOM and many others. They conclude that by using the combination of their own version of the SOM algorithm with the ESOM method gives excellent results in comparison to the other tested techniques.

3.1.2. Intrusion and Anomaly Alerts

Intrusion detection systems suffer from a number of disadvantages. One of the major issue with such systems is the amount of alerts that such systems generate. In order for an IDS to provide a manageable amount of alerts that can be reasonably dealt with by an administrator, a number of alert filtering techniques have been developed. Some of those incorporate the SOM algorithm for various purposes.

Faour et al. [21] employ SOM and Bayesian belief networks in order to automatically filter intrusion detection alarms. SOM in this case is used to cluster attack and normal scenarios, with the Bayesian method used as a classifier. Their system is able to filter 76% of false positive alarms. Faour et al. [22] introduce the combination of SOM and *growing hierarchical* SOM (GHSOM) for the purpose of interesting pattern discovery in terms of possible real attack scenarios. They find that the GHSOM addresses two main limitations of SOM, namely static architecture and lack of hierarchical representation of relations of the underlying data. Shehab et al. [96] extend the previous model by introducing a decision support layer to enable administrators to analyse and sort out alarms generated by the system. They have also shown empirically that GHSOM has the potential to perform better than the rigid-structured original SOM.

Another drawback of existing IDSs is the lack of meaning of generated alerts. Any logical connection between generated alarms is usually omitted. For this purpose a number of researchers started looking into intrusion alert correlation. SOM has also been used within this area, most notably by Smith et al. [98] and Xiao and Han [106]. Smith and colleagues [98] develop a two stage alert correlation model where in the first stage individual attack steps are grouped together and in the second stage a whole attack is grouped together from the groups generated within the first stage. In their work SOM is used for the first stage. Experiments however deem the SOM noticeably worse than an algorithm proposed by the authors. Xiao and Han [106] on the other hand create a system which correlates intrusion alerts into attack scenarios. The authors use an improved ESOM, which enables evolution of the network and fast incremental learning. The output of the system are visual attack scenarios presented to an administrator.

3.1.3. Visualisation

Due to the SOM algorithm's capability of visualising multidimensional data in a mean-ingful way, its use lends itself ideally to its application in visualising computer security problems. Gonzalez et al. [34] use this ability to visualise the self/non-self space that they use for anomaly detection. This visualisation presents a clear discrimination of the different behaviours of the monitored system. Hoglund et al. [41, 40] on the other hand employ visu-alisation of user behaviour. In their work various host based signals are used for monitoring of users. A visual representation is subsequently presented to administrators in order for them to be able to make an informed decision in case of unacceptable user behaviour.

Kumar and Devaraj [61] use SOM along with BPN for visualisation and classification of intrusions. In this system the SOM helps to visualise and study the characteristics of each input feature. Jirapummin et al. [46] also use SOM however in this case for visualisation of malicious network activities using a U-Matrix. In their system this enables to visually distinguish between different types of scanning attacks. Xiao and Han [106] use SOM as a correlation technique that produces visualisations of whole attack scenarios.

Girardin and Brodbeck [30] and later Girardin [29] develop a system that takes away the burden of an administrator to look through logs of audit data. The SOM algorithm is employed to classify events within such logs and present these events in a meaningful way to an administrator. The authors have successfully developed tools to monitor, explore and analyse sources of real-time event logs using the SOM algorithm. In [29], the author uses the developed tools in order to monitor a dataset with known attacks. The paper concludes by stating that the tools are an effective technique for the discovery of unexpected or hidden network activities. Nevertheless the author also states that after analysing network traffic at the protocol level, it is apparent that such information might not be encompassing enough to make complex patterns apparent. A more complex and varied data would possibly enable this.

Yoo and Ultes-Nitsche [107] use SOM for visualisation of computer viruses within Win-dows executable files. Yoo has found that patterns representing virus code can be found in infected files using the SOM visualisation technique (U-Matrix). Their technique discov-ered a DNA-like pattern across multiple virus variations.

3.1.4. Binary Code Analysis

As mentioned in previous section, SOM algorithm has also been used for the analysis of binary code. Yoo and Ultes-Nitsche [107] analysed windows executables by creating maps of EXE files before and after an infection by a virus. Such maps have been subsequently analysed visually and found to have contained patterns, which can be thought of as virus masks. The author states that such masks can be used in the future for virus detection in a similar manner to current anti-virus techniques. The difference being that a single mask could detect viruses from a whole virus family rather than being able to find only a single variant. In 2006, Yoo and Ultes-Nitsche [109] extend their work by testing their proposed SOM based virus detection technique on 790 virus-infected files, which includes polymorphic as well as encrypted viruses. Using their approach the system is able to detect 84% of all infected files however at a quite high false positive rate of 30%. The authors conclude that this technique complements existing signature based anti-virus systems by detecting unknown viruses. Yoo and Ultes-Nitsche [108] also look at packet payload inspection using their binary code analysis technique. In this case the system is implemented as part of a firewall.

Payer et al. [84] investigate different statistical methods, including the SOM, for the purpose of polymorphic code detection. They have observed three different techniques, looking only at packet payload without any other additional information. Their conclusion is that SOM does not provide detection rates on par with their other neural network technique. Bolzoni et al. [9] also look at payload monitoring using SOM by employing a two-tier architecture intrusion detection system. They state that the SOM enables dramatic reduction of profiles, necessary for detection, to be created using this system.

Buffer overflow attack detection has also been tackled, namely by Rhodes et al. [90] and Ramadas et al. [89]. Rhodes and colleagues [90] monitor packet payloads using a multilayer SOM in order to detect buffer overflows against a DNS server. Ramadas and colleagues [89] perform detection using SOM as part of an existing real-time system. Their system is successful at detecting buffer overflow attack for the Sendmail application. Their conclusion is that the SOM algorithm is particularly suitable for buffer overflow detection.

3.1.5. Attacks and Vulnerabilities

Due to SOM's capabilities also as a classification algorithm, a number of researchers have shown its use for the purpose of attack and vulnerability classification. This vital aspect of intrusion detection enables administrators quickly asses the importance of an alert and thus be able to make an informed decision about what action to take.

DeLooze [16] uses the SOM algorithm in order to classify the database of common vulnerabilities and exposures (CVE), based on their textual description. The author argues that attacks that are in the general neighbourhood of one another can be mitigated by similar means. Their system is able to create a map of the common attack classes based on the CVE database.

Venter et al. [101] attempt to tackle the same problem as DeLooze. They also employ the SOM algorithm for the purpose of clustering the CVE database. They state that the advantage of having such a system is to be able to assess vulnerability scanners. Their system distinguishes 7 attack classes, rather than 4, as is the case in DeLooze's work. Their findings show that there is lack of standardisation of naming and categorisation of vulnerabilities, making it difficult to assess and compare vulnerability scanners.

Pan and Li [83] use SOM in combination with RBF in order to classify novel attacks. Their system is largely an IDS which directly classifies an anomaly into one of a number of predefined attack categories.

Doumas et al. [19] attempt to recognise and classify viruses using a SOM and a BPN. The authors have analysed DOS based viruses. They find that the BPN requires fewer steps than the SOM in order to obtain acceptable results, on the other hand the SOM does not require any class information and is still able to obtain clusters of similar patterns.

DeLooze [17] employ an ensemble of SOM networks for the purpose of an IDS as well as for attack characterisation. Genetic algorithms are used for attack type generation, subsequently employed as part of an IDS that is able to discriminate the type of attack that has occurred.

3.1.6. Email and Spam

An important aspect of software security that is increasingly putting burden on businesses and individuals is the issue of spam and malicious email messages. Some authors have approached to tackle the issue of malicious code detection in email attachments, such as the work of Yoo and Ultes-Nitsche [108]. They look at packet payload inspection using their binary code analysis technique for SMTP traffic. Their system is said to be able to detect a variety of existing as well as novel worms and viruses, however policies and probabilities used to tune the system still need significant development.

Others attempt to solve the issue of spam emails with the help of the SOM algorithm. For example the work of Ichimura et al. [44] attempts to classify spam emails based on the results of an open source tool called SpamAssasin. Their system categorises spam into different groups, from which rules are subsequently extracted in order to aid SpamAssasin with detection. This rule extraction is performed using agents and genetic programming. Their system is able to improve the detection of spam emails, however with some false positives.

Cao et al. [11] also attempt to solve the problem of spam emails. They use a combination of PCA and SOM to perform this task. PCA is used in order to select the most relevant features of emails to be fed to a SOM. The SOM is used to classify the observed email into two categories, spam or normal. Their results show a performance of almost 90% in filtering email.

Luo and Zincir-Heywood [71] introduce a SOM based sequence analysis for spam filtering. Their system also uses a *k-Nearest Neighbour* algorithm as a classifier. A comparison of their system with a *Naive Bayesian* filter is performed and the SOM method is found to achieve better results. The authors however state that the efficiency of the SOM approach is not completely elaborated.

As mentioned earlier, Ramadas et al. [89] develop a module for an intrusion detection system which besides other protocols, is able to monitor SMTP traffic. Their system is able to successfully detect buffer overflow attacks.

3.1.7. Other Software Security Problems

Two more pieces of research work are worthy of mentioning in this section. First of all the work of Chan et al. [13], who propose a web policing proxy able to dynamically block and filter Internet contents. Their system employs Kohonen's algorithm for performing real-time textual classification with a classification rate of 64%. Their work is the first instance of using the SOM algorithm for web application security.

The other research work deals with access control. Weipel et al. [105] introduce a SOM based access control technique to determine access rights to documents based on their content. The system is also able to classify the document's access levels and whether incorrect settings are assigned to documents due to SOM's clustering and classification capabilities.

3.2. Hardware Security

In this section, we will focus on the use of the SOM algorithm in the more tactile areas of of security. Kohonen's algorithm hasn't seen as much attention in this area as in software security, nevertheless some areas, such as biometrics, strongly benefit from the algorithm's clustering and classification properties.

3.2.1. Biometrics

In biometrics various feature recognition techniques are necessary in order to classify visual, auditory and haptic signals for the purpose of security and authentication. Due to SOM's success in the image and vision recognition areas, the algorithm has been applied to a number of biometric systems. For example Herrero-Jaraba et al. [39] use the SOM algorithm for human posture recognition in video sequences for the purpose of physical and personal security. Kumar et al. [60] on the other hand use SOM for face recognition. They use the SOM algorithm along with PCA. Monteiro et al. [79] also use SOM for facial recognition, nevertheless, in this case, independent of facial expressions. The authors compare their SOM based approach to other neural based approaches such as MLP and RBF and have shown that they have obtained comparable results. Khosravia and Safabakhsha [53] use a time adaptive SOM for human eye-sclera detection and tracking. Their experiments show that their system could be used for real-time detection. Bernard et al. [7] use SOM for fingerprint pattern classification. The authors state that this method provides an efficient way of classifying fingerprints. Their system provides 88% classification on a standard dataset, which is a good result, nevertheless one which should be increased to at least 98% in order to be comparable to other best approaches. Shalash and Abou-Chadi [95] also use SOM for fingerprint classification. Their system uses a multilayer SOM, which achieves 91% detection accuracy on the same dataset as used in Bernard's work. Martinez et al. [74] look at biometric hand recognition using a supervised and unsupervised SOM with LVQ. Their system performs well in comparison to other methods due to low false positives. The authors state that based on these results, biometric hand recognition can be used for low to medium-level security applications.

3.2.2. Wireless Security

The field of wireless networking and its security is currently a hot topic in computer science. Decreasing costs of wireless technologies enable widespread use of mobile networks in all aspects of our lives. Some work using the SOM algorithm has also been performed in various branches of wireless networking.

The work of Boukerche and Notare [10] for example looks at fraud in analogue mobile telecommunication networks. Their system is able to identify a number of malicious users of mobile phones based on a number of telecommunication indicators such as network characteristics and temporal usage. The authors state that the performance of their detector is able to reduce profit loss of phone operators to between 1% and 10% depending on the performance of their neural model.

Grosser et al. [36] also look at fraud in mobile telephony. The authors observe unusual changes in consumption of mobile phone usage. In their system SOM is used for pattern generation of various types of calls. These patterns are then used to build up a profile of a user, later used as a baseline for unusual behaviour detection.

Kumpulainen and Hatonen [62] develop an anomaly based detection system that looks at local rather than global thresholds, which depend on local variation of data. Their experiments are performed on server log and radio interface data from mobile networks. The authors state that their local method provides interesting results compared to a global method.

Mitrokotsa et al. [78] introduce both an intrusion detection and prevention system. Emergent SOM is used for both visualisation and intrusion detection and a watermarking technique is used for prevention. Their system is implemented in every node of a mobile ad-hoc (MANET) network in such a way that each node communicates between each other in order to compose an IDS for the network. Using ESOM a feature map is created for each node as well as the whole network. In their system the visualisation of the ESOM is exploited for the purpose of intrusion detection.

Avram et al. [3] use SOM for attack detection in wireless ad-hoc networks. Their system monitors network traffic on individual nodes of the network and anlyses it using the SOM algorithm. A number of routing protocols for MANET networks are monitored and it is shown that high detection rates can be achieved to detect different types of network attacks with low amount of false positive alerts.

It is interesting to note that to our knowledge, the SOM algorithm has not been used thus far for security purposes in other areas of wireless communications, notably within the Bluetooth and Radio Frequency Identification (RFID) areas. This is surprising as with the increase of activity in both of those fields, especially RFID, the need for intrusion detection and RFID chip monitoring systems is apparent.

3.2.3. Smartcards

An interesting application of the SOM algorithm can be found in [88]. Quisquater [88] uses the SOM with traditional correlation techniques in order to monitor execution instructions of a smart card processor. The author develops an attack that is able to eavesdrop on processed data by monitoring the electric field emitted by the processor. The author concludes that this type of attack will become increasingly more relevant in the future and should be investigated further.

3.3. Other Security Areas

Numerous other areas of computer security exist. In this section we have selected a subset of those, where the SOM algorithm has been used for a substantial amount of work performed by the developed research work.

3.3.1. Cryptography

Jamzad and Kermani [45] propose that different images have different abilities to hide a secret message within them. They propose a method for finding steganographically suitable images using a combination of a Gabor filter and the SOM. In their system the SOM is used to determine the most suitable image, based on the data supplied to it by the Gabor filter. In contrast Oliveira et al. [82] use SOM as a clustering and categorisation tool for attacking cryptosystems.

3.3.2. Forensics

Forensics can be thought of as a data mining issue. From this point of view a SOM is an ideal candidate for understanding or extracting unknown information form various data sources.

Beebe and Clark [5] state that an issue in forensics text string searching is the retrieval of results relevant to digital investigation. The authors propose the use of SOM for the purpose of post-retrieval clustering of digital forensic text. Experimental results show favourable results for their method, nevertheless a number of issues pertain. Firstly the issue of scale and secondly whether such clustering does indeed help investigators.

Fei et al. [23, 24] also use SOM as a decision support tool for computer forensic investigations. In this case SOM is used for more efficient data analysis, utilising the algorithm's visualisation capabilities. Anomalous behaviour of users is visualised and better understanding of underlying complex data is enabled in order to give investigators better view of the problem at hand.

Oatley et al. [80] provides a thorough analysis and discussion of existing techniques used for forensic investigation of crimes by police. The authors describe the use of Kohonen's SOM across a variety of both digital and non-digital forensics in order to help investigators solve crimes.

3.3.3. Fraud

Kohonen's SOM has been used for fraud detection on a number of occasions. As already mentioned previously the work of Boukerche and Notare [10] looks at fraud in analogue mobile telecommunication networks. Their system is able to identify a number of malicious users of mobile phones based on a number of telecommunication indicators such as network characteristics and temporal usage.

Grosser et al. [36] also look at fraud in mobile telephony. The authors observe unusual changes in consumption of mobile phone users. In their system SOM is used for pattern generation of various types of calls. These patterns are then used to build up a profile of a user, later used as a baseline for unusual behaviour detection.

Quah and Sriganesh [86, 87] use SOM for real-time credit card fraud detection. Their SOM based approach allows for better understanding of spending patterns by deciphering, filtering and analysing customer behaviour. The SOM's clustering abilities allow the identification of hidden patterns in data which otherwise would be difficult to detect.

3.3.4. Home Security

Oh et al. [81] propose the use of the SOM algorithm as part of a home gateway to detect intrusions in real-time. At the moment their system is a traditional SOM based IDS in nature, nevertheless their uniqueness is in an architecture which takes into account various home based appliances interconnected by a gateway and monitored by the proposed IDS.

3.3.5. Privacy

Han and Ng [37] extend the SOM algorithm in such a way that when used for various machine learning and data mining purposes, the algorithm preserves the privacy of parties involved. The authors propose protocols to address privacy issues related to SOM. In their work they prove that such protocols are indeed correct and privacy conscious.

4. Discussion

From the overview of literature of SOM based security research we can draw a number of conclusions. The SOM algorithm is a successful artificial intelligence technique that is applicable across a wide variety of security problems. The algorithm's strengths lie mainly in clustering and visualisation of complex, highly dimensional data that are otherwise difficult to understand. SOM's clustering capabilities enable it to be used as an effective anomaly detector which can be used in real-time systems, depending on the problem at hand. On its own, the algorithm does achieve good performance in many problem areas, however other algorithms, especially ones which are suited for classification, perform better. For this reason the SOM algorithm performs best when coupled with other approaches such as SVM, HMM or PCA or when extended to tackle a particular problem. Selection of ideal parameters for generation of SOM features maps is still a problematic area, nevertheless this issue is tackled by some extended SOM methods.

Looking at areas of security in which the algorithm has been applied in the past, it is apparent that anomaly detection dominates the field. Many other software security problems have been tackled with the help of the SOM as well, nevertheless numerous areas of security have not yet been approached from a SOM point of view. For example the issue of bots and botnet detection, malware classification or radio frequency identification, could benefit from the clustering and visualisation capabilities of the algorithm. Issues such as insider threat and copyright are also thus far to be looked at. Due to SOM's general machine learning nature and numerous advantages, its application in all of the above mentioned security areas could undoubtedly benefit the security areas' research portfolios.

The issue of SOM performance deserves a discussion on its own. Kohonen originally based his SOM algorithm on the biological property of somatotopic map creation in the human brain as described in section 2.1.. It is a known fact that a mammalian brain is a highly parallel structure that is able to process vast amounts of data at the same time. The fact that the SOM algorithm comprises of, usually, a 2D layer of nodes, each of which performing a computation at every step of the algorithm's operation, the usefulness of machines able to perform parallel computation is undisputed. In the last few years, the field of general purpose processors has slowly started to shift towards these types of computational architectures. The introduction of multi-core general purpose CPU's and inclusion of more specialised highly multi-core architectures, such as the CELL/B.E., into home entertainment devices, marks a step forward for algorithms that benefit from parallelism. The SOM algorithm is one of such algorithms and with the increase of parallelism, issues of computational overhead and thus limitations due to complexity of desired map will increasingly be eliminated. This, coupled with the general success of the algorithm within the security field, evidence of sustained interest in extending the work proposed by Kohonen and areas of security still untouched by the algorithm, suggest that still many possibilities lie ahead for researchers in applying SOM and its incarnations to various security problems.

5. Conclusion

In this chapter we have introduced a biologically inspired algorithm called the Self-Organising Map. This algorithm has been used in over a hundred security related research works and has achieved a substantial interest due to its strengths and capabilities as a tool for visualisation, clustering and classification. The area of software security and in particular intrusion detection has seen the largest amount of interest from within research work conducted with the SOM algorithm. Some experimental evidence has shown that the algorithm performs on par with other established computational intelligence techniques in terms of detection and computational overhead performance. Our review of literature has also revealed that some unique uses of the algorithm opened up areas of security which have not been tackled in a similar way before, such as anomaly based detection and classification of viruses.

Some areas of security have as of now been untouched by the algorithm even though the algorithm's capabilities lend themselves ideally for such use. Examples of such areas are radio frequency identification and bot detection.

The original Kohonen's algorithm has been developed over two decades ago. Since then numerous incarnations, versions and adjustments have been proposed, to exploit or improve the functionalities of the algorithm, with encouraging results. The combination of the algorithm with other machine learning approaches have also shown great results. With the increasingly multi-threaded nature of computing in terms of multi-core computing architectures, such as the CELL/B.E. processor, the authors feel that the SOM algorithm and its various incarnations have a bright future.

References

[1] S. Albayrak, C. Scheel, D. Milosevic, and A. Muller, Combining self-organizing map algorithms for robust and scalable intrusion detection, *Computational Intelligence for Modelling, Control and Automation, 2005 and International Conference on Intelligent Agents, Web Technologies and Internet Commerce, International Conference on,* vol. 2, 2005, pp. 123–130.

[2] Morteza Amini, Rasool Jalili, and Hamid R. Shahriari, Rt-unnid: A practical solution to real-time network-based intrusion detection using unsupervised neural networks, *Computers & Security* 25 (2006), no. 6, 459–468.

[3] Traian Avram, Seungchan Oh, and Salim Hariri, Analyzing attacks in wireless ad hoc network with self-organizing maps, *Communication Networks and Services Research, 2007. CNSR '07. Fifth Annual Conference on,* 2007, pp. 166–175.

[4] Jie Bai, Yu Wu, Guoyin Wang, Simon Yang, and Wenbin Qiu, A novel intrusion detection model based on multi-layer self-organizing maps and principal component analysis, *Advances in Neural Networks - ISNN 2006, LNCS,* Springer, 2006, pp. 255–260.

[5] Nicole L. Beebe and Jan G. Clark, Digital forensic text string searching: Improving information retrieval effectiveness by thematically clustering search results, *Digital Investigation* 4 (2007), no. Supplement 1, 49–54.

[6] E. Berglund and J. Sitte, The parameterless self-organizing map algorithm, *Neural Networks, IEEE Transactions on* 17 (2006), no. 2, 305–316.

[7] S. Bernard, N. Boujemaa, D. Vitale, and C. Bricot, Fingerprint classification using kohonen topologic map, *Image Processing, 2001. Proceedings. 2001 International Conference on,* vol. 3, 2001, pp. 230–233 vol.3.

[8] A. Bivens, C. Palagiri, R. Smith, B. Szymanski, and M. Embrechts, Network-based intrusion detection using neural networks, *Intelligent Engineering Systems through Artificial Neural Networks* 12 (2002), no. 1, 579–584.

[9] D. Bolzoni, S. Etalle, and P. Hartel, Poseidon: a 2-tier anomaly-based network intrusion detection system, Information Assurance, 2006. IWIA 2006. *Fourth IEEE International Workshop on,* 2006, pp. 10 pp.+.

[10] Azzedine Boukerche and Mirela Notare, Neural fraud detection in mobile phone operations, *Parallel and Distributed Processing, LNCS,* 2000, pp. 636–644.

[11] Yukun Cao, Xiaofeng Liao, and Yunfeng Li, An e-mail filtering approach using neural network, *Advances in Neural Networks - ISNN 2004, LNCS,* 2004, pp. 688–694.

[12] Alberto Carrascal, Jorge Couchet, Enrique Ferreira, and Daniel Manrique, Anomaly detection using prior knowledge: application to tcp/ip traffic, *Artificial Intelligence in Theory and Practice,* 2006, pp. 139–148.

[13] A. T. S. Chan, A. Shiu, Jiannong Cao, and Hong-Va Leong, Reactive web policing based on self-organizing maps, *Electrical and Electronic Technology, 2001. TENCON. Proceedings of IEEE Region 10 International Conference on,* vol. 1, 2001, pp. 160–164 vol.1.

[14] Sung-Bae Cho, Incorporating soft computing techniques into a probabilistic intrusion detection system, *Systems, Man and Cybernetics, Part C, IEEE Transactions on* {32 (2002), no. 2, 154–160.

[15] Jongho Choy and Sung-Bae Cho, Anomaly detection of computer usage using artificial intelligence techniques, *Advances in Artificial Intelligence. PRICAI 2000 Workshop Reader, LNCS,* Springer, 2001, pp. 31–43.

[16] L. L. Delooze, Classification of computer attacks using a self-organizing map, *Information Assurance Workshop, 2004. Proceedings from the Fifth Annual IEEE SMC* , 2004, pp. 365–369.

[17] _____, Attack characterization and intrusion detection using an ensemble of self-organizing maps, *Information Assurance Workshop, 2006 IEEE,* 2006, pp. 108–115.

[18] Ozgur Depren, Murat Topallar, Emin Anarim, and Kemal M. Ciliz, An intelligent intrusion detection system (ids) for anomaly and misuse detection in computer networks, *Expert Systems with Applications* 29 (2005), no. 4, 713–722.

[19] Anastasia Doumas, Konstantinos Mavroudakis, Dimitris Gritzalis, and Sokratis Katsikas, Design of a neural network for recognition and classification of computer viruses, *Computers & Security* 14 (1995), no. 5, 435–448.

[20] Nancy A. Durgin and Pengchu C. Zhang, Profile-based adaptive anomaly detection for network security, *Tech. Report SAND2005-7293*, Sandia National Laboratories, November 2005.

[21] A. Faour, P. Leray, and B. Eter, A som and bayesian network architecture for alert filtering in network intrusion detection systems, *Information and Communication Technologies, 2006. ICTTA '06.* 2nd, vol. 2, 2006, pp. 3175–3180.

[22] Ahmad Faour, Philippe Leray, and Bassam Eter, Growing hierarchical self-organizing map for alarm filtering in network intrusion detection systems, *New Technologies, Mobility and Security*, Springer, 2007, p. 631.

[23] B. Fei, J. Eloff, H. Venter, and M. Olivier, Exploring forensic data with self-organizing maps, *Advances in Digital Forensics*, Springer, 2005, pp. 113–123.

[24] B. K. L. Fei, J. H. P. Eloff, M. S. Olivier, and H. S. Venter, The use of self-organising maps for anomalous behaviour detection in a digital investigation, *Forensic Science International* 162 (2006), no. 1-3, 33–37.

[25] Stephanie Forrest, A. S. Perelson, L. Allen, and R. Cherukuri, Self-nonself discrimination in a computer, *Research in Security and Privacy, 1994. Proceedings., 1994 IEEE Computer Society Symposium on*, 1994, pp. 202–212.

[26] K. L. Fox, R. R. Henning, J. H. Reed, and R. Simonian, A neural network approach towards intrusion detection, *Proceedings of the 13th National Computer Security Conference,* vol. 10, 1990.

[27] Bernd Fritzke, A growing neural gas network learns topologies, *Advances in Neural Information Processing Systems* 7 (Cambridge MA) (G. Tesauro, D. S. Touretzky, and T. K. Leen, eds.), MIT Press, 1995, pp. 625–632.

[28] _____, Growing self-organizing networks – why?, *ESANN'96: European Symposium on Artificial Neural Networks,* 1996, pp. 61–72.

[29] Luc Girardin, An eye on network intruder-administrator shootouts, ID'99: *Proceedings of the 1st conference on Workshop on Intrusion Detection and Network Monitoring* (Berkeley, CA, USA), USENIX Association, 1999, p. 3.

[30] Luc Girardin and Dominique Brodbeck, A visual approach for monitoring logs, *LISA '98: Proceedings of the 12th USENIX conference on System administration (Berkeley, CA, USA)*, USENIX Association, 1998, pp. 299–308.

[31] Dieter Gollmann, *Computer security*, 1 ed., John Wiley & Sons, February 1999.

[32] Fabio Gonzalez and Dipankar Dasgupta, Neuro-immune and self-organizing map approaches to anomaly detection: A comparison, *Proceedings of the 1st International Conference on Artificial Immune Systems*, 2002, pp. 203–211.

[33] ———, Anomaly detection using real-valued negative selection, *Genetic Programming and Evolvable Machines* 4 (2003), no. 4, 383–403.

[34] Fabio Gonzalez, Juan C. Galeano, Diego A. Rojas, and Angélica Veloza-Suan, Discriminating and visualizing anomalies using negative selection and self-organizing maps, *GECCO '05: Proceedings of the 2005 conference on Genetic and evolutionary computation (New York, NY, USA)*, ACM, 2005, pp. 297–304.

[35] Julie Greensmith, Jan Feyereisl, and Uwe Aickelin, The dca: Some comparison, *Evolutionary Intelligence* 1 (2008), no. 2, 85–112.

[36] H. Grosser, P. Britos, and R. García-Martínez, Detecting fraud in mobile telephony using neural networks, *Innovations in Applied Artificial Intelligence, LNCS,* vol. 3533, Springer, 2005, pp. 613–615.

[37] Shuguo Han and Wee Ng, Privacy-preserving self-organizing map, *Data Warehousing and Knowledge Discovery, LNCS*, 2007, pp. 428–437.

[38] Simon Haykin, *Neural networks: A comprehensive foundation (2nd edition)* , Prentice Hall, July 1998.

[39] E. Herrero-Jaraba, C. Orrite-Urunuela, F. Monzon, and D. Buldain, Video-based human posture recognition, *Computational Intelligence for Homeland Security and Personal Safety, 2004. CIHSPS 2004. Proceedings of the 2004 IEEE International Conference on*, 2004, pp. 19–22.

[40] Albert J. Hoglund, K. Hatonen, and A. S. Sorvari, A computer host-based user anomaly detection system using the self-organizing map, *Neural Networks, 2000. IJCNN 2000, Proceedings of the IEEE-INNS-ENNS International Joint Conference on*, vol. 5, 2000, pp. 411–416 vol.5.

[41] Albert J. Hoglund and Kimmo Hatonen, Computer network user behaviour visualization using self organizing maps, *Proceedings of ICANN98, the 8th International Conference on Artificial Neural Networks* (L. Niklasson, M. Bodén, and T. Ziemke, eds.), vol. 2, Springer, London, 1998, pp. 899–904.

[42] T. Horeis, *Intrusion detection with neural networks–combination of self-organizing maps and radial basis function networks for human expert integration*, Tech. report, University of Passau, 2003.

[43] Pingzhao Hu and Malcolm I. Heywood, Predicting intrusions with local linear models, *Neural Networks, 2003. Proceedings of the International Joint Conference on*, vol. 3, 2003, pp. 1780–1785 vol.3.

[44] T. Ichimura, A. Hara, and Y. Kurosawa, A classification method for spam e-mail by self-organizing map and automatically defined groups, *Systems, Man and Cybernetics, 2007. ISIC. IEEE International Conference on*, 2007, pp. 2044–2049.

[45] Mansour Jamzad and Zahra Kermani, Secure steganography using gabor filter and neural networks, *Transactions on Data Hiding and Multimedia Security III, LNCS*, Springer, 2008, pp. 33–49.

[46] Chaivat Jirapummin, Naruemon Wattanapongsakorn, and Prasert Kanthamanon, Hybrid neural networks for intrusion detection system, 2002 *International Technical Conference on Circuits/Systems, Computers and Communications (ITC-CSCC 2002)* (Phuket, Thailand), 2002, pp. 928–931.

[47] Eric R. Kandel, James H. Schwartz, and Thomas M. Jessell, *Principles of neural science*, McGraw-Hill Medical, January 2000.

[48] Gunes H. Kayacik and Nur A. Zincir-Heywood, Analysis of three intrusion detection system benchmark datasets using machine learning algorithms, *Intelligence and Security Informatics, LNCS*, Springer, 2005, pp. 362–367.

[49] Gunes H. Kayacik, Nur A. Zincir-Heywood, and Malcolm I. Heywood, On the capability of an som based intrusion detection system, *Neural Networks, 2003. Proceedings of the International Joint Conference on*, vol. 3, 2003, pp. 1808–1813 vol.3.

[50] _____, A hierarchical som-based intrusion detection system, *Engineering Applications of Artificial Intelligence* 20 (2007), no. 4, 439–451.

[51] Latifur Khan, Mamoun Awad, and Bhavani Thuraisingham, A new intrusion detection system using support vector machines and hierarchical clustering, *The VLDB Journal* 16 (2007), no. 4, 507–521.

[52] Rahul Khanna and Huaping Liu, System approach to intrusion detection using hidden markov model, *IWCMC '06: Proceedings of the 2006 international conference on Wireless communications and mobile computing (New York, NY, USA), ACM*, 2006, pp. 349–354.

[53] Mohammad H. Khosravi and Reza Safabakhsh, Human eye sclera detection and tracking using a modified time-adaptive self-organizing map, *Pattern Recognition* 41 (2008), no. 8, 2571–2593.

[54] J. Kim and P. Bentley, Evaluating negative selection in an artificial immune system for network intrusion detection, *Proc. of the Genetic and Evolutionary Computation Conference (GECCO)*, July 2001.

[55] Teuvo Kohonen, Automatic formation of topological maps of patterns in a self-organizing system, *Proceedings of the 2nd Scandinavian Conference on Image Analysis (Espoo)*, 1981, pp. 214–220.

[56] ———, Improved versions of learning vector quantization, *Neural Networks, 1990., 1990 IJCNN International Joint Conference on*, 1990, pp. 545–550 vol.1.

[57] ———, The self-organizing map, *Proceedings of the IEEE* 78 (1990), no. 9, 1464–1480.

[58] ———, *Self-organizing maps*, Springer, December 2000.

[59] ———, *Description of input patterns by linear mixtures of som models*, Tech. report, Helsinki University of Technology, Espoo, 2007.

[60] D. Kumar, C. S. Rai, and S. Kumar, Face recognition using self-organizing map and principal component analysis, *Neural Networks and Brain, 2005. ICNN&B '05. International Conference on,* vol. 3, 2005, pp. 1469–1473.

[61] Ganesh P. Kumar and D. Devaraj, Network intrusion detection using hybrid neural networks, *Signal Processing, Communications and Networking, 2007. ICSCN '07. International Conference on,* 2007, pp. 563–569.

[62] Pekka Kumpulainen and Kimmo Hätönen, Local anomaly detection for mobile network monitoring, *Information Sciences* In Press, Uncorrected Proof.

[63] H. Kusumoto and Y. Takefuji, $O(\log_{?2?}m)$ self-organizing map algorithm without learning of neighborhood vectors, *Neural Networks, IEEE Transactions on* 17 (2006), no. 6, 1656–1661.

[64] Hiroki Kusumoto and Yoshiyasu Takefuj, Evaluation of the performance of $o(\log 2m)$ self-organizing map algorithm without neighborhood learning, *International Journal of Computer Science and Network Security* 6 (2006), no. 10, 104–108.

[65] S. C. Lee and D. V. Heinbuch, Training a neural-network based intrusion detector to recognize novel attacks, *Systems, Man and Cybernetics, Part A, IEEE Transactions on* 31 (2001), no. 4, 294–299.

[66] J. Z. Lei and A. Ghorbani, Network intrusion detection using an improved competitive learning neural network, *Communication Networks and Services Research, 2004. Proceedings. Second Annual Conference on*, 2004, pp. 190–197.

[67] Ding Li, Ni Gui-Qiang, Pan Zhi-Song, and Hu Gu-Yu, Ddos intrusion detection using generalized grey self-organizing maps, *Grey Systems and Intelligent Services, 2007. GSIS 2007. IEEE International Conference on,* 2007, pp. 1548–1551.

[68] Peter Lichodzijewski, Nur, and Malcolm I. Heywood, Dynamic intrusion detection using self organizing maps, *The 14th Annual Canadian Information Technology Security Symposium (CITSS)*, 2002.

[69] _____, Host-based intrusion detection using self-organizing maps, Neural Networks, 2002. IJCNN '02. *Proceedings of the 2002 International Joint Conference on*, vol. 2, 2002, pp. 1714–1719.

[70] Guisong Liu and Zhang Yi, Intrusion detection using pcasom neural networks, Advances in Neural Networks - ISNN 2006, *LNCS*, 2006, pp. 240–245.

[71] Xiao Luo and Nur A. Zincir-Heywood, Comparison of a som based sequence analysis system and naive bayesian classifier for spam filtering, *Neural Networks, 2005. IJCNN '05. Proceedings. 2005 IEEE International Joint Conference on*, vol. 4, 2005, pp. 2571–2576 vol. 4.

[72] Zhenying Ma, A genetic som clustering algorithm for intrusion detection, *Advances in Neural Networks ISNN 2005*, 2005, pp. 421–427.

[73] Markos Markou and Sameer Singh, Novelty detection: a review–part 2:: neural network based approaches, *Signal Processing* 83 (2003), no. 12, 2499–2521.

[74] Francisco Martínez, Carlos Orrite, and Elías Herrero, Biometric hand recognition using neural networks, *Computational Intelligence and Bioinspired Systems, LNCS*, 2005, pp. 1164–1171.

[75] John Mchugh, Testing intrusion detection systems: a critique of the 1998 and 1999 darpa intrusion detection system evaluations as performed by lincoln laboratory, *ACM Transactions on Information and System Security* 3 (2000), no. 4, 262–294.

[76] P. Miller and A. Inoue, Collaborative intrusion detection system, Fuzzy Information Processing Society, 2003. NAFIPS 2003. *22nd International Conference of the North American*, 2003, pp. 519–524.

[77] Aikaterini Mitrokotsa and C. Douligeris, Detecting denial of service attacks using emergent self-organizing maps, *Signal Processing and Information Technology, 2005. Proceedings of the Fifth IEEE International Symposium on*, 2005, pp. 375–380.

[78] Aikaterini Mitrokotsa, Nikos Komninos, and Christos Douligeris, Intrusion detection with neural networks and watermarking techniques for manet, *Pervasive Services, IEEE International Conference on*, 2007, pp. 118–127.

[79] I. Q. Monteiro, S. D. Queiroz, A. T. Carneiro, L. G. Souza, and G. A. Barreto, Face recognition independent of facial expression through som-based classifiers, *Telecommunications Symposium*, 2006 International, 2006, pp. 263–268.

[80] Giles Oatley, Brian Ewart, and John Zeleznikow, Decision support systems for police: Lessons from the application of data mining techniques to soft forensic evidence, *Artificial Intelligence and Law* 14 (2006), no. 1-2, 35–100.

[81] Hayoung Oh, Jiyoung Lim, Kijoon Chae, and Jungchan Nah, Home gateway with automated real-time intrusion detection for secure home networks, *Computational Science and Its Applications - ICCSA 2006, LNCS,* 2006, pp. 440–447.

[82] Claudia Oliveira, José A. Xexéo, and Carlos A. Carvalho, Clustering and categorization applied to cryptanalysis, *Cryptologia* 30 (2006), no. 3, 266–280.

[83] Wei Pan and Weihua Li, A hybrid neural network approach to the classification of novel attacks for intrusion detection, *Parallel and Distributed Processing and Applications, LNCS,* 2005, pp. 564–575.

[84] Udo Payer, Peter Teufl, Stefan Kraxberger, and Mario Lamberger, Massive data mining for polymorphic code detection, *Computer Network Security, LNCS,* 2005, pp. 448–453.

[85] Simon T. Powers and Jun He, A hybrid artificial immune system and self organising map for network intrusion detection, *Information Sciences* 178 (2008), no. 15, 3024–3042.

[86] J. T. S. Quah and M. Sriganesh, Real time credit card fraud detection using computational intelligence, *Neural Networks,* 2007. IJCNN 2007. International Joint Conference on, 2007, pp. 863–868.

[87] Jon T. Quah and M. Sriganesh, Real-time credit card fraud detection using computational intelligence, *Expert Systems with Applications* In Press, Corrected Proof (2007).

[88] Jean-Jacques Quisquater and David Samyde, Automatic code recognition for smart cards using a kohonen neural network, *CARDIS'02: Proceedings of the 5th conference on Smart Card Research and Advanced Application Conference (Berkeley, CA, USA),* USENIX Association, 2002, p. 6.

[89] Manikantan Ramadas, Shawn Ostermann, and Brett Tjaden, Detecting anomalous network traffic with self-organizing maps, *Recent Advances in Intrusion Detection, LNCS,* Springer, 2003, pp. 36–54.

[90] B. C. Rhodes, J. A. Mahaffey, and J. D. Cannady, Multiple self-organizing maps for intrusion detection, *Proceedings of the 23rd National Information Systems Security Conference,* 2000.

[91] Helge Ritter, Thomas Martinetz, and Klaus Schulten, it Neural computation and self-organizing maps; an introduction, Addison-Wesley Longman Publishing Co., Inc., Boston, MA, USA, 1992.

[92] Reza Sadoddin and Ali Ghorbani, A comparative study of unsupervised machine learning and data mining techniques for intrusion detection, *Machine Learning and Data Mining in Pattern Recognition, LNCS,* Springer, 2007, pp. 404–418.

[93] S. T. Sarasamma and Q. A. Zhu, Min-max hyperellipsoidal clustering for anomaly detection in network security, *Systems, Man, and Cybernetics, Part B, IEEE Transactions on* 36 (2006), no. 4, 887–901.

[94] S. T. Sarasamma, Q. A. Zhu, and J. Huff, Hierarchical kohonen net for anomaly detection in network security, *Systems, Man, and Cybernetics, Part B, IEEE Transactions on* 35 (2005), no. 2, 302–312.

[95] W. M. Shalash and F. Abou-Chadi, A fingerprint classification technique using multilayer som, *Radio Science Conference, 2000. 17th NRSC '2000. Seventeenth National,* 2000, pp. C26/1–C26/8.

[96] M. Shehab, N. Mansour, and A. Faour, Growing hierarchical self-organizing map for filtering intrusion detection alarms, *Parallel Architectures, Algorithms, and Networks, 2008. I-SPAN 2008. International Symposium on,* 2008, pp. 167–172.

[97] Taeshik Shon and Jongsub Moon, A hybrid machine learning approach to network anomaly detection, *Information Sciences* 177 (2007), no. 18, 3799–3821.

[98] Reuben Smith, Nathalie Japkowicz, Maxwell Dondo, and Peter Mason, Using unsupervised learning for network alert correlation, *Advances in Artificial Intelligence, LNCS,* 2008, pp. 308–319.

[99] Anil Somayaji, Michael Locasto, and Jan Feyereisl, Panel: The future of biologically-inspired security: Is there anything left to learn?, *Proceedings of the 2007 Workshop on New Security Paradigms,* The Association for Computing Machinery, 2008.

[100] A. Ultsch and H. P. Siemon, Kohonen's self organizing feature maps for exploratory data analysis, *Proceedings Intern. Neural Networks (Paris),* Kluwer Academic Press, 1990, pp. 305–308.

[101] H. S. Venter, J. H. P. Eloff, and Y. L. Li, Standardising vulnerability categories, *Computers & Security* In Press, Corrected Proof.

[102] Chun-Dong Wang, He-Feng Yu, Huai-Bin Wang, and Kai Liu, Som-based anomaly intrusion detection system, *Embedded and Ubiquitous Computing, LNCS,* vol. 4808, Springer, 2007, pp. 356–366.

[103] Lei Wang, Yong Yang, and Shixin Sun, A new approach of network intrusion detection using hvdm-based som, *Advances in Neural Networks ISNN 2005,* LNCS, 2005, pp. 488–493.

[104] Wei Wang, Xiaohong Guan, Xiangliang Zhang, and Liwei Yang, Profiling program behavior for anomaly intrusion detection based on the transition and frequency property of computer audit data, *Computers & Security* 25 (2006), no. 7, 539–550.

[105] Edgar Weippl, Werner Winiwarter, and I. K. Ibrahim, Content-based management of document access control, *14th International Conference on Applications of Prolog,* October 2001.

[106] Yun Xiao and Chongzhao Han, Correlating intrusion alerts into attack scenarios based on improved evolving self-organizing maps, *International Journal of Computer Science and Network Security* 6 (2006), no. 6, 199–203.

[107] Inseon Yoo, Visualizing windows executable viruses using self-organizing maps, *VizSEC/DMSEC '04: Proceedings of the 2004 ACM workshop on Visualization and data mining for computer security (New York, NY, USA)*, ACM, 2004, pp. 82–89.

[108] Inseon Yoo and Ulrich Ultes-Nitsche, Adaptive detection of worms/viruses in firewalls, *Proc. of International Conference on Communication, Network, and Information Security (CNIS 2003)* (New York), December 2003.

[109] ———, Non-signature based virus detection, *Journal in Computer Virology* 2 (2006), no. 3, 163–186.

[110] Zhenwei Yu, J. J. P. Tsai, and T. Weigert, An automatically tuning intrusion detection system, *Systems, Man, and Cybernetics, Part B, IEEE Transactions on* 37 (2007), no. 2, 373–384.

[111] Jun Zheng, Ming-Zeng Hu, and Hong-Li Zhang, A new method of data preprocessing and anomaly detection, *Machine Learning and Cybernetics, 2004. Proceedings of 2004 International Conference on,* vol. 5, 2004, pp. 2685–2690 vol.5.

[112] Jun Zheng, Mingzeng Hu, Binxing Fang, and Hongli Zhang, Anomaly detection using fast sofm, *Grid and Cooperative Computing GCC 2004Workshops, LNCS,* 2004, pp. 530–537.

In: Computer Security: Intrusion, Detection and Prevention
Editors: R. D. Hopkins and W. P. Tokere

ISBN: 978-1-60692-781-6
© 2009 Nova Science Publishers, Inc.

Chapter 2

NETWORK MANAGEMENT FOCUSED ON CLIENT COMPUTER

Kazuya Odagiri[1,a] and Naohiro Ishii[2,b]

[1] The University of Electro-Communications, Japan

[2] Aichi Institute of Technology, Japan

Abstract

Recently, P2P system is attracting great attention as one of the next generation network services. While the conventional Client-Server system is a network service putting an important role to the network server, the P2P system is realized on the P2P Network where client computers communicate each other directly. The P2P system is suitable to the current network situation where users are handling large-capacity contents such as moving or streaming data. However, the P2P network is not generally developed yet. Actually, the current network is managed through network infrastructure and network server mainly, and is not sufficient to manage client computers for P2P system. A DACS (Destination Addressing Control System) Scheme has been developed by authors, which is a method to manage the whole network through the management of the client computer. We propose here that DACS Scheme is compatible with P2P system putting an important role to the client computer. The development of the P2P system is described by the developed results of DACS Scheme. We explain the motivation for the research of the DACS Scheme, it's basic principle and security function of the DACS scheme. Then, we explain the new user support realized by DACS Scheme as an example for showing the effectiveness of this scheme.

1. Introduction

Recently, P2P system is attracting great attention as one of the next generation network services. While the conventional Client-Server system is a network service putting an important role to the network server, the P2P system is realized on the P2P Network where client computers communicate each other directly. The P2P system is suitable to the current

---

[a] E-mail address: odagiri@cc.uec.ac.jp
[b] E-mail address: ishii@aitech.ac.jp

network situation where users are handling large-capacity contents such as moving or streaming. However, the P2P network is not generally used yet. Actually, the current network is managed through network infrastructure and network server mainly, and it is not sufficient to manage client computers for P2P system. We think that, if there is a network management scheme to manage communications sent from a client computer (client) effectively, P2P network will be used more generally.

As the studies and technologies on existing network management, various researches and developments such as the server load distribution technology [1][2][3], VPN(Virtual Private Network)[4][5] are carried out. However, these studies and developments are performed forward the specified different goal. Realization of effective management for a whole network is not a purpose. As the study for managing a whole network, there is the study of Opengate [6][7] which controls Web accesses from LAN (Local Area Network) to internet. However, this study has the limited purpose of controlling Web access to internet. As the study for managing a whole network effectively without the limited purpose, there is the study of PBNM (Policy-based network management) [8][9][10][11] in IETF (Internet Engineering Task Force). However, in PBNM, communications sent from many clients are controlled by the mechanism located on the network path. As a network management scheme, DACS (Destination Addressing Control System) Scheme has been developed by authors [16][17][18][19]. DACS Scheme is the scheme to manage the whole network through the communication control of client computer. We propose that DACS Scheme is compatible with P2P system putting an important role to the client computer. We would like to contribute to the development of the P2P system by introducing the developed results about the DACS Scheme. In this article, we explain the study of the DACS Scheme we performed so far as a whole. First, motivation and related studies of this research is explained in section 2. Then, the basic mechanism of DACS Scheme is explained in section 3, and security function as extended function is explained in section 4. In section 5, examples of new user support realized by use of DACS Scheme is described to show the effectiveness of DASC Scheme.

2. Motivation and Related Studies on this Research

As the studies and technologies on existing network management, various studies and developments such as authentication [12][13], the server load distribution technology [1][2][3], VPN(Virtual Private Network)[4][5] and quarantine network [14][15] are performed. However, these studies and developments are performed forward the specified different goal. Realization of effective management for a whole network is not a purpose. As the study for managing a whole network, there is the study of Opengate [6][7] which controls Web accesses from LAN (Local Area Network) to internet. However, this study has the limited purpose of controlling Web access to internet. As the study for managing a whole network effectively without the limited purpose, there is the study of PBNM (Policy-based network management) [8][9][10][11] in IETF (Internet Engineering Task Force). The content of PBNM is described in Figure 1.

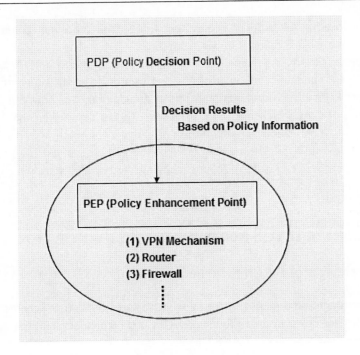

Figure 1. PBNM in IETF.

To be concrete, in the point called PDP (Policy Decision Point), judgment such as permission and non-permission for communication pass is performed based on policy information. The judgment is notified and transmitted to the point called PEP (Policy Enhancement Point) which is the mechanism such as VPN mechanism, router and firewall located on the network path among hosts such as servers and clients. Based on that judgment, the control is added for the communication that is going to pass by. As problems of this method, two points are presented as follows.

Point 1: Communications sent from many clients are controlled by the mechanism located on the network path. Therefore, processing load for that controlling becomes very heavy.

Point 2: The mechanism for communication control needs to be located between each host. Therefore, depending on the network system configuration, configuration change of the network system for adding that mechanism is needed.

Therefore, we proposed a new network management scheme, which overcomes theses problems and has the function which does not exist in existing PBNM, and called it DACS Scheme. The basic principle of DACS Scheme is described as follows. After the client software equivalent to PEP in PBNM is located on a client, the communication sent from the client is controlled through the mechanism of packet filtering and Destination NAT which is the function of this client software. Through that communication control, a whole network is managed. When it is considered at the point that the client software equivalent to PEP is located on the client, there is a study about QOS control by use of PEP located on the client in the studies of PBNM. However, the study for the purpose of managing a whole network effectively by locating the software equivalent to PEP on the client could not be found besides the study of DACS Scheme in past studies.

As the studies of DACS Scheme, we showed the basic principle of DACS Scheme [16], the function to let communication control for each user coexist with communication control for each client [17] and security function [18][19]. In addition, we showed new user support realized by use of DACS Scheme [20][21]. Then, we are forwarding the studies of Web Service function which make it possible to use effectively information in database dispersed on the network and in document medium as PDF file and simple text file [22][23], and the study of new Web Service [24][25][26] for realizing the portal system which each user can create and change.

3. Mechanism of DACS Scheme

3.1. Basic Principle of DACS Scheme

Figure 2 shows the basic principle of the network services by DACS Scheme. At the timing of the (a) or (b) as shown in the following, DACS rules (rules defined by the user unit) are distributed from DACS Server to DACS Client.

(a) At the time of a user logging in the client.
(b) At the time of a delivery indication from the system administrator.

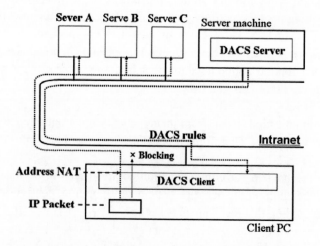

Figure 2. Basic Principle of DACS Scheme.

According to distributed DACS rules, DACS Client performs (1) or (2) operation as shown in the following. Then, communication control of the client is performed for every login user.

(1) Destination information on IP Packet, which is sent from application program, is changed.

(2) IP Packet from the client, which is sent from the application program to the outside of the client, is blocked.

An example of the case (1) is shown in Figure 2. In Figure 2, the system administrator can distribute a communication of the login user to the specified server among servers A, B or C. Moreover, the case (2) is described. For example, when the system administrator wants to forbid an user to use MUA (Mail User Agent), it will be performed by blocking IP Packet with the specific destination information.

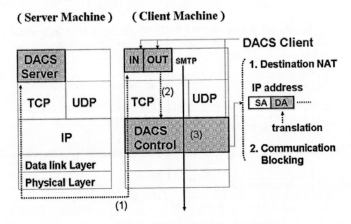

Figure 3. Layer Setting of DACS Scheme.

In order to realize DACS Scheme, the operation is done by DACS Protocol as shown in Figure 3. As shown by (1) in Figure 3, the distribution of DACS rules is performed on communication between DACS Server and DACS Client, which is arranged at the application layer. The application of DACS rules to DACS Control is shown by (2) in Figure 3. The steady communication control, such as a modification of the destination information or the communication blocking is performed at the network layer as shown by (3) in Figure 3.

3.2. DACS Protocol

DACS Protocol is a communication protocol required by DACS Scheme, and can be realized by Phase1 and Phase2 which is separated in the state of DACS Client.

Phase1 Initializing process of DACS Client
Phase2 Steady state process of DACS Client
        a.When DACS rules is applied to DACS Control.
        b.When DACS Server checks whether DACS Client has started.

3.2.1. Initializing Process (Phase1)

The protocol of Phase1 is shown in Figure 4. (S1-S4 indicates the processing sequence by the server side, and C1-C9 indicate the processing sequence of the client side.)

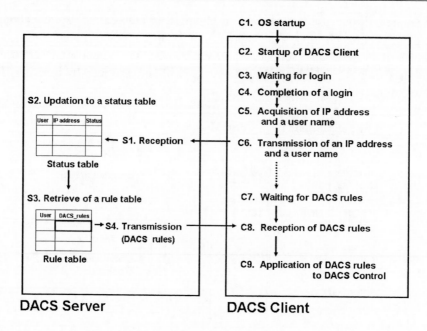

Figure 4. Initializing Process in DACS Protocol (Phase1).

First, when OS starts (C1), DACS Client starts (C2). Then, DACS client is in the status of waiting for user login (C3). When user login is completed (C4), DACS Client acquires the IP address and login user name of the client (C5). Then, DACS Client transmits them to DACS Server (C6). Usually, how to set the IP address to the client has either to set up automatically using DHCP service, or other way in which the customer and the system administrator do manual setting. When a network interface starts, the IP address is set up by a method of either. Therefore, if DACS Client acquires the IP address of the client at the time of user login, there are no problems to acquire the IP address. Although it is how to acquire the IP address and login user name, in the experiment explained later, the IP address is extracted from the practice result message of a command to display network setting information. Moreover, since the user name is set to the environment variable when logged in OS, the user name is acquired through the environment variable. By DACS Scheme, since it is premised on the scheme which performs the user authentication of the client, the checks to the user name is not performed in DACS Server. Incidentally, the LDAP Server (OpenLDAP) is adopted as an authentication server in this experiment. After transmitting the user name and the IP address to DACS Server, processing is performed in DACS Server. The DACS Server registers newly or updates the IP address and DACS Client presence of the client into the status table ,in which a user name is the main key (S2).

Status=0: DACS Client stops.
Status=1: DACS Client starts.

In the next processing, DACS rules of the login user registered into the rule table is extracted (S3), and it transmits to DACS Client (S4). Although DACS Client applies DACS rules to DACS Control (C9) after the reception (C8), it performs actually controlling the communication in DACS Control. In addition, at the time of the end of DACS Client, status is updated to 0.

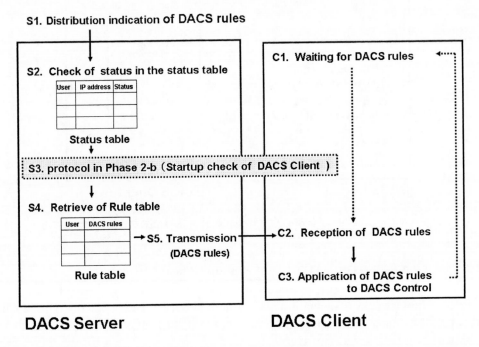

Figure 5. Distribution Process of DACS rules by System Administrator in DACS Protocol (Phase 2-a).

3.2.2. Distribution Process of DACS rules by System Administrator (Phase 2-a)

Next, the protocol in Phase2-a is shown in Figure 5. (S1-S5 shows the processing sequence performed in the server side, and C1-C3 shows the processing sequence in the client side.)

The system administrator gives DACS Server the indication of distributing DACS rules (S1). The DACS rules are applicable to DACS Client of the client to which the specific user logs in. As the sequence, the system administrator registers new DACS rules into a rule table first. Then, the user name used as the candidate for application is given to DACS Server. DACS Server checks the IP address of the client and the startup presence or absence of the client in the status table (S2). When the status is 1, the seizing acknowledgment of DACS Client is performed. When the data in the status table shows an outage (i.e., when status is 0), the startup check of DACS Client is done (S3). When the client is in the status of seizing the presence of DACS Client, DACS rules are transmitted to DACS Client (S5). Then, DACS rules are applied to DACS Control (C3). DACS Client is in the status of awaiting after the application of DACS rules (C1).

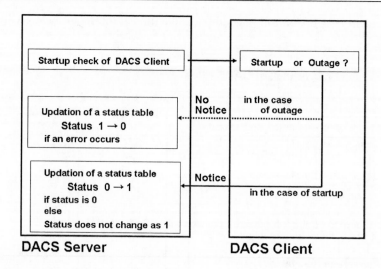

Figure 6. Checking Process of DACS Client startup in DACS Protocol (Phase 2-b)

3.2.3. Checking Process of DACS Client startup (Phase 2-b)

Protocol in Phase2-b is shown in Figure 6. DACS Server checks whether DACS Client has started. The timing which seizes the presence of DACS Client is as follows.

- When carrying out with the fixed interval periodically.
- When carrying out in Phase2-a before a transmission of DACS rules.(When Status is 0 in the status table.)

DACS Client is in the status that the receiving process from DACS Server is awaited. Therefore, when DACS Server asks, there is a response if DACS Client has started and an error occurs if it has stopped. When the error occurs, status is updated from 1 to 0 in the status table. The reason for checking whether DACS Client has started periodically is to improve the system efficiently by the minimum startup check of DACS Client in the sequence (S3) of Phase2-a. Here, the status description of DACS Server and DACS Client is shown in Figure 7. The directional arrow of the dotted line shows the flow of the state transition of DACS Server and DACS Client. The state changes in order as follows; to Active (steady state) from Initializing (initializing status), Off (idle state), and Initializing.

Non-Active (transient status) in DACS Client shows all the statuses that it is not Active, when it does not reach to a steady state after the Off, or Initializing. When DACS Client is in the status of Initializing, status is changed into 1 from 0. Under a steady state (Active), status is not changed from 1 in response to the notice from DACS Client for the startup check. However, when judged with Non-Active as a result of the startup check of DACS Client, status is changed into 0 by DACS Server from 1. Moreover, explanation about the directional arrow (solid line) of DACS Server (Active) and DACS Client (Active, Off, Non-Active) is given. First, there is a directional arrow between DACS Server (Active) and DACS Client (Active) as follows.

- The inquiry to DACS Client from DACS Server.
- The response from DACS Client to the above-mentioned inquiry.
- The transmission of DACS rules from DACS Server to DACS Client.

In the opposite arrow of a dashed line for the directional arrows of solid line from DACS Server (Active) to DACS Client (Off, Non-Active), it is shown that there is no response from DACS Client to the inquiry from DACS Server to DACS Client.

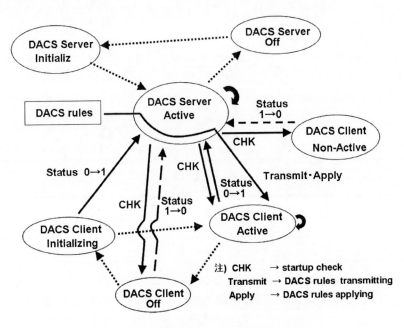

Figure 7. Status description of DACS Scheme.

3.3. Communication Control on Client

The communication control for each user was given. However, it may be better to perform communication control for each client instead of each user. For example, it is the case where many and unspecified users use a computer room, which is controlled. In this section, the method of communication control for each client is described, and the coexistence method with the communication control for each user is considered.

When a user logs in to a client, the IP address of the client is transmitted to DACS Server from DACS Client. Then, if DACS rules corresponding to IP address, is registered into the DACS Server side, it is transmitted to DACS Client. Then, communication control for each client can be realized by applying to DACS Control. In this case, it is a premise that a client uses a fixed IP address. However, when using DHCP service, it is possible to carry out the same control to all the clients linked to the whole network or its subnetwork for example.

When using communication control for each user and each client, communication control may conflict. In that case, a priority needs to be given. The judgment is performed in the DACS Server side as shown in Figure 8.

Although not necessarily stipulated, the network policy or security policy exists in the organization such as a university (1). The priority is decided according to the policy (2). In (a), priority is given for the user's rule to control communication by the user unit. In (b), priority is given for the client's rule to control communication by the client unit. In (c), the user's rule is the same as the client's rule. As the result of comparing the conflict rules, one rule is determined respectively. Those rules and other rules not overlapping are gathered, and DACS rules are created (3). DACS rules are transmitted to DACS Client. In the DACS Client side, DACS rules are applied to DACS Control. The difference between the user's rule and the client's rule is not distinguished.

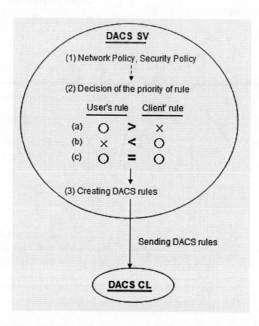

Figure 8. Creating DACS rules in the DACS Server side.

3.4. Network Service Corresponding to DACS Scheme

In this section, network service's corresponding to DACS Scheme is explained. In existing DACS Scheme, information for communication control by a user unit and by a client unit has been maintained as DACS rules on the DACS Server. By applying that information for communication control to DACS Client (DACS Control) located on a client, communication from the client is controlled. As the result, the specific mechanism is not needed on the network server. However, on the network introducing DACS Scheme, if a correspondence list of a client's IP address and user name logging in that client is passed to the network server, it becomes possible to identify which user is sending the communication from a client. As the result, it becomes possible for a program on the network server to perform different processing for each user. Concrete example is the Web Service's correspondence to DACS Scheme.

4. Security Function

4.1. Adaptability for DACS Scheme

In the basic DACS Scheme explained in section 3, it is assumed that DACS Client must be implemented on all clients. When the client which DACS Client is not installed in is connected to the network, each network server can be accessed from that client technically. Depending on network or security policy, access for each network server can be permitted or not permitted. For the purpose of corresponding to the non-permitted case, the function of preventing the communication from the client which DACS Client is not installed in is needed. Even if permitted, the communication needs to be encrypted when a user expects it. For example, in the service of handling information and contents for the specified user such as POP service, communication needs to be encrypted for the purpose of preventing information interception. When communication is tunneled and encrypted, processing for encrypting and decrypting occurs in the server side. The function of tunneling and encrypting only minimum communication is needed for reducing processing load in the server side where communications from a lot of users and clients concentrate.

From here, the security function with the adaptability for DACS Scheme is examined. At first, as the method for preventing the communication from the client which DACS Client is not installed in, access control on the network server side is examined. First, the method of using packet filtering mechanism is considered. By locating packet filtering mechanism on each network server, it is possible to perform access control based on IP address and TCP port. In DACS Scheme, communication control is performed by a user unit. To perform access control by a user unit on the network server, the mechanism, which makes it possible to identify which user is sending communication, is needed. That is, the packet filtering mechanism which corresponds to DACS Scheme is needed. The details of the method for corresponding to DACS Scheme are described in section 3.4. Because access control is performed according to the correspondence list of a client's IP address and a user name logging in that client, processing load comes to be very heavy. Then, the method of each network service's performing access control by a user unit is considered. Each network service is needed to correspond to DACS Scheme. Being same as packet filtering mechanism which corresponds to DACS Scheme, processing load is very heavy. Moreover, it is difficult to make all network service correspond to DACS Scheme. Access control on the network server side is not suitable to DACS Scheme.

Next, as another method to prevent the communication from the client which DACS Client is not installed in, the method of using the mechanism of single sign on operation such as Kerberos is considered. In this method, each network service must correspond to the mechanism of single sign on operation. However, because there is not always the guarantee, this method is not unsuitable to DACS Scheme.

Therefore, as the other method to prevent the communication from the client which DACS Client is not installed in, the method of tunneling and encrypting the communication between the network server and the client which DACS Client is installed in is considered. Essentially, only tunneling is needed to prevent such a communication. By adding the encrypting function, the information interception is prevented. To tunnel and encrypt the communication, there are some methods of tunneling and encrypting under the network layer (third layer) of OSI model by using PPTP and L2TP, IP sec etc. In addition, there are some other methods at the upper layer more than transport layer (forth layer) by using SSL and TLS, SSH etc. The protocol without the function of encrypting like L2TP needs to be incorporated with other encrypting function. In the case of tunneling and encrypting under third layer, all communications between a network server and a client are tunneled and encrypted. On the other hand, in the case of tunneling and encrypting above forth layer, the communication between a network server and a client are encrypted and tunneled by a network service unit. Since the processing to restore the tunneled and encrypted communication is needed in the network server, it is expected to tunnel and encrypt the minimum communication. In comparing the former method with the latter method, the latter method is advantageous to reduce the processing load in the server. However, it is insufficient only to tunnel and encrypt the communications between a network server and a client simply by a network service unit. In DACS Scheme, communication control is performed not only by a client unit but also by a user unit. Depending on the content of network or security policy, it may be needed for one specified users to use one network service with the communication tunneled and encrypted. Also, it may be needed for another specified user to use same network service with the communication not tunneled and unencrypted. This communication control is realized by connecting the function of communication control by a user unit in DACS Scheme and the function of tunneling and encrypting by a network service unit above the forth layer. In addition, because the unspecified number of network services moving on TCP/IP needs to be controlled, the communication will be tunneled and encrypted, not by the method that is effective for only specific network service, but by the method that is effective for the unspecified number of network services. In the method of using SSL and TLS, the communication for the unspecified number of network services is not always tunneled and encrypted. In the method of using the port forwarding function of SSH, it is possible to tunnel and encrypt the communication for the unspecified number of network services. To perform communication control with these requirements satisfied, the function of DACS Scheme is extended as shown in next section.

4.2. Security Function by SSH

In this section, the security function of DACS Scheme is described. The communication is tunneled and encrypted by use of SSH. By using the function of port forwarding of SSH, it is realized to tunnel and encrypt the communication between the network server and the client which DACS Client is installed in. Normally, to communicate from a client application to a network server by using the function of port forwarding of SSH, local host (127.0.0.1) needs to be indicated on that client application as a communicating server. The transparent use of a client, which is a characteristic of DACS Scheme, is failed. The transparent use of a client means that a client can be used continuously without changing setups when configuration change of the network system is done. The function which doesn't fail the transparent use of a client is needed. The mechanism of that function is shown in Figure 9. The changed point on network server side is shown as follows in comparison with existing DACS Scheme. SSH Server is located and activated, and communication except SSH is blocked. In Figure 9, DACS rules are sent from DACS Server to DACS Client (a). By DACS Client which accepts DACS rules, DACS rules are applied to DACS Control in DACS Client (b). The movement to here is same as existing DACS Scheme. After functional extension, as shown in (c) of

Figure 9, DACS rules are applied to DACS SControl. Communication control is performed in DACS SControl with the function of SSH. By adding the extended function, selecting the tunneled and encrypted or not tunneled and encrypted communication is done for each network service. When communication is not tunneled and encrypted, communication control is performed by DACS Control as shown in (d) of Figure 9. When communication is tunneled and encrypted, destination of the communication is changed by DACS Control to localhost as shown in (e) of Figure 9. After that, by DACS STCL, the communicating server is changed to the network server and tunneled and encrypted communication is sent as shown in (g) of Figure 9, which are realized by the function of port forwarding of SSH. In DACS rules applied to DACS Control, localhost is indicated as the destination of communication. In DACS rules applied to DACS SControl, the network server is indicated as the destination of communication. As the functional extension explained in the above, the function of tunneling and encrypting communication is realized in the state of being suitable for DACS Scheme, that is, with the transparent use of a client. Then, by changing the content of DACS rules applied to DACS Control and DACS SControl, it is realized to distinguish the control in the case of tunneling and encrypting or not tunneling and encrypting by a user unit. By tunneling and encrypting the communication for one network service from all users, and blocking the untunneled and decrypted communication for that network service, the function of preventing the communication for one network service from the client which DACS Client is not installed in is realized. Moreover, even if the communication to the network server from the client which DACS Client is not installed in is permitted, each user can select whether the communication is tunneled and encrypted or not. The function of preventing information interception is realized.

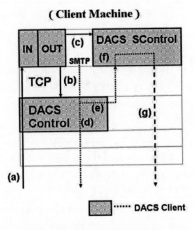

Figure 9. Extend Security Function.

5. Realization of New User Support

In this section, after problems of existing user support is described, new user supports realized by DACS Scheme is explained as an example to show the effectiveness of DACS Scheme.

5.1. Problems of Existing User Support

5.1.1. The problem on User Support for Changing Setups of Client

When the mail boxes located on one network server are relocated on the different network servers, some users must change setups of the client software. In this case, a notice of changing setups of the client is sent by E-mail, a homepage and a document announcement from a system administrator to each user. The user who accepted the notice usually changes setups of the client by oneself. When changing setups can not be done, the user inquires to the network management section. The system administrator replies those inquires through telephone. When the user can not change still, the system administrator goes to the place which the client exists and changes setups of the client. When the system administrator can change the communication server for same host name under the central control freely and easily, the user does not need to change setups of the client.

5.1.2. The problem for Coping with Annoying Communication

It is pointed that, much time and effort are spent to specify which client or user is transmitting annoying communication, when DHCP service is used. As an example of annoying communication, the communication which is sent from the client infected by virus is considered. In this case, the source IP address of annoying communication is specified first. Next, the client having that IP address is found out as the virus infection client by a user or system administrator, and identified which user used that client. The main point of this process is shown as following. When an IP address is dynamically managed using DHCP service, the IP address of the client may be changed according to the lease period of an IP address and the use situation of the client (the period to next use). Therefore, the IP address of the client is not necessarily grasped. As the result, after the source IP address of annoying communication is specified by the network management section, the client having that IP address must be specified among many clients by the user or system administrator. When this process for specifying the virus infection client is simplified, the burden for the user and system administrator is reduced.

As another example, the communication problem using UDP (User Datagram Protocol) such as streaming of the moving picture and the sound which may generate the congestion of the network is described. The congestion of the network becomes the cause of holding down the communication using TCP (Transmission Control Protocol). To cope with this problem, it is necessary to specify which user is using the client at that time. About this point, it can not be specified easily in the scheme of the conventional network. There is no guarantee that the user can certainly be specified. When the user can be specified just after capturing the annoying communication, it is easy to cope with it. Further, when it is possible for the system administrator to block the communication by intensive management of the client, annoying communication is able to be blocked temporarily without specifying the place where the client is physically. To cope with these problems described in the above, the new form of user support by DACS Scheme is examined.

5.2. New User Support

5.2.1. Support at Changing Setups of Client with DACS Scheme

When network configuration is changed, user support by DACS Scheme is compared with user support by Non-DACS Scheme, and an advantage of user support by DACS Scheme is described. User support processes after changing the network configuration are described in Figure10.

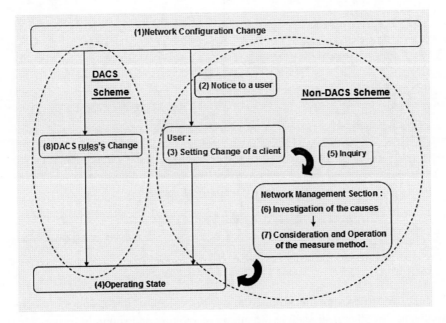

Figure 10. Process introducing DACS Scheme.

When DACS Scheme is not introduced, notification for changing setups is sent to a user in a laboratory (2) after changing the network configuration (1). It is sent by E-mail and a homepage or a document. The user who accepts that notification changes setups of a client (3). If there is no problem in changing setups of the client, it is enabled to start the operating (4). When it is not possible to change setups by some causes, the user inquires to the network management section (5). In the network section, investigation by hearing comprehension for the user or investigation in the field is done (6). If a cause is specified, the coping way are considered, and carried out (7). It is a burden for a system administrator to support each user for every inquiry. When DACS Scheme is introduced, a system administrator has only to change DACS rules (8) at the time of changing the network configuration. After changing DACS rules, communication control corresponding to new network configuration is started at a point in time when the user logs in to a client again (4). Because the system administrator with understanding the policy for using a laboratory network sets DACS rules, a trouble by a cause except an artificial factor such as missing setups of DACS rules does not occur. This process of user support is largely simplified in comparison with the process of user support by Non-DACS Scheme.

5.2.2. Coping with Annoying Communication by DACS Scheme

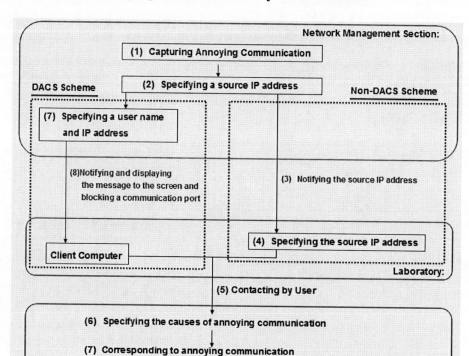

Figure 11. Change of User Support.

To cope with the communication from a virus infection client and the communication with annoyance to other user such as streaming of moving and sound, a system administrator needs to specify which user or client is transmitting the communication to. For example, when there is a direct cause in the client itself such as virus infection, the client must be specified. A user must be specified, when there is a direct cause in user oneself. When the IP address is managed dynamically by DHCP service, much time and effort is spent to specify the client or user. The coping process for annoying communication is described as shown in Figure11 and explained with an example of the user support for a laboratory. A characteristic of this mechanism is the next two processing on Web Server.

(a) User authentication is performed by user information.

(b) Information related to user is searched and extracted from data which is accumulated beforehand.

Processing of (a) is performed after processing of (5) in Figure11. This processing is necessary to perform processing of (b) and becomes essential so that Web Service premises anonymous user. Web page as Personal Portal is generated by the program such as CGI on the Web Server. Because the program is introduced by system administrator and can't usually be changed by a user, the Personal Portal can't always be easy to use for each user or customize for personal use. In this paper, to overcome this problem, two kinds of functions of Web Service based on DACS Scheme, which make each user creates Personal Portal freely and easily, were developed. By using these functions, when each different user inputs same URL on Web Browser, the different information for each user is searched and extracted from database or document medium, and displayed on Web Browser. However, in these functions, it is possible only to send and accept information by a user unit. Because it is necessary to send and accept information by a group unit and by all users unit, these functions are insufficient. In addition, these two kinds of functions are independent with each other. So, to use in actual network, these two kinds of functions need to be integrated as one service, and integrated interface needs to be brought to each user. Therefore, after extending these two kinds of functions of Web Service to send and accept information not only by a user unit, but also by a group unit and by all users unit, DACS Web Service, is proposed, which is realized as the result of having integrated these extended two kinds of functions of Web Service.

At first, annoying communication for other users is captured by communication detection through the mechanism such as F/W or IDS (1). Next, a source IP address of the annoying communication is acquired (2). To here, it is the same thing when DACS Scheme is introduced or not introduced. When DACS Scheme is not introduced, the process of user support is described in the following. Under using DHCP Service, if a whole network is divided into multiple subnetworks, and each subnetwork is assigned to each laboratory, a system administrator can manage scope of the IP address used in a laboratory. If not so, the system administrator can not manage it. In the case of the former, the IP address is notified to the laboratory (3), and the client transmitting the communication is specified (4). In the laboratory, because it is impossible to manage which client uses which IP address, the client is specified after investigating the network setups information of each client. It takes trouble very much. In the case of the latter, it is difficult to specify the client. This is because the system administrator can not know the laboratory using the IP address. Even if the system administrator can know it, because it is needed to investigate the network setups information of each client, it takes trouble very much. After the client is specified, the user of the laboratory contacts a network management section (5). In the situation that a laboratory cooperates with a network management section, the cause specification of annoying communication and coping with it are done (6). On the other hand, when DACS Scheme is introduced, source IP address of the annoying communication needs to be acquired (2) to specify the client first. When a user needs to be specified, a user name is specified from the IP address (7). When a user has a direct cause such as streaming of the moving picture and the sound, the message to notify abnormality is transmitted to the IP address of the client which a user logs in. If a client has a direct cause such as infection by virus, the message to notify abnormality is transmitted to the IP address of the client. The message is displayed in the screen of the client. At the same time, the used port by annoying communication is blocked (8). The user sees the message of the screen, and contacts the network management section (5). In the situation that a laboratory cooperates with a network management section, specification of annoying communication and coping with it are done (6). It is shown that DACS Scheme is effective at the following two points. The first point is that the client which transmits annoying communication is specified simply. The client which has a problem is specified by seeing the message of a screen at a glance. The second point is shown as follows. Because the influence to others is prevented by blocking a communication port of the client, time margin for the cause specification of annoying communication and the coping with it is generated effectively. When the urgent degree such as virus infection is high, DACS Scheme is particularly effective.

6. Conclusion

In this article, we explained the study of the DACS Scheme which is a network management scheme by use of communication control on a client. First, the basic principle and protocol of DACS Scheme are explained. Then, the security function for controlling the communications form the client where DACS CL is not located is explained. As a study to raise the effectiveness of DACS Scheme, new user support realized by DACS Scheme is explained. To be concrete, we explained the promotion of efficiency in user support at the time of network system's configuration change and measures method to the computer virus infection client. As a future plan of this study, after the implementation of DACS system to realize DACS Scheme, we would like to operate this system in practical network.

References

[1] S.K.Das,D.J.Harvey, and R.Biswas,"Parallel processing of adaptive meshes with load balancing," *IEEE Tran.on Parallel and Distributed Systems*, vol.12,No.12,pp.1269-1280,Dec 2002.

[2] M.E.Soklic,"Simulation of load balancing algorithms: a comparative study," *ACM SIGCSE Bulletin*, vol.34, No.4,pp.138-141,Dec 2002.

[3] J.Aweya, M.Ouellette,D.Y.Montuno,B.Doray, and K.Felske,"An adaptive load balancing scheme for web servers," *Int.,J.of Network Management.*,vol.12,No.1,pp.3-39,Jan/Feb 2002.

[4] C.Metz, "The latest in virtual private networks: part I," *IEEE Internet Computing*, Vol. 7, No. 1, pp. 87–91,2003.

[5] C.Metz, "The latest in VPNs: part II," *IEEE Internet Computing*, Vol. 8, No. 3, pp. 60–65, 2004.

[6] Y. Watanabe, K. Watanabe, E.Hirofumi, S.Tadaki,"A User Authentication Gateway System with Simple User Interface, Low Administration Cost and Wide Applicability," *IPSJ Journal*, Vol.42, No.12 pp.2802-2809,2001.

[7] S.Tadaki, E.Hirofumi,K. Watanabe, Y.Watanabe,"Implementation and Operation of Large Scale Network for User' Mobile Computer by Opengate," *IPSJ Journal* ,Vol.46, No.4 pp.922-929,2005.

[8] S.Jha, M.Hassan, "Java implementation of policy-based bandwidth management," *Int. J. Network management*, John Wiley&Sons, Vol.13, isuue.4, pp.249-258, July, 2003.

[9] G.M.Prerez, F.G.Skarmeta, S.Zeber, T.Symchych, "Dynamic Policy-Based Network Management for a Secure Coalition Environment," *IEEE Communications Magazine*, Vol.44, issue.11, pp.58-64, November, 2006.

[10] D.C.Verma, "Simplifying Network Administration Using Policy-Based Management," *IEEE Network*, Vol.16, issue.2, pp.20-26, March-April, 2002.

[11] M.Sugano, S.Tanaka, Y.Sakata, K.Oguma, N.Shiratori, "Application and Implementation of Policy Control Method "PolicyComputing" in Computer Networks," *IPSJ Journal*, Vol.42, No.2, 2001.

[12] K.Wakayama, Y.Decchi, J.Leng, A.Iwata, "A Remote User Authentication Method Using Fingerprint Matching," *IPSJ Journal*, Vol.44, No.2, pp.401-404, 2003.

[13] S.Seno, Y.Koui, T.Sadakane, N.Nakayama, Y.Baba, T.Shikama, "A Network Authentication System by Multiple Biometrics," *IPSJ Journal*, Vol.44, No.4, pp.1111-1120, 2000.

[14] http://www.nec.co.jp/univerge/solution/pack/quarantine/

[15] http://www.ntt-east.co.jp/business/solution/security/quarantine/index.html

[16] K.Odagiri, R.Yaegashi, M.Tadauchi, N.Ishii, "Efficient Network Management System with DACS Scheme : Management with communication control," *Int. J. of Computer Science and Network Security*, Vol.6, No.1, pp.30-36, January, 2006.

[17] K.Odagiri, R.Yaegashi, M.Tadauchi, N.Ishii, "Efficient Network Management System with DACS Scheme", Proc. of Int. Conf. on Networking and Services, Silicon Valley, USA, IEEE Computer Society, July, 2006.

[18] K.Odagiri, R.Yaegashi, M.Tadauchi, N.Ishii, "Secure DACS Scheme, "Journal of Network and Computer Applications," Elsevier. (in printing)

[19] K.Odagiri, R.Yaegashi, M.Tadauchi, N.Ishii, "Extended DACS Scheme implementing Security Function," *Proc. of Int. Conf. on Networking and Services*, Athens, Greece, IEEE Computer Society, June, 2007.

[20] K.Odagiri, R.Yaegashi, M.Tadauchi, N.Ishii, "New User Support in the University Network with DACS Scheme," *Int. J. of Interactive Technology and Smart Education.*

[21] K.Odagiri, R.Yaegashi, M.Tadauchi, N.Ishii, "Simplified Network Management with DACS Scheme," *Proc. of Int. Conf. on Networking and Services*, Athens, Greece, IEEE Computer Society, June, 2007.

[22] K.Odagiri, R.Yaegashi, M.Tadauchi, N.Ishii, "New Web Service Based on Extended DACS Scheme," Int. *J. of Computer Science and Network Security*,Vol.6, No.3,pp8-13,March,2006.

[23] K.Odagiri, R.Yaegashi, M.Tadauchi, N.Ishii, "New Function for Displaying Static Document Dynamically with DACS Scheme," *Int. J. of Computer Science and Network Security*,Vol.6,No.5,pp81-87,May,2006.

[24] K.Odagiri, R.Yaegashi, M.Tadauchi, N.Ishii, "Basic Portal System with the Function of Communication Control Every User,*" J. of Convergence Information Technology.*

[25] K.Odagiri, R.Yaegashi, M.Tadauchi, N.Ishii, "Free Information Usage System on the Network introducing DACS Scheme," *Proc of Int. Conf. on Internet and Web Applications and Services, Mauritius*, IEEE Computer Society, May, 2007.

[26] K.Odagiri, R.Yaegashi, M.Tadauchi, N.Ishii,, "Practical DACS Web Service for User's Free Portal Page Creation," *Proc of Int. Conf. on Web Services*, pp.952-959, July, 2007, Salt Lake City, Utah, USA, IEEE Computer Society, July, 2007.

In: Computer Security: Intrusion, Detection and Prevention   ISBN 978-1-60692-781-6
Editors: R. D. Hopkins and W. P. Tokere   © 2009 Nova Science Publishers, Inc.

Chapter 3

TRENDS, PROBLEMS AND MISCONCEPTIONS IN TESTING NETWORK INTRUSION DETECTION SYSTEMS' EFFECTIVENESS

*Agustin Orfila, Juan M. E. Tapiador and Arturo Ribagorda**
Computer Science Department, Universidad Carlos III de Madrid
28911 Leganes, Madrid, Spain

Abstract

Network Intrusion Detection Systems (NIDS) are hardware or software systems that are used to identify and respond to intrusions in computer networks. An intrusion is a deliberate or accidental unauthorized access to or activity against any of the elements of the network. Evaluation of how effective different intrusion detection technologies are becomes mandatory, in order to know which is the one that better fits in a particular scenario. Nevertheless this is not an easy task. This chapter reviews the main problems regarding testing effectiveness: the absence of standard test methodologies and metrics, the drawbacks of current datasets, the different requirements for testing different technologies, etc. These conditions made evaluation difficult not only for the industry but also for researchers. Scientific proposals are often naïvely compared. We focus on providing evidence of this situation by means of supporting examples. Some guidelines for the future are finally proposed.

Keywords: Network Intrusion Detection; effectiveness evaluation; dataset; metrics;

1 Introduction

Intrusion detection systems (IDS) are defined as software or hardware systems that automate the process of monitoring the events occurring in a computer system or network, analysing them for signs of security problems [1]. A generic model of intrusion detection comprises a set of functions: raw data sourcing, event detection, analysis, data storage and response. The analysis function is the one that has been more studied. It processes data from both event and data storage functions in order to provide a judgement on the input

*E-mail address:adiaz, jestevez, arturo@inf.uc3m.es

(e.g. state the event is intrusive or not). This judgement may feed the response fuction. Researchers focus on looking for algorithms to improve the effectiveness of the analysis module. Thus, testing becomes mandatory for comparison. However this is not an easy task and many times the proposals are naïvely compared. This situation happens because there is no consensus on the evaluation procedure and it is not straightforward to define one. In this chapter we review the main difficulties and misconceptions faced when evaluating IDS effectiveness and the possibilities to overcome them. The problems can be summarized in two groups. The first is the adoption of a common input for IDS testing. The issues comprehend the way a dataset is produced, updated and made public. The second faces how to measure the IDS effectiveness properly given a dataset. Thus, many open questions arise such as choosing a metric that takes into account the essential parameters for the problem at issue, finding the best operating point of an IDS, selecting a practical graphical representation or defining the testing procedures. Although extensive research has faced these questions, current proposals does not adopt any of them and continue providing their results with inherited methodologies from other fields (such as machine learning) in an ad-hoc manner. However, the inner features of intrusion detection demands a customized approximation to the problem. These features are, amongst others, a very low prevalence of attacks, a changing environment (new forms of attack constantly appearing) or the influence of an intruder to pervert evaluation results.

This chapter is organized as follows. First, the main problems for producing an evaluation dataset are exposed. Second, the main metrics and testing procedures found on the state of the art are summarized. Third, a discussion is done analysing numerical examples and putting them into the context of different metrics. Finally the main conclusions are shown.

2   Dataset and evaluation procedure

This section summarizes the main problems faced to produce, update and make public a dataset for intrusion detection effectiveness evaluation. As pointed out in [2] there are many challenges for IDS testing. Let us first review those related to produce a dataset for NIDS effectiveness evaluation. One is the difficulty to produce an appropriate dataset for both signature based and anomaly detectors. The results of testing signature based NIDS (S-NIDS) depends on the number of attack samples and how innovative they are. S-NIDS are effective with known attacks and innefective with novel forms of intrusion because a time is needed to create a new signature to model a novel attack. Thus, for S-NIDS the background traffic is only relevant for detecting false positives and they use to be few in these systems. Conversely, anomaly detectors need normal traffic to build their own models. They require a training phase where the input traffic is clean of attacks (what is not a trivial task) and a testing phase where the normal and abnormal inputs are mixed. Nevertheless, abnormal traffic must be properly documented in order to know if the NIDS is effective at detecting it (a similar situation happens with machine learning based NIDS). Another problem is to find a procedure to produce a dataset that can be publicly distributed, updatable and with a proven relationship with what is expectable in a real scenario. In order to achieve these goals, the first possibility is to record real traffic and analyse it manually. Thus, the traffic features would be ideal (at least as ideal as the scenario where the traffic was recorded) and it could be updatable periodically with new real traffic. However there are privacy and confidentiality problems with this approach. No institution wants to share their real data and the manual process to categorise traffic (intrusive, non intrusive) is not an easy task (because of the great amount of data to process and because of the difficulty of the forensic process itself). One possibility to overcome the privacy problem is to anonimize the traffic [3]. Nevertheless this filtering could eliminate important information for detection and it is always a controversial process. It is also difficult to guarantee that no private data is revealed after the anonimization process. An alternative is to simulate the traffic [4, 5]. Thus, no concerns about privacy have to be taken into account. In addition, the process become repeatable, controllable and documented. Nevertheless, drawbacks appear such as the cost of an in depth simulation and the impossibility to establish how similar the traffic is to the one expected in a real scenario. Questions arise such as the correspondence of the base rate of intrusions with those of a real operating environment or the possible artifacts introduced in the simulation that could help the IDS in the analysis process. Finally there is also a problem with the unit of analysis IDS use [6]. Each IDS analyses the data sources at a certain level (e.g. network layer, transport layer, application layer). Machine learning research proposals use to work at "connection record" level that is a representation of basic features of individual TCP connections, temporal traffic features computed using a two second time window and content features. The reason why many machine learning proposals make use of this particular data strucuture is because it is the basis of the well known KDD'99 dataset [7]. It was built for a machine learning contest [8] and it is based on the recorded traffic simulated on MIT/LL evaluation [4]. This variability on the units of analysis is a serious drawback for evaluation because, as it will be shown in the next section, the most important parameters to measure effectiveness critically depend on the unit of analysis. If different units are used, comparison become undefined. Some different units of analysis can be related (e.g. a TCP flow with the corresponding tcp packets) making conversion possible but this is not the typical case. In this respect, some authors present their results over different units of analysis [9] and it can be seen that NIDS effectiveness depends on it. Beyond this matter, some attacks are not fully characterized by a single event so detection on an event basis is not a well defined problem.

In practice, NIDS are usually tested on KDD'99 or MIT/LL public datasets (sometimes also on proprietary datasets). Many times these datasets are not used in their original form but by means of subsets produced after an ad-hoc filtering process (e.g.[10, 11]). Sometimes a random selection of instances is done and sometimes resampling of normal instances is fulfilled. Unfortunately, no standard procedures are followed making comparison difficult. Although these public benchmarks were produced ten years ago, they are still used due to the absence of new fully documented ones. Available new public traffic datasets [12, 13] lack the preprocessing and documentation phases needed to test IDS (i.e. labelling which packets denote intrusive behaviour) and most of them are anonymized to preserve data privacy. Furthermore, there are additional problems with MIT/LL dataset (and consequently with KDD'99) such as presenting statistically different charachteristics from real traffic, low traffic rates, relative uniform distribution of the four major attack categories, skewed distribution of victim hosts, and flat network topology [6, 14]. In addition, the percentage of attacks in KDD'99 is unrealisticly high (over 80%) both in the provided training and testing datasets. The reason of this high prevalence is that this dataset was built on the

Table 1: Prediction contingency matrix

		Event	
		$\neg I$	I
NIDS	$\neg A$	TN	FN
Report	A	FP	TP

scope of a machine learning contest where the capacity to distinguish between different attack categories was the main goal. The importance of providing a realistic attack base rate for the evaluation process (as explained in the next section) was not taken into account.

3   Metrics

First of all, let us define the main terms and relationships that are used for evaluating NIDS effectiveness. There are different ways to refer to the same concepts in the literature so it is important to adopt a common terminology. Let us suppose a NIDS produces reports on an event (E) basis. The possible reports considered are an alarm (A) or no alarm ($\neg A$). Similarly, let us assume that every event can be categorized as intrusive (I) or non intrusive ($\neg I$). Given a dataset with N events, a general contigency matrix of a NIDS has the form of Table 1, where $N = TP + TN + FP + FN$. Based on these values, accuracy, Hit rate (H), False alarm rate (F) and intrusion frequency are respectively given by $a = \frac{TP+TN}{N}$, $H = \frac{FP}{FN+TP}$, $F = \frac{FP}{TN+FP}$ and $p = \frac{FN+TP}{N}$.

Table 2 summarizes the main relationships, the equivalent terms found in IDS literature and a short explanation of their meaning. Accuracy ($TN + TP/N$) is a worthless measure for the field at issue due to the imbalance class problem. The intrusion base rate is typically very low (how low depends both on the unit of analysis and the scenario). Thus, a system that states that every event is non intrusive would achieve very good accuracy results but it is not at all a good detection system. Consequently other measures are provided to state IDS effectiveness. Most of the research on the analysis function of IDS just shows their results providing H and F (see for instance [15, 11]) and sometimes its graphical tradeoff -the receiver operating characteristic (ROC) [16]. Thus, when trying to compare two threshold IDS -that can be tuned to operate on different pairs (F, H)- (e.g. anomaly detectors), if one of the ROCs stands out the other then it can be stated that the corresponding IDS is more effective under any circumstance. However, if the ROCs crosses it cannot be stated which is more effective. Even in the first situation it would be desirable a way to measure how better is one over the other. In the same manner, non parametric IDS (e.g. signature detectors) can only operate on a single (F, H). If an IDS_1 operates on point (F_1, H_1) and IDS2 operates on (F_2, H_2) then IDS_1 overcomes IDS_2 if $F_1 < F_2$ and $H_1 > H_2$. Otherwise it cannot be stated anything about which is more effective from direct inspection of the ROC. In order to solve this situation other metrics are needed.

In this section, we review the main metrics proposed to measure IDS effectiveness (see Table 3). Once a metric is assumed, the best configuration of an IDS for certain defined conditions and the comparison of IDS become possible. Thus, the most effective IDS is the one that achieves a greatest result according to the metric, for the operating conditions con-

Table 2: Terminology used in this paper. For readibility, we will use the terms listed in the leftmost column

Term	Equivalent terms from IDS literature	Meaning
F	$P(A|\neg I), \alpha$	False positive rate. The probability that there is an alert, A, when there is no intrusion, $\neg I$
H	$P(A|I), 1 - \beta$, Recall	Hit rate (detection rate, or true positive rate). The probability that there is an alert, A, when there is no intrusion, I
FNR	$P(\neg A|I), \beta$	False negative rate. The probability that there is no alert, $\neg A$, when there is an intrusion, I
TNR	$P(\neg A|\neg I), 1 - \alpha$	True negative rate. The probability that there is no alert, $\neg A$, when there is no intrusion, $\neg I$
PPV	$P(I|A)$, "Bayesian detection rate", precision	Positive predictive value. The probability that an intrusion, I, is present when an IDS outputs an alarm, A
NPV	$P(\neg I|\neg A)$	Negative predictive value. The probability that there is no intrusion, $\neg I$, when an IDS does not output an alarm, $\neg A$
p	p(I), B	Intrusion prevalence or base rate. The probablity that there is an intrusion.

sidered. Several performance metrics have been introduced to measure IDS effectiveness. On the one hand the traditional approach to the problem is to compute H and F or PPV and NPV or even precision and recall. On the other hand the new trends are metrics like expected cost [17, 18], economic value [19] or intrusion detection capability [20]. Despite of their contribution to the analysis of IDS, the latter are still rarely applied in the literature when proposing a new analysis engine. As pointed out in [21] this is due to two main reasons. First, each metric is proposed in a different framework (e.g. decision theory, meteorology, information theory, etc.). Second, these metrics assume the knowledge of some uncertain parameters such as the likelihood of an attack, or the costs of responses or failed detections. Furthermore, these uncertain parameters can change during the operation of the IDS and this situation is not fully supported by the metrics. Next we are going to briefly compare the most relevant. Table 3 summarizes the formulas involved in each metric.

The expected cost (M) metric [17], based on decision theory, shows the dependancy of IDS effectiveness on H, F, p and misclassification costs (C_α, C_β). The costs are incurred when, on an event basis, a response is taken and no intrusion is present (C_α) or viceversa, no response is taken and there is an intrusion C_β. These costs and the base rate p depend on the scenario where the IDS is evaluated. The decision to respond or not against a suspicious event is based on the IDS report and on a decision model. Accordingly, a decision (to respond or not) can be taken against the detector report (if M is lower in such a case). The lower M is, the better the IDS is. For a given estimation of p and the cost tradeoff C, a threshold IDS would operate in the operating point (F, H) that minimizes M. For those IDS that can only operate in a single point (F, H), M would be a fixed value. The expected cost is not normalized and its main disadvantages are that C (that is assumed stationary) is

Table 3: Main metrics proposed to measure IDS effectiveness

Name of the metric	Formula	Explanation
Expected Cost (M)	$M = \min\{C(1-H)p, (1-F)(1-p)\} + \min\{CHp, F(1-p)\}$	C_β: cost of not responding to an intrusion C_α: cost of responding to no intrusion $C = \frac{C_\beta}{C_\alpha}$ ($C_\alpha = 1$ when reescaling)
Economic Value (V)	$V = \frac{M_{prob} - M}{M_{prob} - M_{per}}$	L = cost of not responding to an intrusion C = cost of responding $M_{prob} = \min\{p, \frac{C}{L}\}$ $M_{per} = \min\{p, \frac{C}{L}p\} = p\min\{1, \frac{C}{L}\}$ $M = \min\{(1-H)p, \frac{C}{L}((1-F)(1-p)+(1-H)p)\} + \min\{Hp, \frac{C}{L}(F(1-p)+Hp)\}$
Intrusion detection capability (C_{ID})	$(H(X) - H(X\|Y))/H(X)$	$H(X) = -p\log p - (1-p)\log(1-p)$ $H(X\|Y) = -(1-p)F\log\frac{(1-p)F}{(1-p)F+pH} - (1-p)(1-F)\log\frac{(1-p)(1-F)}{(1-p)(1-F)+p(1-H)}$

not an objective measure and it is hard to estimate. Nevertheless, sometimes it is better a rough estimation than no estimation at all as we will discuss in the next section.

Economic value (V) [19] is a normalized metric that measures the reduction in expected cost that an IDS provides over a system that works just based on the knowledge of p, and a cost ratio estimation. Thus, a decision maker that follows this metric should perform according to the IDS report and the decision model in order to maximize V. This decision model considers a response cost C if response actions are taken, regardless an intrusion takes place or not. Conversely, it considers a loss L if no actions are taken and an intrusion happens. Therefore, the costs are not just related with the decision maker mistakes (as in [17]) but directly with the economic consequences of taking actions or not. The main advantage of this approach is that the estimation of $\frac{C}{L}$ is more intuitive and meaningful for a decision maker than the corresponding tradeoff of [17]. Nevertheless an estimation is still needed with this model. It is also straightforward to know if an IDS is worthless and how far it is from a perfect one.

If we do not take any costs into account then the most interesting metric is C_{ID} [20] that is based on an information-theoretic approach. It is simple, sensitive to changes in F for small p values (typical of the intrusion detection field) and with a grounding in information theory. It provides an intrisic measure of IDS effectiveness. Nevertheless, its main drawbacks are two. First, this metric obscures the intuition that is to be expected when evaluating IDS effectiveness [21]. The meaning of the metric (the reduction of the uncertainty on the input to an IDS due to the own IDS capability) is difficult to quantify in practical values of interest such as H or F. Second, it does not take the costs into account (although an extension to support them is pointed out in [22]) what can lead to misleading conclusions.

It is important to note that all these works consider the problem of detection as a binary classification problem (to establish if an event is intrusive or not). However, the consequences of different kinds of attack are usually very different and this is not taken into account by these metrics. Nevertheless, they could be adapted to taxonomies of attacks that distinguish between different attack categories. Proposals that try to classify intrusions according to a taxonomy (e.g. MIT/LL/KDD'99 taxonomy) use to provide the results according to a contingency matrix that considers the attack categories (e.g. [10, 23]).

4 Discussion

Let us first analyze if expected cost, economic value and C_{ID} provide consistent results when a comparison is done. Thus, given two non parametric IDS, we want to analyze if one overcomes the other according to these three metrics. For instance, suppose that the base rate of the test dataset at issue is $p = \frac{25}{60618} = 4.12 * 10^{-4}$. IDS_1 can only operate on $(F_1, H_1) = (0.00779, 0.76)$ and IDS_2 on $(F_2, H_2) = (0.003598, 0.56)$. Directly from (F, H) inspection it is not possible to know which IDS is better because $H_1 > H_2$ and also $F_1 > F_2$. In these conditions, C_{ID} for IDS_1 is 0.3555 and C_{ID} for IDS_2 is 0.2403. Therefore, according to C_{ID}, IDS_1 would clearly overcome IDS_2. However, according to the economic value metric, IDS_2 stands out IDS_1 for $0.0194 < \frac{C}{L} < 0.061$. For instance if $\frac{C}{L} = 0.04$, then $V(IDS_1) = 0$ and $V(IDS_2) = 0.197$. This means that, for this cost relationship, IDS_2 has a value that is almost 20% of the perfect detector while IDS_1 is worthless. An explanatory graphical representation is shown in Figure 1. Analogously, according to the expected cost metric, IDS_2 would also overcome IDS_1 for $17 < C < 50.8$.

From this example we can see that excluding costs may lead to uncertain statements such as concluding that, given a base rate, an IDS overcomes another. A similar problem appears to tune a threshold IDS to its best operating point. In order to know which of the possible operating pairs (F, H) is the best one for a given operating environment, costs play an important role. Imagine, for instance, an IDS that could be tuned to operate on (F_1, H_1) or (F_2, H_2). Then, in order to tune it properly a cost estimation becomes mandatory, as can be deduced from the above disccusion.

It is also important to discuss about the value of p. The previous analysis has considered a fixed value for it. Given a dataset, it has a characteristic p. Nevertheless, in a real scenario the prevalence of attacks p is not going to be exactly the same as the one considered in evaluation conditions and it will be difficult to estimate. Unfortunately, all the metrics depend on p. In fact, there is a new challenge we have not remarked yet in this chapter. An intruder could try to modify, up to a certain extent, the base rate p (e.g. by launching several port scans) in order to distort the conclusions obtained during the evaluation phase. Thus, the evaluation statements would become less useful because they did not take into account an adaptive adversary model. A formal framework for reasoning about how to evaluate IDS effectiveness against adversaries has been recently proposed [21]. The intruder can modify the base rate p by controlling the frequency of attacks. In order to make the evaluation process more robust, they proposed to establish that the best IDS is the one that better performs regarding an adaptive intruder. The solution of a zero-sum game between the

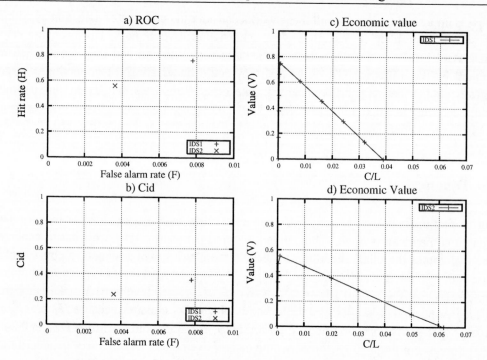

Figure 1: Comparison of the effectiveness of two IDS for a given attack base rate. a) From ROC space is not possible to establish which IDS is more effective. b) C_{ID} metric states that IDS_1 overcomes IDS_2 c) and d) plots show that the most effective IDS depends on the cost relationship

intruder and the IDS provides the new robust better operating point. The main problem of this approach is the need to estimate how much an intruder can modify p.

Finally graphical representations may help the IDS evaluator. The main proposed representations for the field at issue are: the ROC, the value curves and the intrusion detection operating characteristic (IDOC) [21]. As discussed, two are the problems of the ROC. First, it is not possible to know the best operating point directly from it (the costs are not represented). A possible fix to this problem is to use isoline projections onto the ROC (a geometric approach) according to a cost metric [21]. Second, it does not take into account modifications in p. An alternative to ROC curves is to use value curves [19] that represent the economic value vs. $\frac{C}{L}$. As a consequence, there is a curve for each operating point (F, H) and the costs conditions are directly reflected. Once again the problem is that this representation does not take into account (graphically) the changes in p. Finally the intrusion detection operating characteristic (IDOC) represents H vs. PPV for different values of p. Authors claim that the tradeoffs of IDOC are easier to interpret than the tradeoffs of other metrics. The main advantage of this proposal is the possibility of graphically represent different p values in a single plot. The main drawback is that costs and F are not represented explicitly. An obvious conclusion from the previous analysis is that these representations are complementary and they all should be used for an in depth analysis of IDS effectiveness.

It is important to note that there is no standard methodology to test NIDS effectiveness even when a dataset is assumed. Research proposals use ad-hoc procedures. Let us summarize some of the open questions that need to be faced in addition to the election of the dataset and the evaluation metric. First, how to filter a dataset to test the IDS under different operating conditions. Second, how to partionate the database to produce training data and test data for those IDS that need them. In order to validate results, the well known k-fold cross validation, typically used in machine learning, does not accomodate to the intrusion detection problem (although some researchers use it, e.g. [24]). The reason is that, in the field at issue, test conditions should be different in nature from training conditions because new forms of network intrusion constantly appear and this should be reflected in the evaluation procedures. Furthermore, the prevalence of attacks in training and test datasets should be different because it is an expectable situation that the evaluation conditions are different from those expected on a real scenario. An assessment environment for anomaly NIDS has been recently proposed to promote a standard methodology [25] on proprietary datasets. They propose to partition the dataset in three. The first partition would be used for the training set and it must be attack free while the second and the third would compose, respectively, the testing set and the validation set (which must contain attack free and some labeled attacks). They promote the use of the testing subset to tune the IDS and the validation dataset (with different forms of attack from test dataset) to test the NIDS effectiveness.

5   Conclusion

NIDS effectiveness evaluation is a very difficult and multifactorial problem. This chapter has reviewed the main handicaps and misconceptions that a serious evaluation faces as well as the recent advances achieved. The main improvements are related to providing better metrics that fit this particular field. Contrary, the main open questions relate to establish an evaluation framework where a standard methodology is applied. An in-depth study of how to face the unit (or units) of analysis problem is still needed. New documented datasets with different realistic frequency of attacks should be produced, updated and made public. A good simulation framework is probably the best option because the dataset is then under control and it can be fully documented and distributed lacking privacy problems. Once a dataset is considered, a standard methodology should be established to test NIDS under different operating conditions. Results should be reported with more than one of the proposed metrics because each one focuses in a different aspect and a first read can lead to erroneous conclusions. Accordingly, it is also advisable that results are graphically represented under different operating conditions. In addition, it is still an open question to state if NIDS that achieve good results over well-known datasets would also achieve a good behaviour under a real scenario. Similarly, an adversary model that tries to defeat the evaluation results should also be studied deeply in the future to guarantee the robustness of the evaluation process.

References

[1] R. Bace, P. Mell, Nist special publication on intrusion detection system, Tech. rep., NIST (National Institute of Standards and Technology), special Publication 800-31

(2001).

[2] P. Mell, V. Hu, R. Lippman, J. Haines, M. Zissman, An overview of issues in testing intrusion detection, national Institute of Standards and Technologies. Internal report 7007 (2003).

[3] R. Pang, M. Allman, V. Paxson, J. Lee, The devil and packet trace anonymization, SIGCOMM Computer Communications Reviews 36 (1) (2006) 29–38.

[4] R. Lippmann, D. Fried, I. Graf, J. Haines, K. Kendall, D. McClung, D. Weber, S. Webster, D. Wyschogrod, R. Cunningham, M. Zissman, Evaluating intrusion detection systems: The 1998 DARPA off-line intrusion detection evaluation, in: Proceedings of the DARPA Information Survivability Conference and Exposition, IEEE Computer Society Press, Los Alamitos, California, USA, 2000.

[5] H. G. Kayacik, N. Zincir-Heywood, Generating representative traffic for intrusion detection system benchmarking, in: Proceedings of the 3rd Annual Communication Networks and Services Research Conference, CNSR '05, IEEE Computer Society, Washington, DC, USA, 2005, pp. 112–117.

[6] J. McHugh, Testing intrusion detection systems: a critique of the 1998 and 1999 DARPA intrusion detection system evaluations as performed by lincoln laboratory, ACM Transactions on Information and System Security 3 (4) (2000) 262–294.

[7] C. Elkan, Results of the KDD'99 classifier learning contest, http://www-cse.ucsd.edu/users/elkan/clresults.html (September 1999).

[8] C. Elkan, Results of the KDD'99 classifier learning, ACM SIGKDD Explorations Newsletter 1 (2) (2000) 63–64.

[9] K. Wang, S. J. Stolfo, Anomalous payload-based network intrusion detection, in: Proceedings of Recent Advances in Intrusion Detection, RAID '04, Sophia Antipolis, French Riviera Francesa, France, 2004, pp. 203–222.

[10] C. Tsang, S. Kwong, H. Wang, Genetic-fuzzy rule mining approach and evaluation of feature selection techniques for anomaly intrusion detection, Pattern Recognition 40 (9) (2007) 2373–2391.

[11] Y. Li, L. Guo, An active learning based TCM-KNN algorithm for supervised network intrusion detection, Computers & Security 26 (7-8) (2007) 459–467.

[12] P. A. Gutierrez, A. Bulanza, M. Dabrowski, B. Kaskina, J. Quittek, C. Schmoll, A. V. F. Strohmeier, K. Zsolt, Mome: An advanced measurement meta-repository., in: Proceedings of 3rd International Workshop on Internet Performance, Simulation, Monitoring and Measurement. IPS-MoMe 2005, Warsaw, Poland, 2005.

[13] Community resource for archiving wireless data at dartmouth (crawdad), http://crawdad.cs.dartmouth.edu/ (2008).

[14] M. V. Mahoney, P. K. Chan, An analysis of the 1999 darpa/lincoln laboratory evaluation data for network anomaly detection., in: Proceedings of the Sixth International Workshop on Recent Advances in Intrusion Detection, Pittsburgh, EE.UU, 2003, pp. 220–237.

[15] M. S. Abadeh, J. Habibi, C. Lucas, Intrusion detection using a fuzzy genetics-based learning algorithm, Journal of Network and Computer Applications 30 (1) (2007) 414–428.

[16] G. Folino, C. Pizzuti, G. Spezzano, GP ensemble for distributed intrusion detection systems, in: Proceedings of the Third International Conference on Advances in Pattern Recognition, ICAPR 2005, Vol. 3686 of Lecture Notes in Computer Science, Springer, 2005, pp. 54–62.

[17] J. E. Gaffney, J. W. Ulvila, Evaluation of intrusion detectors: A decision theory approach, in: Proceedings of the IEEE Symposium on Security and Privacy, SP '01, IEEE Computer Society, Washington, DC, USA, 2001, pp. 50–.

[18] J. W. Ulvila, J. E. Gaffney, Evaluation of intrusion detection systems, Journal of Research of the National Institute of Standards and Technology 108 (6) (2003) 453–473.

[19] A. Orfila, J. Carbó, A. Ribagorda, Autonomous decision on intrusion detection with trained BDI agents, Computer Communications 31 (9) (2008) 1803–1813.

[20] G. Gu, P. Fogla, D. Dagon, W. Lee, B. Skorić, Measuring intrusion detection capability: an information-theoretic approach, in: Proceedings of the 2006 ACM Symposium on Information, computer and communications security, ASIACCS '06, ACM, New York, NY, USA, 2006, pp. 90–101.

[21] A. A. Cárdenas, J. S. Baras, K. Seamon, A framework for the evaluation of intrusion detection systems, in: SP '06: Proceedings of the 2006 IEEE Symposium on Security and Privacy, IEEE Computer Society, Washington, DC, USA, 2006, pp. 63–77.

[22] G. Gu, P. Fogla, D. Dagon, W. Lee, B. Skorić, An information-theoretic measure of intrusion detection capability, Tech. rep., GIT-CC-05-10, College of Computing, Georgia Tech, Atlanta, Georgia, USA (2005).

[23] D. Tian, Y. Liu, B. Li, A distributed hebb neural network for network anomaly detection., in: Proceedings of the 5th International Symposium on Parallel and Distributed Processing and Applications, ISPA 2007, Vol. 4742 of Lecture Notes in Computer Science, Springer, 2007, pp. 314–325.

[24] D. D. J. Gomez, Evolving fuzzy classifiers systems with genetic algorithms and application to network intrusion detection, Proceedings of the 2002 IEEE Workshop on Information Assurance, United States Military Academy, West Point, NY, 2002.

[25] M. Bermúdez-Edo, R. Salazar-Hernández, J. E. Díaz-Verdejo, P. Garcia-Teodoro, Proposals on assessment environments for anomaly-based network intrusion detection

systems., in: J. López (Ed.), First International Workshop Critical Information Infrastructures Security, CRITIS 2006, Vol. 4347 of Lecture Notes in Computer Science, Springer, Samos, Greece, 2006, pp. 210–221.

In: Computer Security: Intrusion, Detection and Prevention   ISBN: 978-1-60692-781-6
Editors: R. D. Hopkins and W. P. Tokere   © 2009 Nova Science Publishers, Inc.

Chapter 4

RECONFIGURABLE HARDWARE IN MODERN SECURITY SYSTEMS

Issam Damaj[1], Youssef Iraqi[2] and Safaa Kasbah[3]

Dhofar University, P.O. Box 2509, 211 Salalah, Oman

Abstract

The rapid progress and advancement in electronic chips technology provides a variety of new implementation options for system engineers. The choice varies between the flexible programs running on a general purpose processor (GPP) and the fixed hardware implementation using an application specific integrated circuit (ASIC). Many other implementation options present, for instance, a system with a RISC processor and a DSP core. Other options include graphics processors and microcontrollers. Specialist processors certainly improve performance over general-purpose ones, but this comes as a quid pro quo for flexibility. Combining the flexibility of GPPs and the high performance of ASICs leads to the introduction of reconfigurable computing (RC) as a new implementation option with a balance between versatility and speed.

Field Programmable Gate Arrays (FPGAs), nowadays are important components of RC-systems, have shown a dramatic increase in their density over the last few years. For example, companies like Xilinx and Altera have enabled the production of FPGAs with several millions of gates, such as, the Virtex-2 Pro and the Stratix-2 FPGAs. Considerable research efforts have been made to develop a variety of RC-systems. Research prototypes with fine-grain granularity include Splash, DECPeRLe-1, DPGA and Garp. Examples of systems with coarse-grain granularity are RaPiD, MorphoSys, and RAW. Many other systems were also developed, for instance, rDPA, MATRIX, REMARC, DISC, Spyder and PRISM.

The focus of this chapter is on introducing the use of reconfigurable computers in modern security applications. The chapter investigates the main reasons behind the adoption of RC-systems in security. Furthermore, a technical survey of various implementations of security algorithms under RC-systems is included laying common grounds for comparisons. In addition, this chapter mainly presents case studies from cryptography implemented under RC-systems.

---

[1] E-mail address: i_damaj@du.edu.om; With the Dept. of Electrical and Computer Engineering
[2] E-mail address: y_iraqi@du.edu.om; With the Dept. of Computer Science
[3] E-mail address: s_kasbah@du.edu.om; With the Foundation Program

1. Introduction

The rapid progress and advancement in electronic chips technology provides a variety of new implementation options for system engineers. The choice varies between the flexible programs running on a general purpose processor (GPP) and the fixed hardware implementation using an application specific integrated circuit (ASIC). Many other implementation options present, for instance, a system with a RISC processor and a DSP core. Other options include graphics processors and microcontrollers. Specialist processors certainly improve performance over general-purpose ones, but this comes as a quid pro quo for flexibility. Combining the flexibility of GPPs and the high performance of ASICs leads to the introduction of reconfigurable computing (RC) as a new implementation option with a balance between versatility and speed.

GPPs are programmed entirely through software. GPPs have wide applicability; nevertheless they may not match the computational needs of many applications. ASICs are custom designed for particular applications. The architecture of an ASIC exploits intrinsic characteristics of an applications algorithm that lead to a high performance. However, the direct architecture algorithm mapping restricts the range of applicability of ASIC-based systems. ASICs provide precise function needed for a specific task. The designer, by synchronizing each ASIC to execute a job, can produce chips that are fast, cheap and consume less power than programmable or general-purpose processors.

Along with trying to find the right balance between versatility and speed, designers have to face the cost constraint too. In addition to the cost of manufacturing several ASICs, another cost is the cost of design. Since a well designed ASIC can solve a certain problem but not a slightly modified problem, efforts to design the new ASIC cannot make use of all the effort spent on the old ASIC since it is too highly customized to be reused. Thus, the effort expended on the design of an ASIC is almost lost when designing other ASIC, even those which performance of a closely related task.

With reconfigurable computing (RC), a new computation paradigm has emerged over the last decade, which intents to fill the gap between conventional microprocessors and application-specific integrated circuits (ASICs) [1]. All reconfigurable systems share the same basic idea: to benefit from programmable logic, which allows to dynamically adapting the system's functionality to the requirements of the running application. The most popular devices, which actually enabled reconfigurable computing, are Field-programmable Gate Arrays (FPGAs), which were introduced in the mid eighties. Many approaches of reconfigurable systems have been proposed in recent years; some of them are known as hybrids, which combine reconfigurable hardware with a processor core such as the MorphoSys reconfigurable system designed at the University of California Irvine (UCI).

The focus of this chapter is introducing reconfigurable computers as modern supercomputing architectures. The chapter also investigates the main reasons behind the current advancement in the development of RC-systems. Furthermore, a technical survey of various RC-systems is included laying common grounds for comparisons. In addition, this chapter mainly presents case studies implemented under the MorphoSys RC-system. The selected case studies belong to different areas of application, such as, computer graphics, information coding, and signal processing. Parallel versions of the studied algorithms are developed to match the topologies supported by the MorphoSys. Performance evaluation and results analyses are included for implementations with different characteristics.

2. Reconfigurable Computing Systems

2.1. History of Reconfigurable Computing

The first descriptions of computing automata capable of reconfiguration were put forward by John von Neumann in a series of lectures and unfinished manuscripts dating back to the late 40's and early 50's. After the death of von Neumann in 1957, his works on self-reproducing automata were collected and edited by Arthur Burks, who published them in 1966. Although von Neumann is generally regarded as the main developer of the conventional serial model of computing, it seems obvious that during the last years of his life, he was more interested in more complicated computing automata. The earliest electronic computers were built with error-prone vacuum tube technology. In 1959, Jack Kilby invented the monolithic integrated circuit at Texas Instruments, but it was not until the introduction of Intel's 4004 microprocessor that general-purpose computers began to be integrated on the same silicon chip.

In 1963, Gerald Estrin of University of California at Los Angeles proposed a variable structure computer system to achieve performance gains in a variety of computational asks [2]. The central idea was to combine both fixed and variable structure computer organizations, where the variable subsystem could be reorganized into a variety of problem-oriented special purpose configurations.

The first suggestion for a programmable logic device is due to Sven Wahlstrom, who in 1967 proposed the inclusion of additional gates to customize an array of integrated circuitry. However, the silicon "real estate" was an extremely scarce resource in those days. In 1967, Robert Minnick published a survey of microcellular research. He described both fixed cell-function arrays and variable cell-function arrays. In fixed cell-function arrays the switching function of each cell remained fixed, and only the interconnections between cells were programmable. In the case of variable cell-function arrays, the function produced by each cell could also be determined by parameter selection.

In the 70's, interest in and the corresponding financial support for non-serial forms of computation seems to have tapered off. This was most probably caused by the introduction of the first microprocessor - the famous 4004 by Intel - in 1971 and the ever growing number and scope of applications enabled by the expanding market of microprocessors and microcontrollers.

In the eighties, there was a revived interest in both systolic and parallel architectures. This interest was inspired partly by the advances in semiconductor integration technology and the evolution of system design concepts —the seminal work on Very Large Scale Integration (VLSI) design by Carver Mead and Lynn Conway was published in 1980 and partly by new and more demanding applications of supercomputing. An interesting design combining parallelism with reconfigurability was the Texas Reconfigurable Array Computer (TRAC) [3]. In the TRA project, reconfigurability meant the reprogramming of interconnections between individual computing elements.

In the late eighties and early nineties, the first platforms for reconfigurable computing were built. One of the first such platforms was designed at Digital Equipment Corporation's (DEC) Paris Research Laboratory (PRL) and was called Programmable Active Memory (PAM) [4]. The speedups achieved by the PAM project were very impressive and as similar results were reported by other research groups at approximately the same time, one could say that reconfigurable computing had passed its first test. This was also realized by two influential engineering societies, the Association for Computing Machinery (ACM) and the Institute of Electrical and Electronics Engineers (IEEE). These engineering societies began sponsoring two annual conference series about the applications of FPGAs, namely the ACM/SIGDA International Symposium on Field-Programmable Gate Arrays and the IEEE Symposium on FPGA-Based Custom Computing Machines. In Europe, the first International Workshop on Field-Programmable Logic and Applications was held in 1991. Reconfigurable computing would not be possible without the advances in electronics, because large FPGA circuits have enormous silicon overhead; for example a programmable logic device with 50000 usable gates may have well over a million transistors. This demonstrates that the FPGA market has benefited tremendously from advances in semiconductor manufacturing technology.

Xilinx, which was founded in 1984, introduced the world's first FPGA in 1985. Being the first in the FPGA market, Xilinx continued to dominate it well into the nineties, but in recent years Altera Corporation has increased its market share substantially, due to the popularity of its new SRAM -based FPGAs, the FLEX 8000 and FLEX 10K family. The convergence of the theoretical path and the technological path in the nineties may mark the beginning of a promising era for reconfigurable computing. Many influential industry observers feel, that the promises of reconfigurable computing are not just superficial media hype, but that there are real advantages to be gained by applying reconfigurable computing.

2.2. Field Programmable Gate Arrays

FPGAs are a hybrid device between PALs and Mask-Programmable Gate Arrays (MPGAs). Like PALs, they are fully electrically programmable, and they can be customized nearly instantaneously. Like MPGAs they can implement very complex computations on a single chip, with millions of gates devices currently in production. These devices have opened up completely new avenues in high-performance computation, forming the basis of reconfigurable computing. Most current FPGAs are SRAM -programmable. This means that SRAM bits are connected to the configuration points in the FPGA, and programming the SRAM bits configures the FPGA. Thus, these chips can be programmed and reprogrammed as easily as a standard static RAM. Here the programming bit will turn on a routing connection when it is configured with a true value, allowing a signal to flow from one wire to another, and will disconnect these resources when the bit is set to false. With a proper interconnection of these elements, which may include millions of routing choice points within a single device, a rich routing network can be created.

Xilinx, one of the major manufacturers of FPGAs defines them as high density Application Specific Integrated Circuits (ASICs) combining the logic integration of custom Very Large Scale Integration (VLSI) with the time to market and cost advantages of standard products [5].

Another major producer Lucent also stresses the versatility of the FPGA in its publication and of the time to market benefits. In the beginning FPGAs were mostly looked at as being of importance for rapid prototyping of circuits which would later be hardwired and thus of being a design tool to aid profitability rather than being of use directly in applications. That is changing as chips become available with higher gate counts on tools and faster routing and placing tools becoming available [6].

Utilizing high-level programming languages allows a complete picture of structure and functionality of the whole circuit is built up via a text file that is then fed through the appropriate software to produce a layout of gates, known as a net list, and downloaded to the FPGA. This is where the advantages of a system based around FPGAs for rapid prototyping is seen.

2.3. Reconfigurable Systems Generalities

Reconfigurable hardware can be used to provide reconfigurable functional units within a host processor. This allows for a traditional programming environment with the addition of custom instructions that may change over time. The reconfigurable units execute as functional units controlled by a main microprocessor. Registers are used to hold the input and output operands. Thus, the basic architecture of comprises a software programmable core processor and a reconfigurable hardware component. The core processor executes sequential tasks of the application and controls data transfers between the programmable hardware and data memory. Generally, the reconfigurable hardware is dedicated to exploitation of parallelism available in the applications algorithm. This hardware typically consists of a collection of interconnected reconfigurable elements. Both the functionality of the elements and their interconnection is determined through a special configuration program called the context.

State of the art RC-systems are of different architectures. A general classification could be viewed in terms of 4 main categories: granularity, depth of programmability, reconfigurability, and interface coupling. We note at this point that more detailed taxonomies are presented in [7, 8]. These 4 main categories are defined as follows:

2.3.1. Granularity

System granularity is defined by the internal structure of the reconfigurable elements. Computation blocks within the reconfigurable hardware vary from system to system. Each unit of computation can be as simple as a 3-input look up table (LUT), or as complex as a 4-bit ALU. This difference in block size is commonly referred to as the granularity of the logic block. A 3-bit LUT is an example of a very fine grained computational element, and a 4-bit ALU is an example of a quite coarse grained unit. Each element operates at the bit level implementing a Boolean function or a finite-state machine. The finer grained blocks are useful for bit-level manipulations, while the coarse grained blocks are better optimized for standard datapath applications. Several reconfigurable systems use a medium-sized granularity of logic block. A number of these architectures operate on two or more 4-bit wide data words. Examples of fine-grain reconfigurable systems are Splash and DECPeRLe-1, and Matrix is an example of a coarse-grain reconfigurable system.

2.3.2. Depth of Programmability

In terms of depth of programmability, a reconfigurable system may have a singlecontext or multiplecontexts. For single-context systems only one configuration program context may be resident in the system. In this case the systems functionality is limited to the context currently loaded. On the contrary, in multiple-context systems, several contexts can be resident in the system at once. This allows execution of different tasks simply by changing the operating context.

2.3.3. Reconfigurability

Reconfigurability pertains to the ability of the system to overlap execution with loading with new context. In statically reconfigurable systems, reconfiguration of the programmable hardware can occur only if the current execution is interrupted or when it finishes. On the other hand, in dynamically reconfigurable systems reconfiguration can be done concurrently with execution. The interface coupling of a reconfigurable system refers to the level of integration of the core processor and the reconfigurable hardware.

Frequently, the areas of a program that can be accelerated through the use of reconfigurable hardware are too numerous or complex to be loaded simultaneously onto the available hardware. For these cases, it is helpful to use dynamically RC-systems to swap different configurations in and out of the reconfigurable hardware as they are needed during program execution. Accordingly, the run-time reconfigurability is more likely to lead to an overall improvement in performance.

2.3.4. Interface Coupling

An RC-system is tightly-coupled if the core processor and the programmable component reside in the same chip. The system is loosely-coupled, if core processor and programmable logic are implemented as separate devices.

In loosely-coupled systems, an attached reconfigurable processing unit behaves as if it is an additional processor in a multiprocessor system. The host processor's data cache is invisible to the attached reconfigurable processing unit. Thus, a higher delay exists in communication between the host processor and the reconfigurable hardware. Such as, when communicating configuration information, input data, and results. However, this type of reconfigurable hardware does allow for a great deal of computation independence, by shifting large chunks of a computation over to the reconfigurable hardware. The most loosely-coupled form of reconfigurable hardware is that of an external standalone processing unit. This type of reconfigurable hardware communicates infrequently with a host processor. This model is similar to that of networked workstations, where processing may occur for very long periods of time without a great deal of communication.

Each of the addressed styles has distinct benefits and drawbacks. The tighter the integration of the reconfigurable hardware, the more frequently it can be used within an application or set of applications due to a lower communication overhead. The more loosely coupled styles allow for greater parallelism in program execution, but suffer from higher communications overhead.

2.4. Reconfigurable Systems

There has been considerable research effort to develop a variety of RC-systems. Research prototypes with fine-grain granularity include Splash [9], DECPeRLe-1 [10], DPGA [11] and Garp[12]. Array processors with coarse-grain granularity, such as rDPA [13], MATRIX [14], and REMARC [15] form another class of reconfigurable systems. Other systems with coarse-grain granularity include MorphoSys [16], RaPiD [17], and RAW [18]. Other reconfigurable systems with a core control processor and FPGAs as the reconfigurable part are DISC [19], Spyder [20], and PRISM [21]. Other systems include the PipeRench [22].

The Splash and DECPeRLe-1 computers were among the first research efforts in reconfigurable computing. Splash, a linear array of processing elements with limited routing resources, is useful mostly for linear systolic applications. DECPeRLe-1 is organized as a two-dimensional array of 16 FPGAs with more extensive routing. Both systems are fine-grained, with remote interface, single configuration and static reconfigurability.

rDPA, The reconfigurable data-path architecture (rDPA) consists of a regular array of identical data-path units (DPUs). Each DPU consists of an ALU, a micro-programmable control and four registers. The rDPA array is dynamically reconfigurable and scalable. The ALUs are intended for parallel and pipelined implementation of complete expressions and statement sequences. The configuration is done through mapping of statements in high-level languages to rDPA using DPSS (Data Path Synthesis System).

MATRIX is an array of 8-bit basic units (BUs), ALU-multiplication unit and control logic interconnected through a hierarchy of three levels. MATRIX aims to unify resources for instruction storage and computation. The basic unit (BU) can serve either as a memory or a computation unit. The 8-bit BUs are organized in an array, and each BU has a 256-word memory, ALU-multiply unit and reduction control logic. The interconnection network has a hierarchy of three levels and it can deliver up to 10 GOPS (Giga-operations/s) with 100 BUs when operating at 100 MHz.

REMARC consists of a reconfigurable coprocessor, which has a global control unit for 64 programmable blocks (nano-processors). Each 16-bit nano-processor has a 32 entry instruction RAM, a 16-bit ALU, 16 entry data RAM, instruction register, and several registers for program data, input data and output data. The interconnection is two-level (2D mesh and global buses across rows and columns). The global control unit (1024 instruction RAM with data and control registers) controls the execution of the nano-processors and transfers data between the main processor and nano-processors. This system performs well for multimedia applications, such as MPEG encoding and decoding (though it is not specified if it satisfies the real-time constraints).

RaPiD is a linear array (8 to 32 cells) of functional units, configured to form a linear computation pipeline. Each array cell has an integer multiplier, three ALUs, registers and local memory-segmented buses are used for efficient utilization of interconnection resources. It achieves performance close to its peak 1.6 GOPS for applications such as FIR filters or motion estimation.

The Reconfigurable Architecture Workstation (RAW) is a set of replicated tiles, where each tile contains a simple RISC processor, some bit-level reconfigurable logic and some memory for instructions and data. Each RAW tile has an associated programmable switch, which connects the tiles in a wide-channel point-to-point interconnect. When tested on benchmarks ranging from encryption, sorting, to FFT and matrix operations, it provided gains up to 100 times, as compared to a Sun SparcStation 20.

The Dynamically Programmable Gate Arrays (DPGA) is a fine-grained prototype system that use traditional 4-input lookup tables as the basic processing elements. DPGA supports rapid run-time reconfiguration.

Garp is a loosely coupled system with fine granularity. Garp has rows of blocks, which are like the CLBs of the Xilinx 4000 FPGA series. Garp architecture has more than 24 columns of blocks, whilst the number of rows is implementation dependant. The blocks operate on 2-bit data. There are vertical and horizontal block-to-block wires for data movement within the array. Separate memory buses move information (data as well as configuration) in and out of the array. Speedups ranging from 2 to 24 times are obtained for applications, such as encryption, image dithering and data sorting.

MorphoSys: Morphing System features a novel architecture for reconfigurable computing systems. The MorphoSys is primarily targeted to applications with inherent parallelism, high regularity, word-level granularity, and computations with intensive nature. Some examples of such applications are video compression, image processing, graphics acceleration, and security.

The first Processor Reconfiguration through Instruction-Set Metamorphosis (PRISM-I) consists of a board with four Xilinx 3090's plugged into a host system based around a Motorola 68010 system. A C-language-like compiler was created for PRISM-I to automatically translate subroutines to be mapped onto the reconfigurable hardware. Compiled programs run partly on the host processor and partly on the attached FPGA. The second prototype, PRISM-2, brought the host processor and FPGAs closer together, attaching an AMD Am29050 directly to three Xilinx 4010's.

Spyder extended a custom processor with three Xilinx 4010 FPGAs acting as reconfigurable execution units. With Spyder, the programmer is responsible for dividing a program between the main processor and the reconfigurable units and programming each in a special subset of C++ programming language.

DISC - the Dynamic Instruction Set Computer constructs the main processor and reconfigurable component together within the FPGA parts. The first DISC was made with two National Semiconductor CLAy31s FPGAs. A primitive main processor is implemented on a part of one CLAy31, with the majority of the same chip supplying the prototype reconfigurable component. The second CLAy31 served only to control the loading of configurations on the first one. With DISC-2, the main processor is moved onto a separate third CLAy31.

PipeRench is a reconfigurable fabric - an interconnected network of configurable logic and storage elements. By virtualizing the hardware, PipeRench overcomes the disadvantages of using FPGAs as reconfigurable computing fabrics. Unlike FPGAs, PipeRench is designed to efficiently handle computations. Using a technique called pipeline reconfiguration; PipeRench improves compilation time, reconfiguration time, and forward compatibility.

On the industrial level, many RC-systems are currently being produced by different companies like Xilinx [5], Celoxica [23], Elixent [24], Altera [25], Lucent [6], Actel [26], NallaTech [27], Chameleon Systems [28], MorphoTech [29], and Intel [30].

3. Attractions of Reconfigurable Hardware in Security

In recent years, we have witnessed a rapid increase in the number of individuals and organizations using advanced data communications and computer networks for personal and professional activities. Among the variety of new uses of data communications, there are several applications which are highly sensitive to data security. Examples are commercial exchange on the Internet [31], computer networks [32], wireless communications [33], and military [34].

Cryptography is the study of mathematical techniques related to aspects of information security such as confidentiality, data integrity, entity authentication, and data origin authentication. Cryptography is a set of techniques used as a means of providing information security. The main objectives of information security include confidentiality of information content, data integrity to prevent unauthorized alteration of data, authentication, and non-repudiation where an entity is prevented from denying previous commitments or actions [35].

Reconfigurable devices such as FPGAs are a highly attractive option for security, mainly for cryptographic algorithms. RCs provide the flexibility of a dynamic system as well as the ability to easily implement a wide range of algorithms [36].

There are many potential advantages of encryption algorithms implemented in FPGAs. Firstly, algorithm agility; this expression refers to the change of the used cryptographic algorithm during operation. For example, during a session in one of the modern security protocols like SSL, an exchange could be done between 3DES, Blowfish, IDEA, or any other algorithm. As they are reprogrammable, FPGAs seems to be a cheap alternative for traditional hardware with a continuously evolvable area such as security [37]. Secondly, algorithms upload; it is obvious that FPGAs could be upgraded with a new cipher that did not exist (or was not standardized) at design time. Thirdly, algorithm modification; the modification of a standardized security algorithm is possible, for instance, by using S-boxes, permutations, or even as changing the mode of operation. Algorithm modification could be easily done with a reconfigurable hardware. Fourthly, architecture efficiency; in certain cases, a hardware architecture can be much more efficient if it is designed for a specific set of parameters. For example, with fixed keys the main operation in the IDEA cipher degenerates into a constant multiplication which is far more efficient than a general multiplication. Using FPGAs enables the switching to much more efficient implementation in certain specified cases. Last but not least, throughput; although typically slower than ASIC implementations, FPGA implementations have the potential of running substantially faster than software implementations.

An FPGA-based RC-system can be used as an emulator of an actual circuit. Once the FPGA is programmed it could be used in a loosely-coupled style connected to a personal computer for hardware/software co-simulation and/or partitioning. The created simulation environment can be used for the demonstration, characterization, analysis and/or evaluation of the intended functionality. FPGAs are an excellent platform for debugging of a design (semi- or full-custom); the synthesized hardware description can then be transformed into an ASIC implementation.

Due to different reasons, FPGA devices cannot yet be largely used for the delivery of functionality in inexpensive consumer-oriented devices like Personal Digital Assistants (PDAs) and handsets. Although rapidly increasing, currently the physical size of FPGAs is still considered small. FPGAs have relatively expensive prices, high power consumption and low performance; as compared to ASICs. FPGAs obviously can be contemplated on large systems, such as, big transmitters and receivers, repeaters, spectrum scanning devices, and intelligence equipment. In many big systems the primary importance is on versatility, flexibility, and functionality as opposed to cost or power consumption. The following figure shows the basic tradeoffs in hardware design metrics among the three integrated circuit (IC) design technologies.

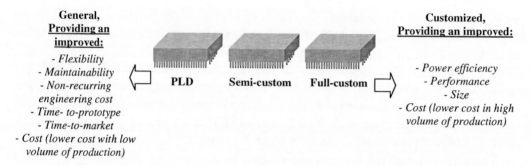

General,
Providing an
improved:
- *Flexibility*
- *Maintainability*
- *Non-recurring*
  engineering cost
- *Time- to-prototype*
- *Time-to-market*
- *Cost (lower cost with low*
  volume of production)

PLD   Semi-custom   Full-custom

Customized,
Providing an improved:
- *Power efficiency*
- *Performance*
- *Size*
- *Cost (lower cost in high*
  volume of production)

Figure. Basic tradeoffs in hardware design metrics among the three integrated circuit design technologies.

In [38] the following is stressed: "for the designer of a secure communications chip, FPGAs offer unprecedented systems design flexibility. The security architect can now experiment with different block or stream ciphers, with different hashing mechanisms, different interfaces with a main host CPU (the master device) until performance is analyzed and evaluated." In such cases, the hardware circuit is realized on an FPGA and the actual behavior can be documented; sound decisions are then possible.

Besides the design metrics shown in the figure, the following should also be considered:

- Speed of real-time operation of the system with its embedded security hardware blocks.
- Ease of integration and embedment of the developed hardware security cores.
- Ease of development.
- Upgradability.
- Correctness through formal development and/or verification.
- Operational dependability on other external components in most systems that are hybrid in nature.
- Physical security (tamper-proof, memory attacks, intrusion detection, etc.).
- Robustness of the cryptography afforded.

Reconfigurable hardware security has been the aim of many research investigations. In [39], the authors presented a large set of cryptographic algorithms implemented under RC-systems. Ploog et al. studied in [40] about how modern smartcards can perform high security operations. The authors emulated the main smartcard algorithms in FPGA hardware and quantified the impact of the main ASIC design parameters on overall speed and silicon area.

Kim et al. presented in [41] the use of FPGAs for a fully-pipelined, 56-bit DES encryption (decryption) and authentication at memory-bus bandwidths. Other implementation for DES was presented by Tom Kean and Ann Duncan from Xilinx in [42]. Prototype designs were realized and tested on the XC6200DS PCI Development System. The IDEA was addressed in [43] by Davor and Mario presenting an FPGA core implementation. The same algorithm was addressed in [44] and [45]. Gao et al. introduced a compact fast elliptic curve crypto coprocessor with variable key size, which highly utilizes the internal SRAM and registers in a Xilinx FPGA [46]. In [47], the authors discuss a reconfigurable hardware implementation of the RSA. Kim et al. [51] presented various architectures (low hardware complexity and high performance versions) of the KASUMI 3GPP block cipher using a Xilinx FPGA. Adam et al. studied in [36] the hardware implementation within commercially available FPGAs of the potential AES candidates. Multiple architectural implementation options were explored for each algorithm. Many wireless security-related algorithms have been implemented and synthesized using FPGAs. These include encryption/decryption algorithms, compression algorithms, hash functions, intrusion detection, authentication, etc. [48 - 62]. In [69 - 72], a large set of cryptographic algorithms were used to test a modern formal development methodologies for FPGAs.

4. Reconfigurable Hardware Implementation of Security Algorithms

4.1. The Advanced Encryption Standard Finalists

The huge progress in network and communications has merged the efforts of both the National Institutes of Standards and Technology (NIST) researchers with that of the international cryptographic community for developing the Advanced Encryption Standard (AES). AES was intended to replace the Data Encryption Standard (DES) which expired in 1998 [73]. One of the requirements on the AES candidates was the possibility of implementing them on hardware, efficiently. Around fifteen candidates algorithms were presented to NIST, only five were selected for inclusion in the AES finalist: MARS, RC6, Rijndael, Serpent and Twofish.

There are four possible options for optimized implementations of the AES finalists in hardware; iterative looping, loop unrolling into a full pipeline, partial pipelining and partial pipelining with sub-pipelining. More about parallelization of security algorithms could be found in [69 - 73].

The key components of the AES finalists are: exclusive OR (XOR), Mod 2^{32} add, Mod 2^{32} subtract, fixed Shift, variable Rotate, Mod 2^{32} multiply, GF(2^8) multiply and lookup tables (LUTs). The Mod 2^{32} multiply and the variable rotate are the most expensive in terms of hardware resources and computation time. Below we give a brief overview and a summary of available FPGA implementations of the AES finalists found in literature.

The key components of the MARS algorithm are XOR, Mod 2^{32} Add, Mod 2^{32} Subtract, fixed Shift, variable Rotate, Mod 2^{32} multiply and LUTs. The MARS algorithm is the most resource intensive due to its use of S-Boxes and the Mod 2^{32} multiply operation. For this reason, no significant effort was concentrated on this algorithm [36].

The key components of the RC6 algorithm are XOR, Mod 2^{32} add, fixed Shift, variable Rotate, Mod 2^{32} multiply. Obviously, Mod 2^{32} multiply is the dominant element of the round function in terms of the required logic resources. The remaining components are simple in structure and require few logic resources.

In [36], the authors designed and implemented RC6 on a Xilinx Virtex XCV1000BG560-4 FPGA. Their results showed that in terms of area, the most optimized solution was when implementing a single round of the RC6 algorithm. In terms of throughput, the best solution was when implementing the 2-stage partial pipelining when operating in feedback mode.

The key components of the Twofish algorithm are: XOR, Mod 2^{32} add, fixed Shift, GF (2^{32}) multiply, and LUTs. These components are considered to be fast operations and can be constructed from simple hardware elements

In [36], the authors designed and implemented the Twofish algorithm on a Xilinx Virtex XCV1000BG560-4 FPGA. The Twofish algorithm couldn't be implemented using a fully pipelined architecture due to the round function overall size, which was caused by the S-Boxes being dependent on the key. In terms of area, the most optimized solution was when implementing a single round of the Twofish algorithm. In terms of throughput, the best solution was when implementing a single stage partial pipelining with one sub-pipeline stage.

The key components of the Serpent algorithm are: XOR, fixed Shift and LUTs. These components are simple in structure requiring few hardware resources for the round function. The Serpent S-Boxes are relatively small and can implemented using combinational logic instead of memory elements.

R. Anderson et al. proposed in [74] the Serpent block cipher as a candidate for AES. They included a complete description of the algorithm with its performance evaluation under different processing systems. Adam et al. in [75] presented an FPGA implementation and performance evaluation of the Serpent. Multiple architecture options of the Serpent algorithm were explored with a strong focus being placed on high-speed implementations. Bora et al. in [76] investigated the possibilities of realizing the Serpent using FLEX10K ALTERA FPGAs series. A high performance encryption (decryption) core of the AES is presented in [77]. The proposed architecture is implemented on a single-chip FPGA using a fully pipelined approach.

Anderson et al. [78], believed that the AES algorithm should be a 32-round Serpent with 256-bit keys for the following reasons: First, Serpent showed that it's the best of the AES finalist in hardware, and it's the only with its fully pipelined architecture that could be fitted into a single chip. Moreover, it was the fastest since it achieved a throughput of 5.04 Gbps versus 2.4 Gbps, 1.94 Gbps, and 1.71 Gbps for RC6, Rijndael and Twofish; respectively. Second, Serpent is the most secure of the other AES finalists.

In [36], the authors designed and implemented Serpent on a Xilinx Virtex XCV1000BG560-4 FPGA. The authors results showed that in terms of area, the most optimized solution was when implementing a single round of the algorithm while operating in feedback mode. In terms of throughput, the best solution was when implementing a full-length pipelined architecture while operating in non-feedback mode.

The key components of the Rijndael algorithm are: XOR, fixed Shift, GF (2^{32}) multiply, and LUTs. These components are simple in structure resulting in few hardware resources of the round function. The Rijndael S-Box is an 8-bit to 8-bit look-up-table. Each round of the algorithm requires sixteen copies of the S-Boxes, resulting in the requirement of significant hardware resources.

Daemen and Rijmen proposed the Rijndael as an AES candidate in [79]. Currently, the Rijndael is known as the AES and available as a Federal Information Processing Standard [80]. In October 2000, the Rijndael algorithm was selected as the new AES. Since that time, extensive work has been done to increase the performance of the algorithm. Many hardware architectures were proposed for further optimization of the algorithm. Almost all were trying to improve the throughput of the algorithm while maintaining acceptable hardware resource requirements.

In [36], the authors designed and implemented Rijndael on a Xilinx Virtex XCV1000BG560-4 FPGA. Obtained results showed that in terms of area, the most optimized solution was when implementing a one round partially pipeline with one sub-pipeline stage. The highest throughput was achieved when implementing a 2-stage loop unrolling architecture while operating in feedback mode where a throughput of 300 Mbps was achieved.

Fischer and Drutarovsky [73] presented a different method of mapping the Rijndael algorithm using Altera low-cost ACEX and high performance APEX FPD families. The first mapping approach was based on 8x8-bit S-Boxes and the second was based on 8-32-bit T-Boxes. Two types of cipher core configurations were assumed: fast configuration and economic configuration. A speed of 612 Mbps, 451 Mbps and a usage of 2493 logic elements (LEs) (30%), 2530 LE (25%) were achieved for the fast configuration with 16 S-Boxes in APEX 20KE200-1 and Flex 10KE200-1 respectively. As for the economic configuration with 8 S-Boxes, the speed was 212 Mbps and the LE usage was 2923 (59%) in ACEX 1K100-1. Faster overall cipher speed (750 Mbps) and very few LE (845; 5%) were achieved in the fast configuration with 16 T-boxes in APEX 1K400-1. The economic configuration with 4 T-Boxes in ACEX 1K50-1 gave a speed of 115 Mbps and a usage of 1213 LE (42%). The 16 S-Boxes implementation was the fastest among other Rijndael cipher implementations in low-cost Altera field programmable devices. Moreover, using the T-boxes approach, it became possible to implement the Rijndael cipher in a circuit as small as ACEX 1K50, and using only 40% of its resources. T-Boxes implementation was 80% faster than the fastest FPD implementation. The advantages of the method using the S-Boxes are very fast encryption but slower decryption and no latency during changing from encryption to decryption. Also, the S-Boxes implementation has the advantage of reducing the memory requirement. On the other hand, the usage of logic elements is high with a low-level of logic sharing. As for the T-Boxes approach, the overall cipher speed for both encryption and decryption is faster. Resource sharing is high and the logic elements being used are very few. The disadvantages of this approach are the high latency when switching from encryption to decryption and vice versa and the memory need for the T-Boxes implementation is increased by at least a factor of 2.

Rodrigues et al. [77] achieved a speed of 4.2 Gbps by implementing the encryptor/decryptor core of the Rijndael algorithm using the fully pipelined approach. The authors proposed a new design optimization to resolve the problem behind the allocation of large amount of memory which is imposed by the fully pipelined approach. The design was implemented on an XCV2600E Xilinx Virtex-E FPGA. The total number of occupied slices was 5677 (22.3%), while the achieved throughput was 4.2 Gbps.

Hodjat and Verbauwhede [81] presented a fully pipelined implementation of the Rijndael encryption processor. The design was implemented on Virtex-II Pro FPGA. A total of 5177 slices were occupied. To achieve the speed of 21.54 Gbps, the authors used the loop unrolling and inner-round and outer-round pipelining techniques with an optimum number of pipeline stages for the byte substitution phase of the algorithm.

In an attempt to improve the hardware complexity and the rate of encryption/decryption of the Rijndael algorithm, Sharma et al., presented a systolic architecture of the algorithm and used short and balanced combinational paths in the design. In brief, the systolic system consists of a bunch of interconnected cells each performs some simple operations. Data flows from the computer memory into this bunch of interconnected cells and then back to memory. The systolic architecture benefits from the similarities of encryption and decryption to provide better performance while maintaining a small chip size. Also, the architecture is highly scalable and regular. For example, one can change the key size from 128 to 192 or 256 bits easily without too much modification in the design. The total number of clock cycles required for encryption or decryption is 40. Thus a throughput of 3.2-Bits per clock cycle was achieved [82].

In [83], Saqib et al. designed a fully pipelined Rijndael implementation for a Xilinx Virtex-XCV2600 FPGA. They proposed two approaches to modify the implementation of the multiplicative inverse in GF (2^8), the most costly step in the algorithm. In the first approach, they used lookup tables to store pre-computed values to allow faster execution time of the algorithm. In the second approach, they tried to reduce the memory requirement by computing the multiplicative inverse using composite field techniques. In the first design, a fast execution time was realized at the price of memory requirement; while in the second design, a reduction in the memory requirement was achieved at the cost of the execution time. The results obtained for both designs are competitive with similar implementations found in [84]. The throughput has increased by 18.5% while the area requirements have decreased by 11.8%.

Mentens et al. in [85] were interested in realizing a compact and a secured implementation of the Rijndael algorithm. In their paper, they implemented an unsecured and a secured architecture on a Xilinx XCV800-4-HQ240 FPGA. The compact nature of their design makes it possible to fit on a smart card. For their secured version, they used the masking algorithm, found in [86], to ensure that secret data are always protected with a fresh mask that is a combination of two masks. A throughput of 41 Mbps was realized for the unsecured design, and 29 Mbps for the secured design. The total number of the configurable logic blocks (CLBs) was 908, 1113 for the unsecured and secured design, respectively.

In [87] the authors presented a description of the Rijndael, its design strategy, and the underlying motivations. Many hardware implementations for the Rijndael have been investigated in the literature. For instance, in [88] the authors proposed a reconfigurable system that uses different algorithms to enhance the randomization of the ciphertext and the security levels in the AES algorithm. Ashruf et al. in [89], investigated several Rijndael implementations based on a suggested processor employing two types of FPGAs from Xilinx and Altera.

4.2. Wireless Security

It is obvious that the implementation efficiency of security schemes is as important as the offered security level itself. Reconfigurable computing, specifically FPGAs have been used for a variety of purposes related to wireless security. FPGAs have been used as both testing and implementation platforms. They have been used to achieve several goals. These include using less power, obtaining high throughput, and reducing the area resources or size.

Many wireless security-related algorithms have been implemented and synthesized using FPGAs. These include encryption/decryption algorithms, compression algorithms, hash functions, intrusion detection, authentication, and error-correcting codes. In designing their schemes on FPGAs, researchers have targeted several wireless systems including wireless local area networks (WLAN), wireless personal area networks (WPAN), Bluetooth, and sensor networks.

The use of FPGA for wireless security has evolved along the evolution of the security solutions proposed. Below, is a list of important and representative works on wireless security based on reconfigurable computing.

The authors in [58] investigated the hardware implementation of two error-correcting codes (ECC) that can allow, if used in wireless communications, more data to be carried over the same spectrum, lower transmission power, and higher data security and compression. The two considered ECC are the Turbo Codes and Low Density Parity Check Codes (LDPC). The paper concluded that LDPCs are more suitable to implementation in hardware because they exhibit much more exploitable parallelism, the computations require operators that are more easily implementable in hardware, and they are more regular and tileable in nature than the other considered ECC. The paper presents a hypothetical LDPC implementation using a commercial FPGA.

The paper in [51] presents three implementations of triple Data Encryption Standard (3DES) algorithm on a configurable platform. The three alternatives are presented in order to study the suitability of 3DES for MAC-level encryption. The MAC processing is handled by a Digital Signal Processor (DSP) and a Xilinx Virtex FPGA chip. The presented results showed that 3DES algorithm is suitable for hardware implementation.

The paper in [65] presents a VLSI implementation for the SAFER+ encryption algorithm. The SAFER+ algorithm is a basic component in the authentication Bluetooth mechanism. The proposed design was captured entirely in VHDL using a bottom-up design and verification methodology. An FPGA device was used for the hardware implementation of the algorithm. The proposed implementation reduced the covered area constraints about 25% comparing with previously proposed implementations in addition to achieving high performance.

In [54], the design and implementation of the KASUMI cryptographic algorithm and confidentiality algorithm (f8) to a hardware chip for 3GPP system is presented. Two architectures are proposed and compared; one low hardware complexity version and one high performance version. The two versions are designed for the ME and RNC switch of the 3GPP system respectively. These architectures were implemented with a Xilinx Virtex-E FPGA chip.

In [66], an area optimized architecture and an FPGA implementation for RC5 is presented. The proposed implementation allocates less area resources compared with the previous conventional architecture. The achieved reduction in area resources ranges between 28% and 33%. The proposed architecture has been designed with pipeline technique, which achieves high speed performance. Comparisons with other related published works proved that the proposed architecture is better in operating frequency and throughput.

The paper in [63] presents a VLSI architecture and the FPGA implementation of the keyed-hash message authentication code (HMAC) for the WTLS security layer of the Wireless Application Protocol (WAP). All the internal components of the design were synthesized placed and routed using Xilinx FPGA devices. The synthesis results for the HMAC proved that the proposed system performs better than conventional hardware implementations in terms of area-delay product.

In [57] two architectures and efficient implementations of the 64-bit KASUMI block cipher are presented. The first one uses the pipeline technique while the second one uses feedback logic. The designs were coded using VHDL and for the hardware implementations, an FPGA device was used. Detailed analysis in terms of performance and covered area are presented. The authors concluded that the proposed implementations outperform any previous published KASUMI implementations in terms of performance.

The paper in [52] presents a compatible design of CCMP and OCB AES cipher using separated encryptor and decryptor for IEEE 802.11i. The implemented OCB and CCMP feature 400 Mbps and 243 Mbps throughput respectively at 50 MHz frequency, which are targeted to Xilinx Virtex FPGA device.

The paper in [67] presents a WLAN security processor that is capable of offloading all security encapsulation in an IEEE 802.11i compliant MAC layer to a reconfigurable hardware accelerator. The proposed design is primarily targeted at WLAN applications, and as such is capable of performing WEP, TKIP, CCMP, and WRAP. The use of dedicated instructions designed for WLAN applications resulted in reduced instruction code footprints in comparison to general-purpose processors, and provided the high throughput necessary for 54 Mbps IEEE 802.11 a/g.

[53] explored in depth the SHA-1 hash function and considered various implementations that have been proposed in the literature. Design aspects of performance and size are considered. A new design is proposed as an alternative approach to increase SHA-1 throughput. To evaluate the proposed SHA-1 design approach, the Xilinx FPGA technology was used. The core was developed for and integrated to a v150bg352 FPGA device. According to the obtained results, the proposed SHA-1 implementation is more than 30% faster than any previously known implementation. Additionally, the introduced area penalty was approximately 7.5% compared to the nearest performing implementation.

The authors in [50] presented a compact and energy-efficient hardware design for the 802.15.4 security processing. The design was argued to offer the best architectural area/power/performance ratios for the low-power wireless devices. Compared to typical WPAN processors, the implemented FPGA prototype and the estimated ASIC implementation provided significantly lower energy consumption and higher performance. The FPGA throughput at the highest security level is 90 Mbps and the energy consumption is 1/190 of an 8-bit microcontroller and 1/5 of an ARM9.

The paper in [56] presents a high-throughput hardware architecture for the 64-bit NESSIE proposal MISTY1 block cipher and its FPGA implementation. The proposed architecture can implement both encryption and decryption modes in the same dedicated FPGA device. The MISTY1 rounds are unrolled and RAM blocks embedded in the considered FPGA devices are used for the implementation of the S-boxes. A 75-stage pipeline is inserted and achieves a maximum throughput of 12.6 Gbps at a frequency of 168 MHz. According to the authors, the proposed architecture achieved the largest throughput-to-area ratio value compared to previously published MISTY1 implementations.

The work in [62] proposed a technique to detect an intrusion and concluded with a review and comparison of existing wireless intrusion detection techniques. The paper explained how to implement the entire functionality on FPGAs. The paper discussed an embedded system for monitoring, detecting and responding to information technology security breaches that occur over a WLAN using the 802.11 protocols.

[67][68] proposes a faster RSA encryption/decryption circuit utilizing high speed multiplier architecture. The most significant aspect of the proposed RSA hardware is that any future proposed efficient adder can be implemented in the proposed multiplier, without changing the original hardware architecture thereby improving its efficiency to a great extent. The coding of the RSA is done in VHDL and the FPGA synthesis is done using Xilinx libraries. The results show that the proposed architecture is faster than RSA hardware implemented using traditional multiplication algorithm.

In [65][66], a scalable architecture is studied for the implementation of the parameterized block cipher RC5. Alternative designs of modulo adders and modulo subtractors are examined in order to exploit the efficiency of the FPGA implementation and to achieve high performance and low area resources. The considered adders-subtractors structures are: Ripple Carry adder/subtractor, Carry Skip adder/subtractor, and Carry Look Ahead adder/subtractor. Some of these structures provide high operating frequency, while others are more suitable for minimized covered area resources.

In [48], manifestation of cryptographic implementation required to address the long term security solution for Robust Secure Wireless Network (RSN) based on fast, efficient and low power FPGA has been demonstrated. The proposed design utilizes low cost and low power Spartan-3 FPGA offering encryption rate of 2699 Mbps for CCMP, hence not only meeting the IEEE 802.11 operating data rates of 54 Mbps and 108 Mbps (Super G Mode), but also the high speed requirement of emerging wireless standard like IEEE 802.11n which will support a data rate of 500 Mbps.

In [61] a reconfigurable architecture for multi-coder data compression is proposed. It consists of three main units and serves three different types of compression: text using Huffman, speech using ADPCM, and image using RLE. The three different types of compression are supported by reconfiguring the FPGA on the fly and loading the particular hardware into the FPGA depending on the type of data. The proposed FPGA implementation has very low area resources.

In [59], a hardware implementation of hash function SHA-512 is proposed. The proposed implementation has been developed using VHDL, and has been synthesized placed and routed in an Altera FPGA device. Compared to old standards MD-5 and SHA-1, the proposed implementation of SHA-512 has higher throughput, lower area-delay product in addition to providing more security.

In [60] the authors have implemented AES algorithm on various platforms and compared the obtained results. The platforms included FPGA Xilinx's XC2VP30 device, Desktop PC and handheld device. Multi-cycle technique was employed to process 128-bits data in 32-bits chunk in both hardware and software. The operations were implemented in serialized and concurrent fashion to meet the IEEE 802.11 operating data rates of 54 Mbps and 108 Mbps (Super G Mode). The results show that the implementation on FPGA supports the required throughput and consumes less power hence suitable for handheld devices.

In [64] the authors proposed a high speed, non-pipelined FPGA implementation of the AES-CCMP cipher for wireless LAN using Xilinx development tools and Virtex-II Pro FPGA circuit. The developed AES CCMP core is aimed at providing high speed with sufficient security. Using their scheme the authors obtained an encryption/decryption data path operating at 194/148 MHz resulting in a throughput of 2.257 Gbps for encryption and

1.722 Gbps for decryption. The authors have compared their proposed scheme with several other sequential implementations and concluded that their implementation of AES is more efficient both in term of speed and throughput on FPGA Virtex-II Pro device.

In [49], FPGAs have been used to implement and test parts of the futuristic aspects of global ambient intelligence networks (GAIN). GAIN is a universal network with embedded sensors, which provide hazards and abnormal event detection.

4.3. Tiny Ciphers

With the evolution of embedded systems there is a growing need for security in devices running on low resources. Standard encryption algorithms can cause a small device to become less efficient in terms of throughput, power consumption, etc. In order to avoid such de-efficiency, system designers could investigate the choice of lightweight ciphers. TEA [90], PRESENT [91], MCrypton [92], Hight [93], SEA [94], and CGEN [95] are of many existing lightweight cryptographic algorithms and are efficiently employed for security in environments where hardware resources are limited. Nevertheless tiny ciphers have smaller structures; they are sufficient and safe enough to be a good choice for security solutions.

In [96], the authors presented an FPGA implementation of the Extended Tiny Encryption Algorithm (XTEA). The development strategy starts by refining the specification into a finite state machine (FSM). A corresponding modified FSM is created accounting for the signals controlling the developed datapath structural components. The created datapath and controller are then described using VHDL. The proposed implementation of the XTEA fits in Altera's STARTIX II FPGA with 485 logic cells (LC) used for combinatorial logic and 306 LCs as Registers. The achieved encryption speed is 16.5 Mbps. A second design is also developed eliminating the delays introduced by the controller, replicates a single round 32 times in a pipelined fashion, and runs at a speed of 6.51Gbps.

The work in [97] analyzed and evaluated the development of a cheap and relatively fast hardware implementation of XTEA. The development uses Verilog hardware description language to describe the design. Many hardware design tools are used for the evaluation process including Altera's Quartus, Xilinx ISE, Mentor Graphics HDL Designer, Leonardo Spectrum, Precision Synthesis , and ModelSim. The targeted hardware systems are the reconfigurable Altera's Stratix II and Xilinx Virtex II Pro FPGAs. The best achieved synthesis was by mapping the design onto a Virtex Pro II FPGA with a tiny area and a speed of 134 Mbps. The mapped design employed 32 rounds, although 16 rounds are assumed to be secure enough.

4.4. Hash Functions under FPGAs

Reconfigurable hardware implementations of hash algorithms have been largely investigated, especially for the mapping onto FPGAs. The main targeted hash algorithms are the MD4, MD5, SHA-1, RIPEMD-160, SHA-2 and Whirlpool. The focus in the proposed designs in the literature is again to achieve high-performance implementations.

In [98], a parallel MD4 FPGA implementation is proposed. The suggested design implements arithmetic, logic and circular shift operations using a pipelined parallel processor running with a speed of 5.44 Mbps occupying only 252 CLE slices.

The work in [99] presents several pipelined designs of the MD5. The fastest fully-pipelined design achieved a throughput of 5.8 Gbps and occupied 11498 slices and 10 BRAMs on a Xilinx Virtex-II. A compact MD5 designed by [100] occupies only 630 slices and one BRAM; the design runs with a throughput of 744 Mbps on a Xilinx Virtex-II.

A fast reconfigurable hardware implementation of the SHA-1 is reported in [101] achieving a throughput of 899.8 Mbps occupying 1550 slices on a Virtex-II XC2V3000. In [102], ways to produce a compact SHA-1 are investigated. The proposed design uses carry look-ahead addition to minimize delays with carry propagation. The resultant implementation reduces the number of operands in a round by pre-computing addition of constants and words; it also eliminates the final round. The achieved throughput is 462 Mbps occupying an area of 2200 slices on a Virtex XCVlOOO-6. In [103], techniques to economize the use of resources are presented. The proposed design employs multiplexers to implement switching matrices; the throughput achieved is 114 Mbps and the area occupied is 10500 logic cells in an Apex EP20K1000. In [104], a pseudo-random number generator is used in the implementation of the SHA-1. The final purpose of the implementation is to create a VLSI architecture, but it is initially described in VHDL and synthesized for FPGAs for testing. The developed design can run at 233 Mbps occupying an area of 2600 slices on a Virtex XCV300.

The work in [38] proposed implementations of the RIPEMD-160 hash algorithm under Altera EPF10K50SBC356-1. The design achieves a throughput of 84 Mbps occupying 1964 logic elements. In [105], a RIPEMD-160 FPGA implementation on Xilinx V300E achieves a rate of 89 Mbps occupying 2008 slices.

A fast FPGA implementation of the SHA-2 is proposed in [106]. The implementation achieves a throughput of 1466 Mbps on a Xilinx Virtex-II device occupying 4107 slices. The proposed design for an SHA-2 (512-bit) implements a two-step unrolled implementation. Various implementations of the SHA-2 are also presented in [107] with trials to enhance execution time by pipelining computations.

In [108], three versions of the SHA-2 algorithm were implemented under FPGAs, namely, the SHA-2 (256), (384) and (512). The design compares three implementations in terms of operating frequency, throughput and area-delay product. Among the three implementations, the (256) version consumes least hardware resources (1060 slices), achieving a throughput of 326 Mbps on a Xilinx V200PQ240-6.

In [109], an FPGA implementation is also presented for SHA-2 (384) and (512). The design uses shift registers for message scheduler and compression block to save execution time and resources. In addition, BRAMs are used to store the compression function constants. Both the (384) and (512) versions run with a speed of 479 Mbps occupying 2914 slices and 2 BRAMs.

A fast Whirlpool core has been reported in [110] implemented on a Xilinx Virtex-4. The implementation achieves a throughput of 4896 Mbps and occupies 13210 slices. In [111], another fast core Whirlpool is reported achieving a throughput of 4480 Mbps on a Xilinx XCVI000 occupying 5585 slices. In [111], three additional different Whirlpool designs are presented. The proposed designs, present mini boxes by using Boolean expressions, referred to as BBs (Boolean expressions Based) and by using FPGA LUTs, referred to as LBs (LUT Based). The proposed mini boxes enhance the throughputs reaching the reported 4480 Mbps.

The work in [112] investigates saving hardware resources by using LUT-based RAM for Whirlpool state. The throughput achieved is 382 Mbps occupying 1456 slices on a Virtex-2P XC2VP40.

5. Rapid Prototyping of Security Algorithms for FPGAs

Besides the many important requirements for a successful hardware implementation, ease of development and correctness of the implementation are two vital issues. FPGAs continue to grow in size and currently contain several millions of gates. At the same time, research effort is going into higher-level formal hardware synthesis methodologies for reconfigurable computing that can exploit FPGA technology. [69 - 72] present a methodology to design massively parallel algorithms with applications from cryptography. The method takes a step-wise refinement approach to the development of correct reconfigurable hardware circuits from formal specifications. A functional programming notation is used for specifying algorithms and for reasoning about them. The specifications are realized through the use of a combination of function decomposition strategies, data refinement techniques, and off-the-shelf refinements based upon higher-order functions. The off-the-shelf refinements are inspired by the operators of Communicating Sequential Processes (CSP) and map easily to programs in Handel-C (a hardware description language). The Handel-C descriptions are directly compiled into reconfigurable hardware.

The addressed algorithms in [69 -72] are the International Data Encryption Algorithm (IDEA), the Serpent, the KASUMI, and the F8 from the Third Generation Partnership Project (3GPP). Several reconfigurable hardware implementations are developed with different performance characteristics by applying different refinements to each algorithm. Reconfigurable hardware implementations are compiled to Celoxica's two million gate FPGA-based RC-1000 reconfigurable computer. Performance analysis and evaluation of these implementations are included.

The work in [69] investigated the synthesis of highly parallel reconfigurable hardware implementations of the IDEA algorithm. Important aspects for hardware implementations of cryptographic algorithms like correctness, reliability along with efficiency are stressed through the application of the proposed development model. The different refined designs includes the cipher, decipher, and the key scheduler. A first fully-pipelined design required 88 computing cycles yielding an average throughput of 25.4 Mbps. The second design occupied the minimum area among the different designs with 5650 slices.

[70] carried out a case studying the KASUMI algorithm for 3GPP. The testing of the realized reconfigurable circuits allowed the ciphering with KASUMI in a throughput of 32 Mbps with an occupied area of 5594 slices. In [71], the rapid development of the F8 stream cipher is presented based-on the KASUMI block cipher. The study challenges the adopted high-level multi-stage hardware design methodology with the tight restrictions that are usually implied for wireless circuits. The requirements for the F8 algorithm were to have a circuit with a maximum of 10000 equivalent gates to perform at 2 Mbps [113]. A proposed design meets the speed requirement by running at a speed of 2.86 Mbps, although the area doesn't meet the requirement by occupying 11590 slices (139121 gates). The high cost in hardware resources arises from the applied systematic rules blinding possibilities for intuitive ad hoc optimizations. Optimized hardware realization of the F8 [113] noted a throughput of 2

Mbps with 12210 gates. High-speed implementations were presented in [114] reporting maximum speed of 167.07 Mbps.

Hardware designs for the Serpent algorithm are developed in [72]. A fully-pipelined design failed to compile under the used RC-system, with its large gates count. The maximum achieved parallelism was in running a design with 2 parallel rounds and a third performing the remaining 29 rounds sequentially. The implementation has a throughput of 12.21 Mbps occupying an area of 19198 slices. A design with its sequential single fold implementation achieved throughput of 12.15 Mbps with an area of 12291 slices.

6. Conclusion

In conclusion, reconfigurable computing has attracted much attention among researchers working in security. FPGAs in particular have been used to increase the throughput, reduce power consumption, and reduce area and resources of the proposed security related algorithms. This chapter introduces the use of reconfigurable computers in modern security applications. The chapter also investigates the main reasons behind the adoption of RC-systems in security. Furthermore, a technical survey of various implementations of security algorithms under RC-systems is included laying common grounds for comparisons. Case studies were also presented including reconfigurable hardware implementation of the AES finalists, wireless security algorithms, tiny ciphers, hash algorithms, and rapid prototyping of security algorithms for FPGAs.

References

[1]   M. Gokhale; W. Holmes; A. Kopser; S. Lucas; R. Minnich; D. Sweely; D.Lopresti; Building and Using a Highly Programmable Logic Array. *IEEE Computer*, 1991, 81-89.

[2]   Estrin G.; Bussell B.; Turn R.; Bibb J. *IEEE Transactions on Electronic Computers*. 1963: 12, 747-755.

[3]   Lipovksi G.; Malek M. *Parallel Computing: Theory and Comparisons*, John Wiley & Sons: New York, 1987.

[4]   Bertin P.; Roncin D.; Vuillemin J.; *Introduction to Programmable Active Memories*, ftp://ftp.digital.com/pub/DEC/PRL/research-reports/ PRL-RR-3.pdf

[5]   Xilinx. http://www.xilinx.com.

[6]   Lucent, *FPGA Data Book*, www.alcatel-lucent.com.

[7]   Radunovic B.; Milutinovic V. *A survey of reconfigurable computing architectures*. *Workshop on Field Programmable Logic and Applications*, 1998.

[8]   Radunovic B. An overview of advances in reconfigurable computing systems. *Hawaii International Conference on System Sciences*, 1999, 3, 3039.

[9]   M. Gokhale; W. Holmes; A. Kopser; S. Lucas; R. Minnicha; D. Sweely; and D.Lopresti. *IEEE Computer*. 1991, 81-89.

[10]   P. Bertin, D. Roncin; J. Vuillemin. *Introduction to Programmable Active Memories, in Systolic Array Processors*, Prentice-Hall: Englewood Cliffs NJ, 1989; 300-309.

[11] E. Tau; D. Chen; I. Eslick; J. Brown; and A. DeHon. A first generation DPGA implementation. *Canadian Workshop of Field-Programmable Devices*, 1995.

[12] J. Hauser; J. WawrzynekGrape. A mips processor with a re-configurable coprocessor. *IEEE Symposium on FPGAs for Custom Computing Machines*. 1997.

[13] R. Hartenstein; R. Kress. A datapath synthesis system for the reconfigurable datapath architecture. *Asia and South Pacific Design Automation Conference*. 1995, 479-484.

[14] E. Mirsky and A. DeHon. Matrix: A re-configurable computing architecture with configurable instruction distribution. *IEEE Symposium on FPGAs for Custom Computing Machines*. 1996, 157-66.

[15] T. Miyamori and K. Olukotun. A quantitative analysis of reconfigurable coprocessors for multimedia applications. *IEEE Symposium on Field Programmable Custom Computing Machines*, 1998.

[16] Lu G.; Singh H.; Lee M.; Bagherzadeh N.; Kurdahi F.; Filho E.; and Alves V. *The MorphoSys Dynamically Reconfigurable System-on-Chip*. Workshop on Evolvable Hardware. 1999, 152-160.

[17] C. Ebeling; D. Cronquist; and P. Franklin. Configurable computing: The catalyst for high-performance architectures. *IEEE Conference on Application-specific Systems*, 1997, 364-72.

[18] J. Babb; M. Frank; V. Lee; E. Waingold; R. Barua; M. Taylor; J. Kim; S. Devabhaktuni; and A. Agrawal. The RAW benchmark suite: computation structures for general-purpose computing. *IEEE Conference on Application-specific Systems*, 1997, 134-43.

[19] M. Wirthlin and B. Hutchings. A dynamic instruction set computer. *IEEE Workshop on FPGAs for Custom Computing Machines*. 1995, 99-107.

[20] C. Iseli and E. Sanchez. A C++ compiler for FPGA custom execution units synthesis. *IEEE Workshop on FPGAs for Custom Computing Machines*, 1995, 173–179.

[21] L. Agarwal, M.Wazlowski, and S. Ghosh. An asynchronous approach to efficient execution of programs on adaptive architectures utilizing FPGAs. *IEEE Workshop on FPGAs for Custom Computing Machines*. 1994, 101-110.

[22] Cadambi S.; Weener J.; Goldstein S.; Schmit H.; Thomas D. Managing pipeline-reconfigurable FPGAs. *Symposium on Field Programmable Gate Arrays*, 1998, 55-64.

[23] Celoxica. www.celoxica.com.

[24] Elixent. www.elixent.com.

[25] Altera. http://www.atera.com.

[26] Actel. www.actel.com.

[27] NALLATECH. www.nallatech.com.

[28] Tag X.; Aalsma M.; and Jou R.; A compiler directed approach to hiding configuration latency in chameleon processors. *Conference on Field-Programmable Logic and Applications*, 2000.

[29] MorphTech. www.morphotech.com.

[30] Intel. www.intel.com.

[31] J. Wilson. Data security hits home. *IEEE Micro*, October 1995.

[32] C. Kaufman, R. Perlman, and M. Speciner. *Network Security*. Prentice Hall, 1995.

[33] R. Nichols and P. Lekkas. Wireless *Security: Models*, Threats, and Solutions. McGraw-Hill, 2002.

[34] P. Alexander. External intrusion detection systems for critical facilities. In *Proceedings of the IEEE 1990 International Carnahan Conference on Security Technology Crime Countermeasures*. IEEE, October 1990.

[35] Menezes, P. van Oorschot, and S. Vanston. *Handbook of Applied Cryptography*. CRC Press, fifth edition, August 2001.

[36] Elbirt, W. Yip, B. Chetwynd, and C. Paar. An FPGA-based performance evaluation of the AES block cipher candidate algorithm finalists. *IEEE Transactions on Very Large Scale Integeration (VLSI) Systems*, 9(4):545, August 2001.

[37] S. Chappel. Rapid development of reconfigurable systems. In *12th International Workshop on Rapid System Prototyping*, pages 44–49, 2001.

[38] R. Nichols and P. Lekkas. Wireless Security: Models, Threats, and Solutions. McGraw-Hill, 2002.

[39] F. Rodriguez-Henriquez, N.A. Saqib, A. Diaz-Perez, C. Koc, *Cryptographic algorithms on reconfigurable hardware*, Springer, New York, 2006.

[40] H. Ploog and D. Timmermann. FPGA based architecture evaluation of cryptographic coprocessors for smartcards. In *IEEE Symposium on FPGAs for Custom Computing Machines*, pages 29 –293. IEEE, 1998.

[41] Kim, S. Steele, and J.G. Koller. A fully pipelined, 700 MBytes/s DES encryption. In *IEEE Ninth Great Lakes Symposium on core VLSI*, pages 386–387. IEEE, 1999.

[42] T. Kean and A. Duncan. DES key breaking, encryption and decryption on the XC6216. In *IEEE Symposium on FPGAs for Custom Computing Machines*, pages 310– 311. IEEE, 1998.

[43] D. Runje and M. Kovac. Universal strong encryption FPGA core implementation. In *Proceedings of Design, Automation and Test in Europe*, pages 923–924, 1998.

[44] O. Mencer, M. Morf, and M.J. Flynn. Hardware software tri-design of encryption for mobile communication units. In *Proceedings of the 1998 IEEE International Conference on Acoustics, Speech and Signal Processing*, volume 5, pages 3045–3048, 1998.

[45] Michalski, K. Gaj, and T. El-Ghazawi. An Implementation Comparison of an IDEA Encryption Cryptosystem on Two General-Purpose Reconfigurable Computers. In Field-Programmable Logic and Applications: *13th International Conference*, FPL, *Lecture Notes in Computer Science*, pages 204 – 219, Lisbon - Portugal, 2003. Springer.

[46] [46] L. Gao, H. Lee, and G. Sobelman. A compact fast variable key size elliptic curve cryptosystem coprocessor. In *Seventh Annual IEEE Symposium on Field-Programmable Custom Computing Machines FCCM '99*, pages 304–305. IEEE, 1999.

[47] M. Shand and J. Vuillemin. Fast implementations of RSA cryptography. In Kenneth L. Pocek and Jeffrey M. Arnold, editors, *11th Symposium on Computer Architecture*, Windsor, Canada, pages 252–259, November 1993. Available From: ftp://ftp.digital.com/pub/DEC/PRL/research-articles/SV93.ps.Z.

[48] Arshad Aziz and Nassar Ikram, Hardware implementation of AES-CCM for robust secure wireless network, *Proceedings of the 5th Annual ISSA Information Security Conference (ISSA)*, pp. 44 -51, 2005.

[49] Ferriere, D. Long, L.E. and Jankowski, T.M., Configurable sensor networks: an academic experience provides a future glimpse at improved infrastructure safety and

security, in *IEEE Conference on Technologies for Homeland Security*, pp: 270-273, 2007.

[50] Hamalainen, P.; Hannikainen, M. and Hamalainen, T.D., Efficient hardware implementation of security processing for IEEE 802.15.4 wireless networks, in *48th Midwest Symposium on Circuits and Systems*, Vol 1, pp: 484-487, 2005.

[51] Hamalainen, P.; Hannikainen, M.; Hamalainen, T. and Saarinen, J., Configurable hardware implementation of triple-DES encryption algorithm for wireless local area network, in *Proceedings of IEEE International Conference on Acoustics, Speech, and Signal Processing, ICASSP*, Vol. 2, pp: 1221-1224, 2001.

[52] Ho Yung Jang; Joon Hyoung Shim; Jung Hee Suk; In Cheol Hwang; and Jun Rim Choi, Compatible design of CCMP and OCB AES cipher using separated encryptor and decryptor for IEEE 802.11i, in *Proceedings of the 2004 International Symposium on Circuits and Systems, ISCAS,* Vol. 3, pp: 645-648, 2004.

[53] Kakarountas, A.P.; Theodoridis, G.; Laopoulos, T. and Goutis, C.E., *High-Speed FPGA implementation of the SHA-1 hash function, in intelligent data acquisition and advanced computing systems: technology and applications, IDAACS*, pp: 211-215, 2005.

[54] Kim, H. W., Y. Choi, M. Kim and H. Ryu, Hardware implementation of 3GPP KASUMI Crypto Algorithm. In *Proceedings of the International Technical conference on circuits/systems, computers and communications, ITC-CSCC*, 2002.

[55] Kitsos, P.   Sklavos, N. and Koufopavlou, O., Hardware implementation of the SAFER+ encryption algorithm for the Bluetooth system, in *IEEE International Symposium on Circuits and Systems, ISCAS,* Vol. 4, pp: 878-881, 2002.

[56] Kitsos, P.; Galanis, M.D. and Koufopavlou, O., A RAM-based FPGA implementation of the 64-bit MISTY1 block cipher, in *IEEE International Symposium on Circuits and Systems, ISCAS*, Vol. 5, pp: 4641-4644, 2005.

[57] Kitsos, P.; Galanis, M.D. and Koufopavlou, O., High-speed hardware implementations of the KASUMI block cipher, in *Proceedings of the 2004 International Symposium on Circuits and Systems, ISCAS* Vol. 2, pp: 549-552, 2004.

[58] Levine, B.; Reed Taylor, R. and Schmit, H., Implementation of near Shannon limit error-correcting codes using reconfigurable hardware, in *IEEE Symposium on Field-Programmable Custom Computing Machines,* pp: 217-226, 2000.

[59] Li, H. and Miao, C., Hardware Implementation of Hash Function SHA-512, in *Proceedings of the First international Conference on innovative Computing, information and Control* – Vol. 2. ICICIC. pp 38-42, 2006.

[60] Parikh, C. and Patel, P., *Performance evaluation of AES algorithm on various development platforms, in IEEE international symposium on consumer electronics, ISCE,* pp: 1-6, 2007.

[61] R. Seshasayanan and K. K. Senthil Kumar, Reconfigurable architecture For WTLS, in Annual India Conference, pp: 1-4, 2006.

[62] Raja, P. C. K.   Suganthi, VLSI approach to wireless security mechanism, in *IEEE International Conference on Personal Wireless Communications, ICPWC*, pp: 429-433, 2005.

[63] Selimis, G.   Sklavos, N. and Koufopavlou, O., VLSI implementation of the keyed-hash message authentication code for the wireless application protocol, in *Proceedings*

of the 2003 10th IEEE International Conference on Electronics, Circuits and Systems, ICECS, Vol. 1, pp: 24-27, 2003.

[64] Sivakumar, C. and Velmurugan, A., High speed VLSI design CCMP AES cipher for WLAN (IEEE 802.11i), in *International Conference on Signal Processing, Communications and Networking, ICSCN*, pp: 398-403, 2007.

[65] Sklavos, N.; Fournaris, A.P. and Koufopavlou, O., WAP security: implementation cost and performance evaluation of a scalable architecture for RC5 parameterized block cipher, in *Proceedings of the 12th IEEE Mediterranean Electrotechnical Conference, MELECON* Vol. 2, pp: 795-798, 2004.

[66] Sklavos, N.; Machas, C. and Koufopavlou, O., Area optimized architecture and VLSI implementation of RC5 encryption algorithm, in *Proceedings of the 2003 10th IEEE International Conference on Electronics, Circuits and Systems, ICECS*, Vol. 1, pp: 172-175, 2003.

[67] Smyth, N. McLoone, M. and McCanny, J.V., Reconfigurable hardware acceleration of WLAN security, in *IEEE Workshop on Signal Processing Systems*, SIPS, pp: 194-199, 2004.

[68] Thapliyal, H.; Kamala, R.V. and Srinivas, M., RSA encryption/decryption in wireless networks using an efficient high speed multiplier, in *IEEE International Conference on Personal Wireless Communications, ICPWC*, pp: 417-419, 2005.

[69] Abdallah, I. Damaj, "Reconfigurable hardware synthesis of the IDEA cryptographic algorithm," *Proceedings of Communicating Process Architectures* 2004, Jan F. Broenink and Gerald H. Hilderink (eds.), IOS Press, Oxford, United Kingdom. 5 – 8 September, 2004. P 387 – 416.

[70] Damaj, Higher-level hardware synthesis of the kasumi cryptographic algorithm, *Journal of Computer Science and Technology* **22** (1) (2007) 60{70}.

[71] Damaj, "Synthesizing The F8 cryptographic algorithm for programmable devices," *The Fourth IASTED International Conference on Advances in Computer Science and Technology*, Langkawi, Malaysia, 2 – 4 April 2008. P 68 – 73.

[72] Damaj, "Parallel Algorithms Development for Programmable Devices with Application from Cryptography," *International Journal of Parallel Programming*, Elsevier, 2007, I 6 V 35 P 529 – 572.

[73] V. Fischer and M. Drutarovský. Two methods of Rijndael implementation in reconfigurable hardware. *Proc. Workshop Cryptographic Hardware and Embedded Systems CHES* 2001, pp. 77-92, 2001.

[74] R. Anderson, E. Biham, and L. Knudsen. Serpent: A proposal for the advanced encryption standard. In *Proceedings of the First Advanced Encryption Standard (AES) Conference*, Ventura - CA, 1998.

[75] Elbirt and C. Paar. An FPGA implementation and performance evaluation of the Serpent block cipher. In *Proceedings of the 2000 ACM/SIGDA eighth international symposium on Field programmable gate arrays*, pages 33 – 40, New York - USA, 2000. ACM Press.

[76] P. Bora and T. Czajka. Implementation of the SERPENT algorithm using ALTERA FPGA devices. Public Comments on AES Candidate Algorithms - Round 2, October 2000.

[77] F. Rodriguez-Henriquez, N. A. Saqib, A. and Diaz-Perez. 4.2Gbit/s single-chip FPGA implementation of AES algorithm. *Electronics Letters*. v39 i15. 1115-1116.

[78] R. J. Anderson, E. Biham, L. R. Knudsen: The case for Serpent. *AES Candidate Conference* 2000: 349-354

[79] J. Daemen and V. Rijmen. AES Proposal: Rijndael. http://csrc.nist.gov/CryptoToolkit/aes/rijndael/Rijndael-ammended.pdf, September 1999.

[80] National Institute of Standards and Technology. *Announcing the advanced encryption standard AES. Technical report*, Federal Information Processing Standards Publication 197, November 2001.

[81] Hodjat and I. Verbauwhede. A 21.54 Gbits/s fully Pipelined AES processor on FPGA. *12th IEEE Symposium on Field-Programmable Custom Computing Machines.* 308-309, 2004.

[82] S. Sharma and T. S. B. Sudarshan. Design of an efficient architecture for advanced encryption standard algorithm using systolic structures. *International Conference of High Performance Computing (HiPC2005),* 2005.

[83] N. A. Saqib, F. Rodr´ıguez-Henr´ıquez, and A. D´ıaz-P´erez. Two Approaches for a single-chip FPGA implementation of an encryptor/decryptor AES core. In FPL 2003, volume 2778 of *Lecture Notes in Computer Science*, pages 303–312. Springer-Verlag Berlin Heidelberg, 2003.

[84] M. McLoone and J.V McCanny: High Performance FPGA Rijndael Algorithm Implementations. In C. Koc, D.Naccache, and C. Paar, editors, CHES2001, LNCS 2162, pp. 65-76, Springer-Verlag, 2001.

[85] N. Mentens, L. Batina, B. Preneel, and I. Verbauwhede. An FPGA implementation of Rijndael: trade-offs for side-channel security. In *IFAC Workshop* - PDS 2004, Programmable Devices and Systems, Elsevier, pp. 493-498, 2004.

[86] M. L. Akkar and C. Giraud. An implementation of DES and AES, secure against some attacks. In: Proceedings of 3rd International Workshop on Cryptographic Hardware and Embedded Systems (CHES)(C. K. Koc, D. Naccache and C. Paar, Eds.). number 2162 In : *Lecture Notes in Computer Science*. Springer-Verlag. Paris, France. pp.309-318. 2001.

[87] J. Daemen and V. Rijmen. *The design of Rijndael.* Springer-Verlag New York, Inc., 2002.

[88] M. Jing, C. Hsu, T. Truong, Y. Chen, and Y. Chang. The diversity study of AES on FPGA application. In *Proceedings of the IEEE International Conference on Field-Programmable Technology*, pages 390–393. IEEE, December 2002.

[89] R. Ashruf, G. Gaydadjiev, and S. Vassiliadis. Reconfigurable implementation for the AES algorithm. In *Proceedings of ProRISC* 2002, pages 169–172, November 2002.

[90] D. Wheeler and R. Needham. TEA, a tiny encryption algorithm. In B. Preneel, editor, *Proceedings of FSE* 1994, *LNCS*, volume 1008, pages 363–366, Springer-Verlag, 1994.

[91] Bogdanov, L. R. Knudsen, G. Leander, C. Paar, A. Poschmann, M. J. B. Robshaw, Y. Seurin and C. Vikkelsoe, "PRESENT: An ultra-lightweight block cipher," In Cryptographic Hardware and Embedded Systems - CHES 2007, *Lecture Notes in Computer Science*, Springer, Volume 4727, P 450 – 466, 2007.

[92] Lim and T. Korkishko. mCrypton - A lightweight block cipher for security of low-cost RFID tags and sensors. In J. Song, T. Kwon, and M. Yung, editors, Workshop on Information Security Applications - WISA'05, *LNCS*, volume 3786, pages 243-258, Springer-Verlag, 2005.

[93] Hong, J. Sung, S. Hong, J. Lim, S. Lee, B.-S; Koo, C. Lee, D. Chang, J. Lee, K. Jeong, H. Kim, J. Kim, and S. Chee. HIGHT: A new block cipher suitable for low-resource device. In L. Goubin and M. Matsui, editors, *Proceedings of CHES 2006, LNCS*, volume 4249, pages 46–59, Springer-Verlag, 2006.

[94] 41. F.-X. Standaert, G. Piret, N. Gershenfeld, and J.-J. Quisquater. SEA: A scalable encryption algorithm for small embedded applications. In J. Domingo-Ferrer, J. Posegga, and D. Schreckling, editors, Smart Card Research and Applications, *Proceedings of CARDIS 2006, LNCS*, volume 3928, pages 222–236, Springer-Verlag.

[95] M.J.B. Robshaw. Searching for compact algorithms: cgen. In P.Q. Nguyen, editor, *Proceedings of Vietcrypt 2006, LNCS*, volume 4341, pages 37–49, Springer, 2006.

[96] W. El-Ghazzawi, R. Saraeb, I. Damaj, "Hardware Development of the Extended Tiny Encryption Algorithm," *ACS/IEEE International Conference on Computer Systems and Applications*, Dubai/ Sharjah, United Arab Emirates, 8 – 11 March, 2006.

[97] Damaj, S. Hamadeh, H. Diab, "Efficient Tiny Hardware Cipher under Verilog," High Performance Computing and Simulation Conference, as a part of the 22nd *EUROPEAN Conference on Modelling and Simulation*, Nicosia, Cyprus, 3 – 5 June 2008.

[98] M. B. Sherigar, A. S. Mahadevan, K. S. Kumar, and S. David. A pipelined parallel processor to implement MD4 message digest algorithm on Xilinx FPGA. In VLSID '98: *Proceedings of the Eleventh International Conference on VLSI Design: VLSI for Signal Processing*, page 394, Washington, DC, USA, 1998. IEEE Computer Society.

[99] Joux. Multicollisions in iterated hash functions. application to cascaded Constructions. In Advances in Cryptology - CRYPTO 2004, 24th Annual International CryptologyConference, Santa Barbara, California, USA, August 15- 19, 2004, Proceedings, volume 3152 of *Lecture Notes in Computer Science*, pages 306-316. Springer, 2004.

[100] J. P. Tillich and G. Zemor. Group-theoretic hash functions. In Algebraic Coding, First French-Israeli Workshop, Paris, France, July 19-21, 1993, Proceedings, volume 781 of *Lecture Notes in Computer Science*, pages 90-110. Springer, 1993.

[101] J.M. Diez, S. Bojanic, Lj. Stanimirovicc, C. Carreras, and O. Nieto-Taladriz. Hash algorithms for cryptographic protocols: FPGA implementations. In *Proceedings of the 10th Telecommunications Forum*, TELFOR2002, Belgrade, Yugoslavia, May 26 -28, 2002.

[102] T. Grembowski, R. Lien, K. Gaj, N. Nguyen, P. Bellows, J. Flidr, T. Lehman, and B. Schott. Comparative analysis of the hardware implementations of hash functions SHA-1 and SHA-512. In ISC '02: *Proceedings of the 5th International Conference on Information Security*, Springer-Verlag, pages 75-89, London, UK, 2002.

[103] Y. K. Rang, D. W. Kim, T. W. Kwon, and J. R. Choi. An efficient implementation of hash function processor for IPSEC. In *Proceedings of 2002 IEEE Asia-Pacific Conference on ASIC*, pages 93-96, Taipei, Taiwan, Aug 2002.

[104] N. Sklavos and O. Koufopavlou. On the Hardware Implementations of the SHA-2 (256, 384, 512) Hash Functions. In *Proceedings of IEEE International Symposium on Circuits and Systems*, ISC AS 2003, volume 5, pages V-153-V-156, Bangkok, Thailand, 2003.

[105] W. Ng, T. S. Ng, and K. W. Yip. A unified architecture of MD5 and RIPEMD-160 hash algorithms. In *Proceedings of IEEE International Symposium on Circuits and Systems*, ISCAS 2004, volume 2, pages 11-889- 11-892, Vancouver, Canada, 2004.

[106] R. P. McEvoy, F. M. Crowe, C. C. Murphy, and W. P. Marnane. Optimisation of the SHA-2 family of hash functions on FPGAs. *ISVLSI* 2006, pages 317- 322, 2006.

[107] Satoh and T. Inoue. ASIC-Hardware-Focused Comparison for Hash Functions MD5, RIPEMD-160, and SHS. In *ITCC '05: Proceedings of the International Conference on Information Technology: Coding and Computing (ITCC'05)* - Volume /, pages 532-537, Washington, DC, USA, IEEE Computer Society, 2005.

[108] N. Sklavos and O. Koufopavlou. On the Hardware Implementations of the SHA-2 (256, 384, 512) Hash Functions. In *Proceedings of IEEE International Symposium on Circuits and Systems,* ISC AS 2003, volume 5, pages V-153- V-156, Bangkok, Thailand, 2003.

[109] M. McLoone and J.V. McCanny. Efficient Single-Chip Implementation of SHA-384 and SHA-512. In *Proceedings. 2002 IEEE International Conference on Field-Programmable Technology, FPT02,* volume 5, pages 311-314, Hong Kong, December 16-18, 2002.

[110] M. McLoone, C. McIvor, and A. Savage. High-Speed Hardware Architectures of the Whirlpool Hash Function. In *FPT'05,* pages 147-162. IEEE Computer Society Press, 2005.

[111] P. Kitsos and O. Koufopavlou. Eflficient Architecture and Hardware Implementation of the Whirlpool Hash Function. *IEEE Transactions on Consumer Electronics,* **50**(1):208-214, February 2004.

[112] N. Pramstaller, C. Rechberger, and V. Rijmen. A Compact FPGA Implementation of the Hash Function Whirlpool. In FPGA '06: Proceedings of the international symposium on Field Programmable Gate Arrays, pages 159-166, ACM Press, New York, NY, USA, 2006.

[113] J. Alcantara, A. Vieira, F. Galvez-Durand, and V. Alves. A methodology for dynamic power consumption estimation using VHDL descriptions. *Symposium on Integrated Circuits and Systems Design,* pages 149 – 154, September 2002.

[114] K. Marinis, N. Moshopoulos, F. Karoubalis, and K. Pekmestzi. On the hardware implementation of the 3GPP confidentiality and integrity algorithms. *Lecture Notes in Computer Science,* 2200, 2001.

In: Computer Security: Intrusion, Detection and Prevention   ISBN: 978-1-60692-781-6
Editors: R. D. Hopkins and W. P. Tokere   © 2009 Nova Science Publishers, Inc.

Chapter 5

PERFORMANCE FOR CRYPTOGRAPHY: A HARDWARE APPROACH

Athanasios P. Kakarountas[1,*] and Haralambos Michail[2,†]
[1]University of Central Greece, Lamia, GR-35100 Greece
[2]Department of Electrical & Computer Eng. University of Patras,
Patras, GR-26500, Greece

Abstract

Cryptography can be considered as a special application of coding schemes. High speed execution of Encoding and Decoding processes is crucial in the majority of the so-called security schemes. In fact, the characteristics of a cryptographic algorithm in terms of throughput are usually the most important requirement to adopt the algorithm in a security scheme. As the need for higher security increases, the market urges for strong cryptographic protocols that will offer the desired degree of privacy. However, most of the algorithms now and forthcoming are complex and do not seem to be efficient for performance-oriented purposes. In this chapter, an algorithmic approach for designing high-speed cryptographic primitives is presented. Setting as target the high throughput, a complete methodology for developing various types of cryptographic primitives, focusing on hardware (without however excluding software, or a combination of them) is offered. The application of the proposed design approach also highlights the effect of designing for supercomputing on a critical application, such as cryptography. Parallelism and code transformation are few of the techniques that will be used for achieving the desired target, the implementation of the ever best proposed cryptographic primitives in terms of speed and throughput.

Introduction

Security has been more critical than ever since sensitive details have become widely available through various types of networks. All the organizations (or even the citizens) that possess such information need to feel protected from eavesdroppers, thieves or generally anyone who

---

* E-mail address: kakarountas@ieee.org;
† E-mail address: michail@ece.upatras.gr;

tries to illegally acquire the sensitive data. Thus it is important to store the data safely and in a such way that will discourage anyone from getting access to it.

Furthermore, it is also necessary to feel secure, not only for storage issues, but also for circulating the data through a safe communication channel. Especially in our times, because communication is conducted at high speeds, it is critical to be able to establish quickly a secure channel and transmit sensitive data in a way that only authorized persons can access.

Cryptography is a significant weapon in our quest to protect our treasure: the sensitive data. Seen as a process, we can assume that cryptography is nothing more than a simple mathematic function that transforms one set of numbers (or characters, objects etc) to another. This means that it is used to change comprehensible data (messages) to a seemingly corrupted group of numbers (characters), at least for those not knowing the inverse function to reproduce the initial message. Implementations of simple mathematic functions in computer hardware can be realized either by using software (the most common way) or by creating a custom hardware component. The optimization of such implementations is generally limited on how someone can use or select the appropriate hardware or create the fastest execution code by using the appropriate instructions.

It can be said that the latter is the case in most current solutions that concern cryptography. Many implementations exist, however few of them can satisfy the requirement for high performance; most of the implementations achieve this goal through uncounted use of redundancy. Although cost and performance are joint design parameters, there is no explicit way to develop cost effective implementations and at the same time achieve the desired high throughput (performance).

On the other hand, if cryptography is seen as an algorithm then it can be assumed that the tools that we have in hand to optimize their performance are enriched by many techniques well known from basic algorithm theory. The last three years there is a push to treat cryptography primitives as basic iterative algorithms. Then, optimization is based on various types of transformations, or the use of special properties of the algorithm or the hardware platform it will be embedded in.

The scope of this chapter is to highlight the techniques that can be used to guide the designers to elegant, cost-effective, high-performance implementations of cryptographic primitives. The chapter is organized in three parts. In the first part, a thorough presentation of the current status of cryptography is given, considering hash functions, block ciphers and the upcoming elliptic curves based cryptography. In the second part, several algorithmic optimization techniques are listed and from those a methodology to produce high performance implementations is formed. The methodology is generic; it is focused on hardware implementations. However it can be used also for software-oriented implementations with slight modifications. In the last part, a simple example is given in order to exhibit the benefits of the presented methodology.

So let us begin our quest by recalling the saying in Sun Tzu's *The Art of War*, "Learn the field of the battle, otherwise your army will be defeated".

Status of the Market

The most common cryptographic components are the block ciphers and the hash functions. In the last decade there has also been a growing interest in Elliptic Curves Cryptography (ECC).

The combination of the above offers complete solutions for a number of applications, forming special cryptographic schemes.

Concerning the simple hash functions, they are widely used for data integrity and user authentication. Nowadays many applications like the Public Key Infrastracture (PKI) [1], IPSec [2], Secure Electronic Transactions (SET) [3], and the 802.16 [4] standards incorporate authenticating services. Hash functions are also required for authentication to Virtual Private Networks (VPN's) [2]. Digital signature algorithms like DSA [5] that are used for authenticating services like electronic mail, electronic funds transfer, electronic data interchange, etc. are based on hash functions. Hashes are also used to identify files on peer-to-peer file sharing networks [6].

Hash functions are further used in signed code systems such as Microsoft's Windows Update [7] to ensure the integrity and authenticity of downloaded programs and patches. Hashes are also used to periodically check on-disk code integrity in systems such as Tripwire [8]. Last but not least, the US federal government in 2004 came up with a new plan to help secure electronic voting [9], employingSHA-1 so as to achieve a higher level of security and therefore more confidence in e-voting than ever before.

Hash functions are widely used in practical signature schemes [10], in web protocols such as SSL [11], providing security in networks and mobile services and also in electronic passwords management [12]. They are also the main modules that exist in the HMAC implementations that produce Message Authentication Codes (MAC's) [13]. It has also to be mentioned that both TLS [14] and IPSec standards suggest an HMAC mechanism based on a collision resistant hash function. Moreover, hashing functions are deployed in the Diffie-Hellman [15] protocol key exchange.

As far block ciphers are concerned, the most well known is Advanced Encryption Standard (AES) [16], which replaced the old Data Encryption Standard (DES). Since NIST adopted AES algorithm as basic standard for symmetric cryptography, AES became the main symmetric algorithm in many communication protocols and applications. The AES algorithm has broad applications, including mobile phone, cellular phones, smart cards, RFID tags, WWW servers and automated teller machines (ATMs). The main wireless protocols [17-18] adopted AES algorithm as the basic security mechanism [19] which provides to system authentication, authorization and data integrity. AES can serve as a good example of how block ciphers are structured.

As far as the ECC is concerned, since N. Koblitz [20] and V. Miller [21] presented Elliptic Curve Cryptography (ECC) independently in 1985, ECC is now considered a mature public-key cryptosystem and has withstood a large number of attacks. Extensive research work is being carried out regarding the underlying mathematics, security and efficient implementations. ECC offers the highest strength per bit and the smallest key size compared to any other public-key cryptosystem. This fact relies on the underlying mathematical problem of ECC, i.e. the discrete logarithm problem in the group of points over elliptic curves. Among the various fields that elliptic curves can be defined on, integer fields F_p and binary polynomial fields F_m^2 are considered to be the most appropriate ones for an efficient and secure implementation.

The latter cryptographic algorithms are based on simple functions that can be easily implemented in various ways. The most common way is the algorithm's implementation in software, as this development approach is the most cost-effective. Although this solution is ideal for inclusion in common PCs or widely used platforms (i.e. mobile phones) it lacks of high performance characteristics. Hence, it is practically impossible to rely only on software implementations to manage cases in which there is a need to develop a server-based system that services numerous requests from a significantly high number of clients. This is a key indication that hardware implementation needs to be considered. On the other hand, it is not advisable to implement the whole security scheme in hardware, as the cost becomes extremely high, without needing to do so.

Thus a combination of software-hardware co-design can be considered ideal for developing low-cost but high-performance cryptosystems. This chapter will not focus on how to combine the two design approaches; surely this would go beyond the scope of the book. The main focus will be concentrated on how to modify the algorithms of the cryptographic components, to achieve the highest performance. Then, having the best possible components, their combination has better probabilities to achieve the desired characteristics, as dictated by the targeted application.

Consider the following: all of us know what security suites are used by our friends, but do we know what security suite is used by large enterprises, organizations, etc.? Well, this should be an indirect answer to all of them that may argue with the claim that high-performance implementations need to be applied to hardware. In fact, after spending a short time in your favourite Internet search machine, you will be amazed to discover that a vast number of hardware cryptographic primitives are available commercially, and more amazed when you discover the clients of the vendors of these cryptographic components.

High Performance and How to Achieve It

There is a big variety of choices that can be made at early stages of the design/development process to help us achieve the desired performance. The most obvious selection is the use of the best performing hardware, either a microprocessor running the appropriate code, or a hardware programmable device (i.e., FPGA, PLD, etc).

In fact, this was the trend until 5 years ago. Until then, there was no need for current communication speeds, nor were the clients-users of a service so many. In the last five years, there has been an effort to go beyond the common implementations (simply porting the algorithm to the available platform). Next follows a short list of the techniques that we have in hand and can help us improve our designs of cryptographic components. Recall that in this chapter, the implementation is based on algorithmic enhancement. Also, notice that from hereafter when there is a reference to 'code' it either means code written in any programming language to implement the cryptographic algorithm, or the code description of the hardware implementation of the algorithm, using one of the commonly used Hardware Description Languages (HDL).

A) Loop unrolling

This is a typical algorithmic transformation, usually used to break short loops to a sequence of instructions. This allows higher execution time as there is no need to branch back to the start of the loop. This technique is ideal for software implementations of short code blocks that are frequently used. Furthermore, seen from the hardware design approach, it is a common technique when there are obvious dependencies between the inputs and the outputs.

B) Variable pre-computation

Another typical transformation is to pre-compute a frequently used variable at the beginning of the code block and then use it when needed. This eliminates unnecessary calculations of values that are already available.

C) Numerical system change

A most sophisticated technique is to move the calculations to an alternative number system, which benefits our implementation. For example, especially in hardware implementations where large integer multiplications are frequent, the use of Residue Number System (RNS) renders the multiplication to become a parallel addition of the operands.

D) Logical transformation

A technique mainly used for applications in data access and storage management for embedded programmable processors, is the logical transformation. This means that a code block may produce exactly the same output as another code block, benefiting however the system in several characteristics, like speed, power dissipation, memory size etc.

E) Resource redundancy (Parallelism)

The use of redundant hardware was prohibited in the past mainly due to the high cost. However, nowadays there are multi-core processors available in the market. Thus, it is advisable to use all the provided processing power that is offered from your system. Until now, the use of simple processing platforms limited the achieved performance. Now it is possible to create easily a System-on-a-Chip, using the appropriate special purpose hardware and several processors and memory modules. Furthermore, the analysis of a cryptographic algorithm may prove that one process may be executed from one processing core and another process by another processing core, increasing thus significantly the system's performance.

F) Use of small memories (Look-up Tables) instead of complex descriptions

When the complexity of the algorithm is high, it is common to try to substitute the code block with a static memory that associates the input (as address) to the appropriate output (data stored). However, this technique is rarely used as there are few cryptographic algorithms on which this technique can apply.

The latter are the most important techniques that we have in hand to develop performance-efficient implementations of cryptographic components. In the next section follows a methodology that combines the aforementioned in favour of our design.

A Methodology to Achieve High Performance

The presented methodology is based on the latter algorithmic transformations allowing simultaneous spatial and temporal transformations. Spatial transformations are those that manipulate and re-order the position of the available resources in order to generate the same output. Temporal transformations are those that manage values strongly joint to time and sequence of appearing.

A major advantage of applying a transformation on the algorithm is the capability to know explicitly the penalty this action requires to be paid. Usually the penalty of the transformations' application is paid in area (cost) although power dissipation has to be considered in some cases. In the following paragraphs, the flow of the design methodology is presented in full detail.

In Fig. 1, the flow of the design methodology is illustrated. Initially, the algorithm is explored and in case there is the need for a vast number of heavy arithmetic operations to be executed, the appropriate number system is selected. For example in cases that multiplication is the dominant it is advisable to exploit the characteristics of RNS. After having determined the targeted number system, the next steps are those of the code transformation.

At the first step, the algorithm is unfolded, using the round un-roll technique and allowing more operations to be performed in one single clock cycle. The second step comprises the application of the pre-computation transformation. At this step, units responsible for the calculation of intermediate values (stored in temporary variables) are partitioned appropriately, in order to allow parallel execution and to disjoin in space several dependencies. The two latter steps of the methodology refer to the spatial transformation and define the first phase of the transformations. During this phase, throughput can be increased even by 100%, with a negligible area cost. At this step, logical transformations should be considered. The third step of the methodology, aims at a higher level of abstraction, applying pre-computation technique on constant or once-calculated values and thus achieving data pre-fetching. Such values are the constants of the hashing and the message schedules. Also at this step, the use of memory components is advised to substitute bulk and complex components, that unnecessarily degrade the performance of the system.

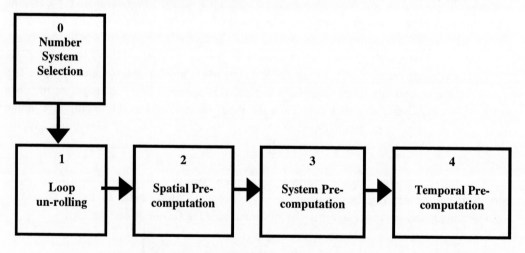

Figure 1. Methodology steps to implement high-speed cryptographic components.

Finally at the fourth step, temporal pre-computation of dependant signals is performed. The two latter steps of the methodology are focused on time transformation of the algorithm and aim dependencies of signals at the RT and system level of abstraction.

A step-by-step example follows of the methodology's application in a real system.

Example

Let's consider as an example of the presented methodology the hardware implementation of SHA-1 hash function. Let's define the target characteristics: high performance (at least 2 Gbps) and low cost. We should consider also alternative implementations to support the final decision.

The initial process of a hashing algorithm is message padding. A Padding Unit is found in every existing implementation of hash functions and it is responsible for dividing the input data (message) in Message schedules (message blocks scheduled to be processed sequentially). Usually the division of the message is made in blocks of 512 bits (ie. SHA and MD algorithms). However, although this unit is illustrated in Fig. 2, it is common to implement it in software, since no security issues arise. This is also the case of the proposed implementations in this work.

Two consecutive operational blocks of SHA-1 are shown in Fig. 3. The critical path is located on the computation of the a_t value (three addition stages and a multiplexer) which determines the highest delay to produce the output data.

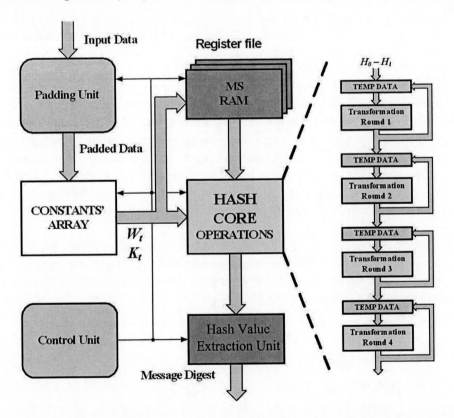

Figure 2. Typical hash core architecture with 4 pipeline stages including a single operation block.

The first step of the methodology is to unfold the iterative block of code. The number of operations that should be unrolled must be decided having in mind the targeted performance. An analysis that was made for SHA-1 hash function has been conducted in order to determine the best ratio Throughput/Area. As illustrated in Fig 4 this ratio presents its maximum when two operations are partially unrolled.

Unfolding the expressions of a_t, b_t, c_t, d_t, e_t, as they were described in [22], it is observed that a_{t-1}, b_{t-1}, c_{t-1}, d_{t-1} values are assigned directly to outputs b_t, c_t, d_t, e_t respectively. In Eq. (2) the expressions of a_t, b_t, c_t, d_t, e_t, are defined.

$$
\begin{aligned}
e_t &= d_{t-1} \\
d_t &= c_{t-1} \\
c_t &= ROTL_{30}\left(b_{t-1}\right) \\
b_t &= a_{t-1} \\
a_t &= ROTL_5\left(a_{t-1}\right) + f_t\left(b_{t-1}, c_{t-1}, d_{t-1}\right) + e_{t-1} + W_t + K_t
\end{aligned}
\tag{2}
$$

where $ROTx(y)$ represents rotation of word y to the left by X bits and $f_t(z,w,v)$ represents the non-linear function associated to the round.

The partial unrolling is based on the basic concept that was previously mentioned. At the first operation block of Fig. 3 except of the output a_{t-1}, the rest of the outputs b_{t-1}, c_{t-1}, d_{t-1} and e_{t-1} derive directly from the inputs a_{t-2}, b_{t-2}, c_{t-2}, and d_{t-2} respectively. This means consequently that also c_t, d_t and e_t can be derived directly from a_{t-2}, b_{t-2} and c_{t-2} respectively. Furthermore, due to the fact that a_t and b_t calculations require the d_{t-2} and e_{t-2} inputs respectively, which are stored in peripheral registers, these calculations can be performed in parallel.

In Fig. 5, the consecutive SHA-1 operation blocks of Fig. 4, have been modified so that a_t and b_t are calculated in parallel. The gray marked areas on Fig. 5 indicate the parts of the proposed SHA-1 operation block that operate in parallel. Now the critical path in Fig. 5 is increased by an extra addition level consisting by four addition stages. Although, at a first glance this reduces the maximum operation frequency, the result is higher throughput as it is increased significantly since the message digest is now computed in only 40 clock cycles.

The modified expressions of a_t, b_t, c_t, d_t and e_t, are described from Eq.3. It can be assumed that area requirements are increased significantly. Thus, the cost-effective constraint seems to be violated. However this is not valid since the introduced hardware is only a small percentage of the SHA-1 core.

$$
\begin{aligned}
e_t &= c_{t-2} \\
d_t &= ROTL_{30}\left(b_{t-2}\right) \\
c_t &= ROTL_{30}\left(a_{t-2}\right) \\
b_t &= ROL_5\left(a_{t-2}\right) + f_t\left(b_{t-2}, c_{t-2}, d_{t-2}\right) + e_{t-2} + W_{t-1} + K_{t-1} \\
a_t &= ROL_5\left(b_1\right) + f_t\left(a_{t-2}, c_{t-2}, ROTL_5\left(b_{t-2}\right)\right) + d_{t-2} + W_t + K_t
\end{aligned}
\tag{3}
$$

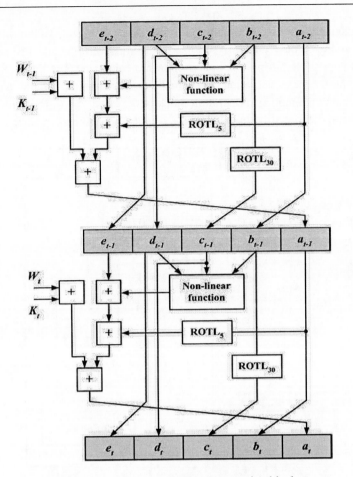

Figure 3. Two consecutive SHA-1 operation blocks.

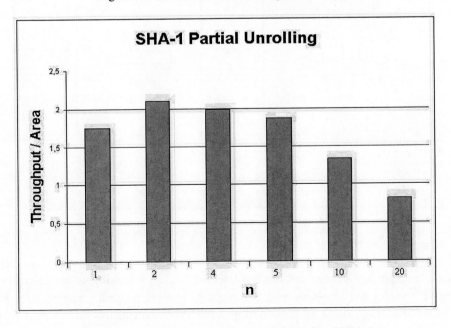

Figure 4. Effect of unrolling the operation blocks of SHA-1.

Afterwards, the spatial pre-computation technique can be used. Taking into consideration the fact that some outputs are derived directly from several inputs respectively, we can assume that it is possible during one operation to pre-calculate some intermediate values that will be used in the next operation. This technique is applied on the partially unrolled operation block and the modified operation block is shown in Fig. 6. From Eq. 3, it is derived that the maximum delay is still observed on the calculation of the a_{t+1} value.

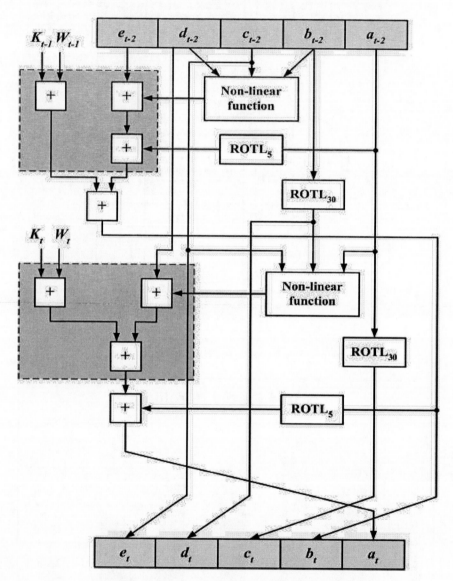

Figure 5. Two unrolled SHA-1 operation blocks.

The outputs c_{t+1}, d_{t+1}, e_{t+1} are derived directly from the a_{t-1}, b_{t1}, c_{t-1}, values respectively, and also the output b_{t+1} is computed much sooner than a_{t+1}. It is possible to pre-calculate some intermediate values and move the pipeline registers to an appropriate intermediate point to store them. Thus, Eq. (3) is transformed to generate the intermediate values e^{*}_{t-1}, d^{*}_{t-1}, f_{t1}, f_{t2}, that are illustrated in Fig. 6.

The new operation block now consists of two units, the "Pre-Computation" unit which is responsible for the pre-computation of the values that are needed in the next operation and the "Post-Computation" unit which is responsible for the final computations of each operation. Applying the transformation to the operation block, the critical path is shortened by one adder level, which contributes approximately 20% to the overall maximum delay.

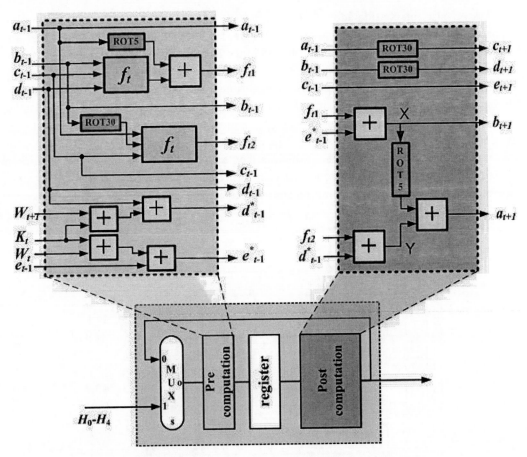

Figure 6. Partially unrolled operation block with pre-computed values.

The proposed operation block in Fig. 6 computes in one clock cycle the result of two operations and its critical path consists of three addition stages and a multiplexer. This means that from the application of the first two steps of the proposed methodology, a 100% increment of throughput in the implementation of the SHA-1 hash function has already been achieved.

At the third step of the proposed methodology, a system-level pre-computation is to be applied to achieve data pre-fetching. Notice that all W_t values can be computed and be available for adequate time before needed to be consumed. Also the values of the constants K_t are known a priori. The latter give us the potential of pre-computing the sum $W_t + K_t$ outside of the operation block.

The sum is then saved into a register that feeds the operation block and thus the externally (regarding the operational block) pre-computed sum $W_t + K_t$ is available at the beginning of each tth operation. Consequently the addition is performed sooner than the time it is really needed and the result is pre-fetched at the operational block. So, it is valid to write:

$$e_{t+3} = c_{t+1} = ROTL_{30}(a_{t-1}) \qquad (4)$$

Taking also in consideration that the constant values W, K can be externally pre-computed, the temporal pre-computation technique can be applied. Values X and Y that are shown in Fig. 6 are going to be pre-calculated in the axis of time. In order to apply this new technique for the pre-computation of the value X, instead of adding $e_{t+3} + K_{t+4} + W_{t+4}$ at the $t+5$ operation (in order to calculate one of the sub-sums needed for the computation of a_{t+5}), during the operation $t+1$ we perform the addition $K_{t+4} + W_{t+4} + ROT_{30}(a_{t-1})$, which is then saved into the register h^*. At the next operation, that is operation $t+3$, the pre-computed sum represents the value $K_{t+4} + W_{t+4} + c_{t+1}$. Finally at the $t+5$ operation the pre-referred sum represents the value $K_{t+4} + W_{t+4} + e_{t+3}$ which is then added with the output of the non-linear function so as to calculate the intermediate value of X_{t+3}. The value of X_{t+3} is used at the same operation in order to calculate the a_{t+5} and b_{t+5} values.

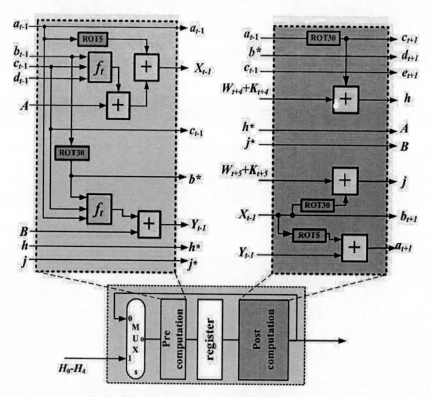

Figure 7. Partially unrolled operation block with pre-computed values and pre-fetching of $W+K$ values.

The result of the pre-calculation of value X, is that now the value of b derives directly from the rotated value of X as shown in Fig. 7. So, it is valid to write the following equation:

$$d_{t+3} = b^*_{t+1} = ROTL_{30}(X_{t-1}) \qquad (5)$$

These facts, gives us the opportunity to apply the temporal pre-computation technique also for the calculation of the value Y. To be more detailed at the $t+1$ operation, the addition $K_{t+5} + W_{t+5} + ROT_{30}(X_{t-1})$ is performed. At the next operation, which is the $t+3$ operation, the previous sum represents the value $K_{t+5} + W_{t+5} + b_{t+1}$ (equal to b_{t+3}). Finally at the $t+5$ operation the pre-referred sum represents the value $K_{t+5} + W_{t+5} + d_{t+3}$ which is added with the output of the second non-linear function so as to calculate the value of Y_{t+3} (this value is noted as Y_{t-1} in Fig. 7 because Fig. 7 describes $t+1$ operation). Y_{t+3} is then used at the "Post-Computation" unit of the same operation so as to calculate the value of a_{t+5}. The delay for the calculation of value Y_{t-1} in Fig. 7 is two addition stages and a non-linear function (delay of two logical gates).

The new critical path of the SHA-1 implementation in Fig. 7 is located on the computation of values X and Y. This means that the new critical path has been reduced to two addition stages, a non-linear function and a multiplexer. The critical path is shortened by one adder level, which contributes approximately 30% to the overall maximum delay whereas two gates (non-linear function) contribute much less.

Table 1. Performance Characteristics of the Implementations Resulting from the Presented Methodology

Implementation	SHA-1		
	Op. Frequency (MHz)	Throughput (Mbps)	Area CLBs
[23] [a]	42.9	119.0	1004
[24] [a]	-	427.0	-
[25] [a]	86.0	530.0	-
[26] [a]	38.6	900.0	1550
[27] [a]	72.0	460.8	518
[28] [a]	72.0	1842.2	878
[29] [a]	64.0	1024.0	1480
[30] [a]	71.0	1731.2	1018
From Methodology [a]	61.0	3150.0	1112
[31] [b]	-	1024.0	851
[32] [b]	-	3541.0	4258
From Methodology [b]	91.0	4715.0	1212
[29] [c]	72.5	1160.0	1484
From Methodology [c]	63.7	3290.0	1175
[33] [d] (Commercial IP)	134.6	847.9	647
[34] [e] (Commercial IP)	-	2010.0	1078 (LUTs)

[a] Virtex FPGA family   [d] Virtex 4 FPGA family
[b] Virtex II FPGA family   [e] Virtex 5 FPGA family
[c] Virtex-E FPGA family

To exhibit the benefits of applying the proposed design methodology, the above implementation was realized and compared to other existing implementations proposed either by academia or industry. The results from the latter implementations are showed in Table 1, for a variety of FPGA families. The highest increase observed for SHA-1, is about 160%; a gain in throughput compared to a non-optimized implementation with four pipeline stages (implemented in the same technology). This non-optimized implementation is the one described and presented in [27].

As it is proved from the results in Table 1, it can be said that the proposed methodology always leads to the best performing implementations. However, in order to meet the initial design requirements, we have to select the implementation with a high performance but also with the lowest cost. As it can be easily derived from Table 1, the implementation of SHA-1 for the XILINX Virtex family is ideal, as this family is the cheapest of all and outperforms the aimed throughput (more than 2 Gbps).

Conclusion

In this chapter, a new methodology was proposed for increasing throughput of almost all cryptographic primitives. The methodology is generic and can be used in a wide range of cryptographic algorithms that are currently in use or will be deployed in the future in the case that high throughput implementations are needed.

The methodology consists of five steps and can lead to significant increase of throughput (about 160% for SHA-1 as was shown in a step-by-step example). Furthermore, other characteristics can be improved (integration area, memory use, etc.). The results derived from their implementation in FPGA technologies confirm the theoretical results of the proposed implementation.

Acknowledgements

The authors would like to thank Prof. Costas E. Goutis for being their mentor in research and life. We would also like to thank the beloved Angie and Maria, as well as our families. Finally, we would like to express our gratitude to all our colleagues who helped us create this work, either by offering precious information and review comments, or by encouraging us to continue when the spirit was tired. So thank you Dimitris, Helen, George, Apostolis, Thanos, George and Vassilis.

References

[1]   SP 800-32., "Introduction to Public Key Technology and the Federal PKI Infrastructure", NIST, US Dept of Commerce,2001.
[2]   SP800-77, "Guide to IPSec VPN's", NIST, US Dept of Commerce., 2005.
[3]   Larry Loeb "Secure Electronic Transactions: Introduction and Technical Reference", Artech House Publishers, 1998.
[4]   D. Johnston and J. Walker, Overview of IEEE802.16 Security, *IEEE Security and Privacy*, May-June 2004.

[5]   FIPS 186, (DSS), "Digital Signature Standard (DSS)", FIPS Publication 180-1, NIST, US Dept of Commerce, 1994.

[6]   FileSharing Talk. Web page, available at http://www.filesharingtalk.com.

[7]   Microsoft, "Internet Explorer 6: Digital Certificates," Jan. 2005, http://www.microsoft.com/windows/ie/ie6/using/howto/security/digitalcert/using.mspx.

[8]   G.H. Kim and E.H. Spafford, "The Design and Implementation of Tripwire: A File System Integrity Checker," in 2nd ACM Conf. Computer and Communications Security, pp. 18-29, 1994.

[9]   C. Biever, "US boosts e-voting software security", NewScientist.com news, http://www.newscientist.com/article.ns?id=dn6593, 2004.

[10] Mironov, Hash functions: "Theory, attacks, and applications", Microsoft Research, Silicon Valley Campus, October 24, 2005.

[11] Stephen Thomas, "SSL & TLS Essentials: Securing the Web", John Wiley and sons Publications, 2000.

[12] R. Morris and K. Thompson, "Password security: A case history," *Communications of ACM*, vol. 22(11), pp. 594-597, 1979.

[13] FIPS 198-1, "The Keyed-Hash Message Authentication Code (HMAC)", FIPS Publication 180-1, NIST, US Dept of Commerce, 2007.

[14] IETF, The Internet Engineering Task Force, Web page, available at http://www.ietf.org.

[15] RM. St. Johns, "Diffie-Helman USM Key Management Information Base and Textual Convention",*RFC* **2786**,March 2000.

[16] National Institute of Standards and Technology (NIST). *FIPS-197*: *Advanced Encryption Standard*, November 2001.

[17] IEEE Standard for Wireless LAN Medium Access Control (MAC) and Physical Layer (PHY) Specification (1999).

[18] IEEE Standard 802.11i-2004: "Standard for Information technology - Telecommunication and information exchange between systems-Local and metropolitan area networks-Specific requirements", July 2004.

[19] Azzedine Boukerche "Handbook of Algorithms for Wireless Networking and Mobile Computing", Chapman & Hall/CRC, 28 November 2005. R. L. Rivest, "The MD5 Message digest Algorithm", IETF Network Working Group , *RFC* **1321**, 1992.

[20] N. Koblitz, "Elliptic curve cryptosystems", *Math. Comp.*, **48**, pp. 203 – 209, 1987.

[21] V. Miller, "Use of elliptic curves in cryptography", In advances in Cryptology, CRYPTO – '85, Springer *LNCS* **218**, pp. 47 – 426, 1986.

[22] FIPS 180-1, "Secure Hash Standard ", *FIPS Publication* **180-1**, NIST, US Dept of Commerce, 1995.

[23] S. Dominikus, "A Hardware Implementation of MD4-Family Hash Algorithms", *IEEE International Conference on Electronics Circuits and Systems (ICECS'02)*, pp.1143-1146, 2002.

[24] R. Hoare, P. Menon, and M. Ramos , "427 Mbits/sec Hardware Implementation of the SHA-1 Algorithm in an FPGA",*IASTED International Conference on Communications and Computer Networks*, pp.188 – 193., 2002.

[25] T.Grembowski, R.Lien, K.Gaj, N.Nguyen, P.Bellows, J.Flidr, T.Lehman and B.Schott, "Comparative analysis of the Hardware implementations of hash functions Sha-1 and Sha-512", In ISC, *Lecture Notes in Computer Science (LNCS)*, vol. 2433 , pp. 75–89.,Springer,2002.

[26] J.M. Diez,, S. Bojanic,, C. Carreras, and O. Nieto-Taladriz, "Hash Algorithms for Cryptographic Protocols: FPGA Implementations", TELEFOR, 2002.

[27] G. Selimis, N. Sklavos, and O. Koufopavlou, "VLSI Implementation of the Keyed-Hash Message Authentication Code for the Wireless Application Protocol", *IEEE International Conference on Electronics Circuits and Systems (ICECS'03)*, pp.24.-27, 2003.

[28] N. Sklavos,E. Alexopoulos, and O.Koufopavlou, " Networking Data Integrity: High Speed Architectures and Hardware Implementations", *IAJIT Journal*, Vol.1, No.0, pp.54-59, 2003.

[29] R.Lien, T.Grembowski, K.Gaj, "A 1 Gbit/s Partially Unrolled Architecture of Hash Functions SHA-1 and SHA-512", *Lecture Notes in Computer Science (LNCS)*,Vol. 2964, pp. 324-338,Springer , 2004

[30] N. Sklavos, P. Kitsos, E. Alexopoulos, and O.Koufopavlou, "Open Mobile Alliance (OMA) Security Layer: Architecture, Implementation and Performance Evaluation of the Integrity Unit", *New Generation Computing: Computing Paradigms and Computational Intelligence*, Springer-Verlag, Vol. 23, No 1, pp. 77-100, 2005.

[31] Yiakoumis, M. Papadomanolakis, H.Michail, A.Kakarountas, and C.Goutis, "Maximizing the hash function of authentication codes", *IEEE Potentials magazine*, Vol. 25, No.2, pp. 9-12, March/April 2006.

[32] Y. K. Lee, H. Chan and I.Verbauwhede, "Throughput Optimized SHA-1 Architecture Using Unfolding Transformation", IEEE 17th International Conference on Application-specific Systems, *Architectures and Processors (ASAP'06)* pp. 354-359, 2006.

[33] CAST Inc., Web page, available athttp://www.cast-inc.com/cores.

[34] Helion Technology Ltd, Data Security Products,Web page, available at http://www.heliontech.com/auth.htm.

In: Computer Security: Intrusion, Detection and Prevention   ISBN: 978-1-60692-781-6
Editors: R. D. Hopkins and W. P. Tokere   © 2009 Nova Science Publishers, Inc.

Chapter 6

FAST FACE DETECTOR AND RECOGNITION FOR BIOMETRICAL SECURITY SYSTEMS

Jose M. Chaves-González, Miguel A. Vega-Rodríguez,
Juan A. Gómez-Pulido and Juan M. Sánchez-Pérez[1]
Univ. Extremadura, Dept. Technologies of Computers and Communications,
Escuela Politécnica, Campus Universitario s/n, 10071, Cáceres, Spain

ABSTRACT

This chapter explains the process which involves building a simple but fast face recognition system using computer vision and image processing techniques. Face recognition is included in biometrical identification methods, which are based on the study and evaluation of biometrical features, such as fingerprints, iris, voice, handprint, DNA… or as we are concerned in this chapter, human face. There are a huge amount of applications which use face recognition, but the more common ones are related to authentication, surveillance, criminal detection and, in general, security systems. We have developed a face recognition using a feature-based method. In general, a generic face recognition system is divided into three stages. In the first one, the detection of the face from a simple image is done. The second step consists in the segmentation of the facial principal components and the feature extraction from the face regions. Finally, in the third stage the recognition or verification of the human face is done. Among the different techniques of face recognition, we explain in this chapter a geometrical technique. The recognition using this technique is very fast, because it is based on the extraction of local features of the human face to do the recognition –which is a very fast feature extraction method. To perform the most robust geometrical face recognition, we use 31 different facial features. These features are calculated from the different geometrical regions located in the segmentation stage (eyebrows, eyes, pupils, nose, tip of the nose, mouth and the four sides of the face –the forehead, the chin and the left and right sides) using an improvement of K-means clustering algorithm. Therefore, the input to the system is a single photograph of the face of the person who wants to be authenticated by the system; whereas the output of the system will depend on the

---

[1] {jm, mavega, jangomez, sanperez}@unex.es

application that we give to the system. In identification problems, the system will give back the determined identity from a database of known individuals, but in verification problems, the system will confirm or reject the claimed identity of the input face. To summarize, in this chapter we overview the different techniques of face recognition and we study in depth the steps and basis to build a fast and functional face recognition based on geometrical features. Finally, in the future work section we point out the way to improve the face recognition to build a more robust security system.

Keywords: face recognition, face detection, facial segmentation, feature extraction, biometrical identification.

1. INTRODUCTION

The strong need for user-friendly authentication systems which are impossible to copy, forge or simply lose (just like cards, passwords, keys, etc) took, quite a lot years ago, to the introduction of biometrical analysis techniques in identification systems. These systems are based on the lecture of physical characteristics from the person who is going to be identified. There are a lot of biometrical characteristics which can perfectly identify a person, but the industry focused on 7 different technologies, which are: iris recognition, retina recognition, finger prints, hand geometry, face recognition, handwriting recognition and voice recognition. Each technology has been developed in a different and specific area, but not a lot of them have become a functional and profitable security and identification system. However, face recognition (that is from an image of a human face) is one of the technologies which is being more researched and developed nowadays. Although face recognition is a very complex problem, this field is really interesting, because its range of application is really wide. There are a huge number of applications which use face recognition techniques [16], such as can be seen in table 1, although the most common ones are dedicated to authentication, surveillance, criminal detection and, in general, security systems.

Table 1. Areas where face recognition techniques are applied nowadays

Areas	Scientific applications
Biometrics	Drivers' licences, entitlement programs, national ID, passport, voter registration, welfare fraud
Smart cards	User identification, stored value security
Access control	Facility access, vehicular access
Law enforcement and surveillance	Advanced video surveillance, CCTV control, portal control, post-even analysis, shoplifting and suspect tracking and investigation
Information security	Desktop logon, application security, data security, data encryption, intranet security, internet access, medical record, secure trading terminals

A general statement for all face recognition applications can be formulated as follows: Given still or video images of a controlled or uncontrolled scene, the system may identify or verify one or more people in the scene using a stored database of well-known faces.

In our case, we have developed a biometrical face recognition system oriented to access control (identification or verification) using a method based on geometrical features of human face [2], [7]. In this type of systems, local (eyes, nose, mouth…) and global (position of each feature in the face) information is hold in a model which makes easy the identification and provides an efficient search.

Different designs give names to different kinds of face recognition system. There are several types of face recognition systems depending on how they are developed [16], [17], but for all of them, the first stage involves the face detection and the last one is a decision system which depending on the function given to the face recognition system performs different tasks. If the system is dedicated to identification, the face recognition will perform the task to discover the person who is being evaluated in that moment (this task involves a lot of comparisons between the face which is being examined and the faces which are saved in the database). On the other hand, if the system is configured for verification, the face recognition will check if the person who is being recognised really is who he/she assures to be (in this case only a comparison is performed). Finally, if the system was dedicated to detection, it would try to find one or several people in various still images or in a video (and this involves also a big number of comparisons).

In the following sections of the chapter, we will explain in depth the different stages performed in the development of the face recognition system. Thus, in section 2 we will explain the different parts and main features of the system build. The first stage of the system, the face detection, is detailed in section 3. In the next section (4) we will talk about the facial segmentation process, explaining which parts of the face have been located and the way it was made. After that, in section 5, we will enumerate and discuss the different facial features which have been extracted, and we will explain the representation chosen to hold the information which represents the face of a person. After that, the decision system which is used and the results which are obtained with it are presented in section 6. Finally, in section 7, the conclusions and the future lines which can be followed from the work described in this chapter are expounded.

2. GENERAL CHARACTERISTICS OF THE SYSTEM

In general, any face recognition system is divided, at least, into three different stages [16]. The first one is always the stage of face detection (it is necessary to separate the face from the rest of the scene before any other operation). The following step is related to the facial feature extraction from the principal components segmentation or facial regions (the facial features are very important, because they are the elements which discriminate each face from the others). In the last stage it is performed the recognition or verification of the face which is being processed. This last stage can be divided into two other stages: the comparison of the features obtained in the second step and the decision system which determines the acceptance threshold for the positive identification of the face which is being processed.

Figure 1 summarizes the different stages described before, where we can see the principal steps followed by a face recognition based on geometrical facial features.

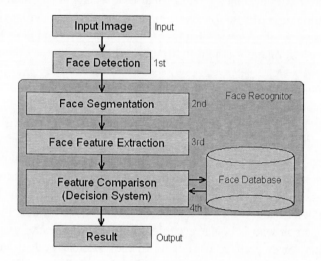

Figure 1. Face recognition principal stages.

Therefore, the face recognition described in this chapter is a face recognition based on facial geometrical features. This kind of systems, although they are neither the easiest to develop nor the most resistant ones when the face presents some occlusion, they are the fastest ones in the recognition, so, we chose the geometrical face recognition thinking in the performance of our system because the images that our system manages are typical images of a face recognition which is situated in the entrance of a restricted area, where occlusions and image conditions are under control, making easier the recognition task. For the development of our first prototype, we have used a face database which can be easily obtained for research purpose from the Internet (AR face database [8]) and which is widely used among scientific community, because it includes a quite big quantity of images (over 4000 colour images) with very high quality (768 by 576 pixels and with 24 bits of depth). We have to point that high quality images are necessary in geometrical face recognitions, so this AR database (figure 2 shows some samples) is a very appropriate face database for testing our face recognition.

Figure 2. Some AR face database samples.

Different techniques have been used in the development of the system. For example, in face detection and segmentation a pixel clustering technique has been used for classifying pixels according to their colour (to apply after that complex pattern recognition algorithms to find and fix the border of the principal parts of the face).To extract facial features, we have used a method based on geometrical feature extraction over a region map generated in the segmentation stage (figure 1). The system manages more than 30 different facial features to be the most robust and reliable face recognition that can be possible. Finally, the decision system chosen for the last stage of the recognition (figure 1) is based on the Euclidean distance. This system gives us the distance between the feature vector of the person which is being evaluated and the different feature vectors of the people which are held in the system face database (in case that the system is configured for identification). For the creation of these vectors, the system applies different weights depending on the importance of the feature which is being evaluated. At the end of the process, the feature vector which is closer to the vector of the person which is being evaluated is the winner. However, only if the distance between the winner vector and the applicant vector does not exceed which is established by the acceptance threshold, the identification of the system will be considered as a positive identification.

3. STAGE 1: FACE DETECTION

Face detection stage consists in closing the face in a box, or what is the same, finding the four sides (forehead, chin, left side and right side) which border the face of the person who is being identified. There are a lot of face detection methods [15], but among the most used ones, we can find in the specific bibliography those which use colour skin for face detection, and not only in the RGB colour space [9], [10], which is the most used one. Quite a lot different colour spaces have been used with success for finding faces in images through the skin colour. Among these colour models we can emphasize for their importance the HSV colour space [5], [14] and the YCbCr colour model [6], [11] which are the most accurate ones for finding skin colour, such as several studies about skin colour detection reveal [1], [12].

Our system uses the colour information of the image, and the clustering algorithm called K-means [3], [13] to perform the face detection stage. An example of the output given by our face recognition system for a face detection operation can be seen in figure 3, where besides we can see the face recognition' main window interface.

The main window of the application (figure 3) includes two important sections. The input zone, which includes the main menu and the zone situated in the bottom left corner. Using these buttons and controls, the application can be managed. Basically, there are controls to perform the different stages of face recognition, such as: the face detection, the face segmentation (full or choosing only some parts) and the identification or verification stages (these two last operations will require that face database is loaded). However, most of the window is occupied by three pictures, two of reduced dimensions in the top left corner and a bigger one that occupies almost the half of the window. One of the small pictures (the first one) shows the original image which is being processed and the final result for the detection over it. The other small picture contains a processed image of the face once the K-means algorithm is applied with K equal to 7 (which provides a detailed map of the regions which divide the face). As we can see, the application is oriented to research, more than to the final user, because it shows middle information which is very useful to check how the system is evolving, but it is useless for a final user. Thus, we can consider the biggest image of the application as the work picture, where we study the final results given by the detection over a determined map of pixels obtained with the K-means clustering algorithm. In figure 3, the main image shows the final result for face detection in a map of pixels obtained from the K-means algorithm when K is equal to 3 (face is associated to one class –pink colour in the main picture of figure 3–, the hair and the darkest parts of the image are associated to other class – white colour– and the background of the image and in general, the more brilliants parts are associated with a third class –colour black in the main picture of figure 3–).

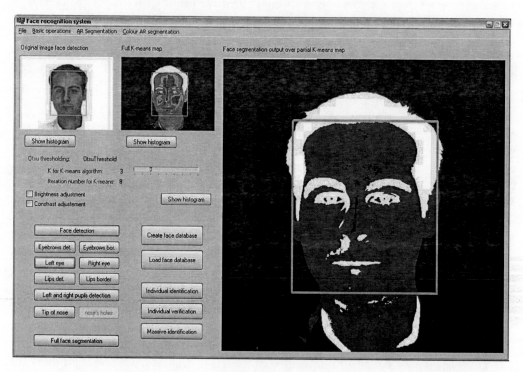

Figure 3. Face detection example using the build face recognition system.

K-means algorithm is a clustering method that classifies any data into K classes. In our case, these data are the pixels of an image. We have to point that in this method it is necessary to establish the value for K before the algorithm execution, so we try some values (K=2, K=3 ... K=8) using our problem and we discovered that for left, right and top sides, with K equal to 3 (one class for the background and the lightest areas of the image, another to the hair and the darkest ones and another for skin colour) was enough to find those borders. However, for the chin border detection, it was necessary much more precision, because the colour of the lowest zone of the face is similar to the colour of the neck. For this reason, K-means algorithm was configured with 7 classes to detect with high precision the bottom border of the face. The final result can be observed in figure 3, where we can see that the face is nicely closed into a box with a lot of accuracy. It is really important that face detection is done with the more precision as possible, because the piece of image which is contained in the box which borders the face will be the start point for the following stage of the recognition, where the segmentation of the principal parts of the face will be performed.

4. STAGE 2: FACE SEGMENTATION

Face segmentation consists in detecting the principal areas of the face. It is recommended to perform the most complex segmentation as possible [2], because with more face components detected, we will be able to extract more facial characteristics in the next stage of the recognition, and this means a more reliable and powerful system. Our face recognition segments the eyebrows, the eyes, the pupils, the tip of the nose and the lips [7]. In figures 4 and 5 we can see two examples of face segmentation. Both examples are divided into three images (explained from left to right): the first contains the map of classes obtained by the K-means classifier algorithm with a value for K equal to 7 (which is used for detecting some of the most complex parts of the face), the second shows the result of the segmentation applied over a pixel map generated with K=3 for the K-means algorithm (used in the detection of the easiest areas) and the third image presents the final result of the segmentation over the original image, where the principal parts of the face are perfectly detected and bordered.

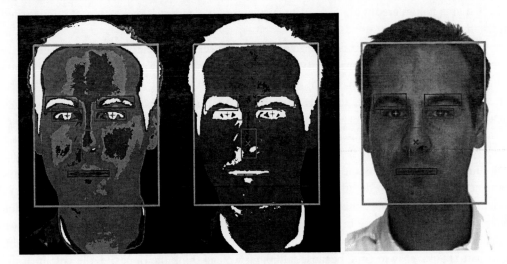

Figure 4. Male face segmentation example.

Face segmentation stage is performed after face detection, which means that the face is delimited by a box when the segmentation process starts. All the available contextual information is studied before starting the detection of a concrete part of the face, therefore important information, such as the position occupied by different parts in the face or the symmetry of the face, is taking into account before starting the detection of a concrete part of the face. For example, it is well known that the eyebrows, if exist, are placed between the top border of the face and, at the most, the half of the face, where the eyes are more or less placed. Besides, we know that the eyes are a symmetrical pair which is above the nose, which vertical position is between the eyes. Finally, between the nose and the chin are situated the lips, in the lower third of the face. Therefore, it is logical and widely recommended to search each part of the face in its appropriate area. Thus, the system performs a limited search which increases the speed and the performance of the face recognition.

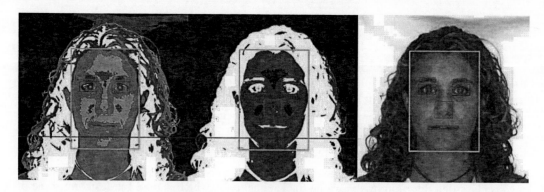

Figure 5. Female face segmentation example.

Furthermore, to carry out a more efficient detection of each part of the face, the detection process is divided into two stages. In the first stage, the system finds the area of the image where the part of the face that is being searched can be placed. After that, in a second step, the detected area is bordered with the best precision possible and, if it makes sense, it is labelled as a part of the face.

The first detection stage is performed through a restricted search of typical patterns in concrete areas using different maps (with different number of classes depending on the area with is being scanned and the details which are required for that zone) generated by the K-means algorithm. Therefore, the detection of each part of the face is done using the same method (pattern recognition in concrete areas of K-means maps), but with different parameters and configurations. Thus, for finding the eyebrows the pattern which is used is a slightly curved segment of the class which represents the hair on the image. For the eyes detection, the system scans the appropriate zones looking for circumference approximations, and once the eyes are bordered, the pupils are searched inside the box which closes each eye looking for a very representative black point rounded by the colour of the class which represents the iris of the eye in the K-means map. In case that we are looking for the lips, we should search a symmetrical segment in the lower area of the face, starting from the chin. This part is quite easy to find, because, although we can think the opposite, the colour of the lips is quite different to the skin colour (which is surrounded). For this reason, as we can see in figures 4 and 5, pixel maps which are obtained from K-means classifier make a very clear difference in the area where lips are situated. Finally, the last element which is detected by our face recognition is the tip of the nose. This element is searched at the end of face segmentation because it is one of the most difficult parts to find. However, it is a very relevant element for identification, because the tip of the nose is a very static part of the face (we cannot move very much our nose, and even less its tip). We know that the nose is between the eyes and the lips, and more specifically between the top border of the lips and the bottom border of the eyes. Besides, the tip of the nose vertical position is, with quite a lot precision, in the half line that separates the two eyes. Therefore, we can conclude that the search area is quite reduced. But, in addition to this, we have the advantage that the tip of the nose is one of the areas with presents more brightness in the face. This fact is immediately detected by K-means clustering method, which gives a quite accurate position of the tip of the nose for not very high values of K.

In conclusion, looking for the appropriate patterns in the precise and studied areas of the face, our system performs a quite accurate face segmentation process of the principal parts of the face (eyebrows, eyes, pupils, nose, tip of the nose and lips). The final result can be observed in figure 4 (which gives an example of male face segmentation) and figure 5 (which gives an example of female face segmentation –easier to do than male segmentation, because women normally has a cleaner face than men–). Once this stage is concluded, the next step consists in the selection and extraction of the facial features which will be the significant information that the system will use to perform the face recognition.

5. STAGE 3: FACE FEATURE EXTRACTION

The choice of an appropriate set of facial features which provides the maximum discrimination and identification rates is a very important part in the development of any face recognition system. The more number of distinctive facial features, the more robust and reliable will be the face recognition, because the facial features are going to be the relevant information that the system will use to perform the identification of different individuals. Moreover, if the system includes a good set of features, we will be able to guarantee the good operation of the system in case that some of the features will be disabled. This situation can take place if, for example, any feature is wrong due to some error caused in the face segmentation stage. If this occurs, there will be other features that have importance enough to identify the person. Therefore, we have used all the available information from the segmentation stage to develop a system which includes the best number of distinctive facial features as can be possible. Figure 6 shows a representation of the facial features which have been extracted for face recognition from the different geometrical points which were obtained in the previous segmentation stage.

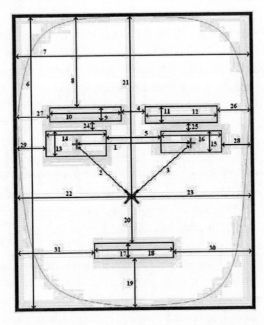

Figure 6. Geometrical features chosen for the face recognition system.

The facial features which can be observed in figure 6, and which are the base for our geometrical face recognition system, are explained in detail in the following paragraphs.

1. *Inter pupils distance.* This feature is very representative for the recognition of a person, because it does not suffer a lot of changes for the same person, but it is different in different people. Therefore, this feature is very valuable for the recognition system and the weight that it has in the feature vector is quite high.

2. *Distance between the tip of the nose and the left pupil.* The tip of the nose is one of the most static elements of human face. For this reason this feature is very valuable in face identification systems. Therefore, distances between the pupils and the tip of the nose has a high weight in the feature set of our face recognition system.

3. *Distance between the tip of the nose and the right pupil.* This feature is similar to the previous one. Obviously, it is necessary that the person who is going to be identified keeps the eyes opened and does not have sunglasses. If for any circumstance, the system cannot find the pupils of the person, this feature and the previous one are invalidated for the recognition.

4. *Inner distance between the eyebrows.* This feature takes the distance that separates both eyebrows in a person. The eyebrows are quite dynamical elements in the face of an individual, so, it is desirable that the person keep the face relaxed when the recognition is taking place. However, we cannot have any guarantee that the person is going to collaborate with the system, so this feature has a low weight in the feature vector of the system.

5. *Inner distance between the eyes.* This feature is more constant and static than the previous one (obviously it is only valid if the eyes are uncovered), so its weight in the feature vector is middle-high.

6. *Face height.* This feature holds the distance between the forehead (which is the first area regularly free of hairs of the face) and the chin. This feature works very well if the individual to identify does not have a beard, because if he has, the precision when the chin is detected is lower. All in all, the face height is a valid feature, so we have included to the feature vector with a medium weight.

7. *Face width.* It is similar to the previous one. This feature saves the maximum face width (although in the figure 6 the width is represented through the forehead to improve the figure's legibility). The importance of this feature is also moderate.

8. *Forehead height.* It is the distance between the top border of the face (established in the face detection stage) and the top border of the eyebrow line (in case that the two eyebrows are not at the same level, the one situated upper on the face determines the eyebrow line). This feature has a quite low value, because it depends on the hairstyle of the person and if he/she has his/her eyebrows relaxed or not. Therefore, this feature has a low weight in the feature vector.

9. *Left eyebrow height.* This feature holds the distance between the top and the bottom borders of the left eyebrow. It is possible that this feature suffers some variation, so, it has a medium importance in the feature vector.

10. *Left eyebrow width.* It saves the distance between the left and the right borders of the left eyebrow. This feature is similar to the previous one and it has a medium weight in the feature vector.

11. *Right eyebrow height*. The eyebrows in a person can be different. That is why we have features for the left and for the right eyebrows. Otherwise, this feature and the one for the left eyebrow are similar, so they have the same weight (medium) in the feature vector.

12. *Right eyebrow width*. It is equivalent to feature 10 (but for the right eyebrow). Medium weight.

13. *Left eye height*. This feature refers to the height of the left eye (from the top to the bottom border established in the face segmentation stage). The disadvantage is that people can have the eye more or less opened, so this feature has a medium-low importance in the feature vector of the face recognition system.

14. *Left eye width*. This feature is similar to the previous one, but they have different importance, because the width of the eye depends less than the eye height on the opened or closed that the eye is, so this feature has a medium weight in the feature vector of the system.

15. *Right eye height*. This feature is equivalent to 13. It takes the height of the right eye. The two eyes of a person are usually different, so, it is necessary to have the measurements for both eyes. Equal to the other eye, this feature has a medium-low importance for the same reasons.

16. *Right eye width*. This feature is similar to the one referred to the left eye. Equal to that one, this feature has a medium importance.

17. *Lips height*. This feature saves the height from the top border of the upper lip to the bottom border of the lower lip. So, in this feature is saved the height of the lips, if we suppose that the mouth is closed. However, the mouth is the part of the face that can suffer more variations in a person. It would be desirable that all people to be recognized have always the face relaxed, with the mouth closed, but we cannot assure this fact, so this feature has a low weight in the face recognition system.

18. *Lips width*. It takes the maximum width distance of the mouth. This feature can suffer a lot of distortions too, so its weight is also low in the feature vector.

19. *Distance between the lips and the chin*. This feature holds the distance from the bottom border of the lips to the bottom border of the face. The lower part of the face is quite unstable, so the weight of this feature for the system is medium-low.

20. *Distance from the lips to the tip of the nose*. Using this feature, the distance between the top border of the lips and the tip of the nose is saved. As we said before, the tip of the nose is a very reliable feature, but moreover, the upper lip (which determines the top border of the lips) is also a very static part of the face. Therefore, this feature has a medium-high weight in the feature vector of the system.

21. *Distance from the tip of the nose to the top border of the face*. Although the tip of the nose is a very reliable part of the face for the recognition, the top border of the face is not very reliable, because depends on the hairstyle of the person who is being recognized, so the weight of this feature for the recognition system is low.

22. *Distance from the tip of the nose to the left side of the face*. This feature saves the distance between the tip of the nose and the left border of the face (which was found in the detection stage). The discrimination value of this feature is medium.

23. *Distance from the tip of the nose to the right side of the face*. This feature is symmetrical to the previous one, so, it has the same importance for the recognition.

24. *Distance between the left eyebrow and the left eye*. This feature saves the distance between the bottom border of the left eyebrow and the top border of the left eye. Due to the variations that both eyebrows and eyes can suffer for the same individual, the weight of this feature in the vector feature has a middle-low value.

25. *Distance between the right eyebrow and the right eye*. This feature is similar and has the same weight for the recognition than the previous one.

26. *Distance from the right eyebrow to the right side of the face*. This feature saves the distance between the right border of the right eyebrow and the right border of the face (found in the face detection stage). The weight of this feature for the recognition is middle.

27. *Distance from the left eyebrow to the left side of the face*. It is similar to the previous one and with the same importance for the recognition. This feature saves the distance between the left border of the left eyebrow and the left border of the face (which was found during the face detection stage).

28. *Distance from the right eye to the right side of the face*. As we can see in figure 6, this feature takes the distance between the right border of the right eye and the right border of the face (which was found in the face detection stage). It has a medium weight in the feature vector.

29. *Distance from the left eye to the left side of the face*. It is similar to the previous one. It holds the distance between the left border of the left eye and the left border of the face. Similar features have similar weights, so it has a medium weight in the feature vector.

30. *Distance from the lips to the right side of the face*. This feature saves the distance between the right border of the lips and the right border of the face (as always, the border found in the face detection stage). The importance in the feature vector is only middle-low, because as we said for other features, the lips are one of the more dynamic parts of the face.

31. *Distance from the lips to the left side of the face*. This feature is symmetrical to the previous one. It has the same middle-low weight just for the same reasons.

As we can see in the previous paragraphs and in figure 6, the face recognition system uses a big number of geometrical facial features. The reason for this high number is to try that our system is the most reliable and robust as possible. In case that one or some of the features fail for a person, due to some error in the segmentation stage or because the user does not help in the recognition process (e.g. hiding some part of the face), some other features exist and should be enough to recognize the person. However, we have to point that the described system is a face recognition application oriented to the identification of individuals who want to access to a restricted area. Therefore, the system can be configured to force people to make easy the identification. If the system detects that there is any problem in the detection of some part of the face (caused for example because the individual is wearing sunglasses), the system can request the user that he/she repeats the identification process relaxing the face and showing all the facial parts. If problems in the identification continue, the system can reject that individual, refusing him/her for the access to the restricted area. But this is an extreme situation. The user usually collaborates with the system, because he/she wants to be identify, so the application has to be designed to support all the casual difficulties that can appear, and since the features are saved in a very efficient way for each individual in a face database (each individual is represented for a feature vector where each cell is a number which occupies not much space and it is very fast to operate with), we try to give the system the most complete feature set to increase its identification power.

Thus, the features used for the recognition are grouped for each individual in a vector of features (which are simple numerical values). As we pointed in the description of the features, a weight is given to each one according to its reliability and its importance for the recognition. Therefore, some features with low importance will be not taken into account if the most important features are available, but on the other hand, if some representative feature cannot be used, there will be other valid features that although are less relevant, working all together are able to identify a concrete individual. However, the task of deciding the parameters necessary to identify a person is done in the following and last stage of the recognition (decision system). In conclusion, the aim of the feature extraction stage is to provide the system with all the recognition information which can be obtained so that the decision system performs a precise and reliable work.

6. DECISION SYSTEM AND OBTAINED RESULTS

The decision system is the last stage in every face recognition system (figure 1) [16]. Using the different features obtained in the previous stage (face feature extraction), the recognition decides if the individual who is being examined is really who he/she assures to be (verification case) or in case of identification, the system recognizes the person through the association with one of the individuals saved in the face database. To determine the identity of a person, the decision system uses the feature vector obtained in the feature extraction stage. The work of the decision system is to compare the feature vector of the individual who is being identified with the feature vectors held in the face database which are necessary.

In case that the system performs *verification*, only a comparison between two vectors will be necessary. The user will provide his/her identification, and the biometrical system will determinate if this one is true or false (the system verifies it) comparing the feature vector held in the system for that individual with the feature vector generated by the system just in the moment of the verification. Otherwise, if the system performs an *identification* task, the person to be identified does not reveal his/her identification. The system will extract the features of that person and once the feature vector is generated, this one is compared with feature vectors of the individuals that are saved in the face database. The feature vector which is more similar (taking into account an acceptance threshold) to the one which is being examined will give the identification to the person who is being identified.

The classifier used to build the decision system is the Euclidean distance. The feature vector which obtains a smaller distance with the feature vector which is being compared will be the one which gives the identification to the person who wants to be identified. However, that distance has to be smaller than the *acceptance threshold* determined by the recognition system so that it is considered that the two feature vectors represent the same person. The smaller the acceptance threshold is configured, the more restrictive the system is. If we have a restrictive system, we force the feature vector of the individual to be identify to be very similar with the feature vector for the same individual if we want that the recognition is positive. It is very important to give a reasonable and appropriate value to the threshold, because if it takes a too low value, a lot of *false rejections* will occur. On the other hand, if the threshold takes a too high value, a lot of *false acceptances* will happen. A good recognition system will minimize both false rejections and false acceptances, but false acceptances are usually unacceptable in a critical face recognition system.

False rejections are normally preferable to false acceptances in every security system, because if a false rejection happens, it is always possible to perform a new identification, but in case of a false acceptance, the system has made a very serious security mistake. Therefore, we have performed an adjustment of the acceptance threshold so that the false acceptance rate is minimal, because we have designed our system to be placed in the entrance of a restricted area, and as we have explained previously, with this kind of application, false acceptances are not desirable.

We have tested our system using a face database which is freely available from the Internet for research purposes [8]. Specifically, we have selected a set of AR face database composed of 20 men and 20 women. We have used a total of 80 different images (2 for each person of the database). This is the first version of our face recognition system, and that is the reason of why this is a software prototype (and not a hardware version using a camera and real people whose key to enter in a restricted area is their own face) and why we have not considered a priority objective to build a perfect face recognition system, with a great acceptance rate. The objective of this work is to develop a complete, easy and functional in a real case, biometric face recognition system. In a real face recognition system for the identification of people who want to access to a restricted area, if someone does not satisfy enough conditions to be recognized (because of some occlusion or some inappropriate facial expression), it is possible to require the person to correct his/her pose and to uncover all the parts of the face before a new identification. However, using still images for the testing, there is not possibility of corrections in the pose of the person if there is any problem in the face detection or face segmentation stages. Even so, and in spite of that there was not the fundamental objective, we have perform some tests (using 2 different images of 20 men and 20 women) and we have fixed the system with still images, giving an optimum value to the acceptance threshold so that the false acceptance rate is zero. This means that for our 40 testing individuals, it is possible that there are some errors in the identification and an individual that should pass cannot do it, but any person who does not have the access granted is going to trick the system. We consider that this fact is really important, so the results obtained by our face recognition system for our testing set of still images are 78.75% of right identification rate, 21.25% of false rejection rate and 0.0% of false acceptance rate. These results have been obtained using a very restrictive acceptance threshold (Threshold 1 column in table 2).

Table 2. Some results obtained with the face recognition system.

	Threshold 1	Threshold 2	Threshold 3
Right identification rate	78.75%	85%	90.75%
False rejection rate	21.25%	11.25%	3.75%
False acceptance rate	0.0%	3.75%	5.5%

If we fix the threshold in a more flexible way, the face recognition system reaches a quite higher right identification rate (Threshold 2 and 3 columns in table 2), but some false acceptances occur, and we have considered this fact intolerable for our system. In conclusion, the acceptance threshold has been configured with a very restrictive value so that no false acceptance happens, because this ensures that the identification is the most reliable and restrictive possible, such as it has to be in a real security system.

7. CONCLUSIONS AND FUTURE WORK

In this chapter we have explained the stages in the development of a biometrical face recognition system based on the extraction of facial geometrical features. Among the different approaches for face recognition [16], [17] we chose this one because it is one of the faster solutions that we can find in the literature. We have tried to do a very complete segmentation stage of the principal components of the face so that the system can be done with a lot of features, giving to the system more power of recognition. Moreover, a weight has been assigned to each feature depending on the stability and reliability for the face recognition, so the more important features are more relevant in the recognition process, but all features have their influence on the recognition process.

Although the main objective of this work was to build a complete and functional face recognition system, we can say that the results obtained for this first version of the system have been quite good, because although we have not reached a very high right identification rate, we are able to reduce the false acceptance rate to zero (maintaining a reasonable right identification rate), which is very important in biometrical security systems. As a nearby future work, we have planned to improve the right detection rate of this face recognition system, studying other classification and segmentation methods which provide more accurate results [17]. Moreover, other line of research will be to develop a hybrid system with geometrical techniques and principal component analysis (PCA) [4], [18] which provides more robustness and reliability to the system. Finally, it is desirable to build a real physical biometrical identification system for the access, for example, to a laboratory. Thus, we will take advantage of the study and we will use the system in an appropriate environment, having at the end a useful and functional biometrical face recognition security system.

ACKNOWLEDGEMENTS

This work has been partially funded by the Spanish Ministry of Education and Science and FEDER under contract TIN2005-08818-C04-03 (the OPLINK project). José M. Chaves-González is supported by research grant PRE06003 from Junta de Extremadura (Spain).

REFERENCES

[1]   Albiol, A., Torres, L., Delp, E.J. Optimum Color Spaces for Skin Detection. IEEE International Conference on Image Processing 2001 (ICIP 2001). Vol 1, pp: 122-124, October 2001

[2]   Campadelli, P., Lanzarotti, R., Lipori G. Face and facial feature localization. 13th International Conference on Image Analysis and Processing. ICIAP 2005. vol 1, pp: 1002-1009, Oct. 2005

[3]   Forsyth, D., Ponce, J. Computer Vision: A Modern Approach. Prentice-Hall, 2003

[4]   Hui-Yuan Wang, Xiao-Juan Wu, Weighted PCA space and its application in face recognition, International Conference on Machine Learning and Cybernetics, 2005, vol 7, pp: 4522-4527, Aug. 2005

[5]   Ikeda, O. Segmentation of faces in video footage using HSV color for face detection and image retrieval. Proc. 2003 International Conference on Image Processing, ICIP 2003. vol. 3, pp: III - 913-916, Sept. 2003

[6]   Jinfeng Y., Zhouyu F., Tieniu T., Weiming H. Adaptive skin detection using multiple cues. International Conference on Image Processing, ICIP'04. vol. 2, pp: 901-904. Oct. 2004

[7]   Karungaru, S., Fukumi, M., Akamatsu, N. Feature extraction for face detection and recognition. 13th IEEE International Workshop on Robot and Human Interactive Communication. ROMAN 2004. vol. 1, pp: 235- 239, Sept. 2004

[8]   Martinez, A.M., Benavente, R. The AR Face Database. CVC Technical Report #24, Jun. 1998

[9]   Naseem, I., Deriche, M. Robust human face detection in complex color images. IEEE International Conference on Image Processing, 2005. ICIP 2005. Vol. 2, pp: II - 338-341, Sept. 2005

[10]   Pham-Ngoc, P-T, Jo K-H. Multi-face Detection System in Video Sequence. The 1st International Forum on Strategic Technology, pp: 146-150, Oct. 2006

[11]   Phung, S.L., Bouzerdoum, A., Chai, D. A novel skin color model in YCbCr color space and its application to human face detection. Proc. 2002 International Conference on Image Processing. vol 1, pp: I-289 - I-292. Sept. 2002

[12]   Phung, S.L., Bouzerdoum, A., Chai, D. Skin segmentation using color pixel classification: analysis and comparison. IEEE Transactions on Pattern Analysis and Machine Intelligence, Vol. 27, No. 1, pp.: 148-154, January 2005

[13]   Shapiro, L.G., Stockman, G.C. Computer Vision. Prentice-Hall, 2001

[14]   Sigal, L., Sclaroff, S., Athitsos, V. Skin color-based video segmentation under time-varying illumination. IEEE Transactions on Pattern Analysis and Machine Intelligence, vol. 26, n° 7, pp: 862 – 877, July 2004

[15]   Yang, M-H., Kriegman, D.J., Ahuja, N. Detecting Faces in Images: A Survey. IEEE Transactions on Pattern Analysis and Machine Intelligence, Vol. 24, No 1, pp: 34-58, January 2002

[16]   Zhao, W., Chellappa, R., Rosenfeld, A., Phillips, P.J., Face Recognition: A literature survey. ACM Computing Surveys, Vol 35, No 4, pp: 399-458, December 2003

[17]   Zhao, W.Y., Chellappa, R. Image-based Face Recognition: Issues and Methods. Image Recognition and Classification, Ed. B. Javidi, M. Dekker, pp: 375-402, 2002

[18]   Xudong, X., Kin-Man, L. An efficient method for face recognition under varying illumination. IEEE International Symposium on Circuits and Systems, 2005. vol 4, pp: 3841-3844, May 2005

In: Computer Security: Intrusion, Detection and Prevention   ISBN: 978-1-60692-781-6
Editors: R. D. Hopkins and W. P. Tokere   © 2009 Nova Science Publishers, Inc.

Chapter 7

MORPHEUS: A WORD-ORIENTED STREAM CIPHER

Nikos Komninos

Algorithms & Security Group,
Athens Information Technology
GR-190 02, Peania, Greece

Abstract

One of the most important information security objectives is confidentiality, which is usually achieved by encryption schemes or encryption algorithms. Even though there are plenty of encryption algorithms in the literature where some of them have become standards, encryption comes along with the application implemented. In this paper, an efficient word-oriented stream cipher, also referred to as Morpheus, for both hardware and software devices, is proposed. Morpheus was created to protect multimedia context for applications such as Games-On-Demand or IPTV, where data are usually streamed over different kinds of networks. Morpheus behaves very well in all known statistical tests and is resilient to known attacks for both synchronous and self-synchronous encryption modes.

Keywords. Stream cipher, encryption, self-synchronous, synchronous.

Introduction

Stream ciphers are considered more appropriate than block ciphers, and in some cases mandatory (e.g. in some telecommunications applications), when buffering is limited or when characters must be individually processed as they are received. Because they have limited or no error propagation, stream ciphers may also be advantageous in situations where transmission errors are highly probable.

The European Network of Excellence for Cryptology (ECRYPT) funded within the Information Society Program (IST) has launched the eSTREAM project, a stream cipher contest whose purpose is to identify new stream ciphers that might become suitable for widespread adoption. The eSTREAM project has defined mainly two categories, or profiles in the project context, for software and hardware applications. Some have emphasized the importance of including an authentication method and as such two further profiles have been proposed which combine authentication methods in stream ciphers for software and/or hardware applications.

The incentive for the Morpheus design, a stream cipher with high throughput for hardware and software applications, was due to the selection of cryptographic primitives in a Games-on-Demand system. In such systems, a vendor possesses a number of terminals (simple PCs or Content Delivery Networks-CDN), which run various games, and several subscribers can play these games remotely by just having a set-top-box and a plain, or High Definition TV (HDTV). An illustration of such a system is shown in Figure 1.

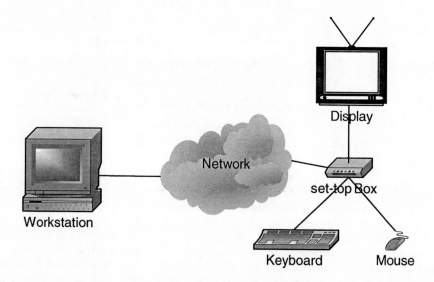

Figure 1. Games-on-Demand system.

In a Games-on-Demand system the vendor wishes to keep the communication with its subscribers private. Since stream data is exchanged between the set-up box and the workstation, a stream cipher is a suitable class of encryption algorithm for such applications. The cipher must encrypt individual characters, usually binary digits, of a plaintext message one at a time, using an encryption transformation which varies in time. The two communicating parties have different characteristics and therefore different capabilities, since the workstation can efficiently implement the cipher in software and the set-top-box can efficiently implement it in hardware.

Current stream ciphers, including those in the eSTREAM project, do not provide high flexibility to software and hardware applications. In this paper we propose Morpheus, a stream cipher that can be efficiently used for both software and hardware applications since it uses simple mathematical operations, such as eXclusive-OR, addition modulo 2^w, lookup table and fixed rotations that can be implemented efficiently in both software and hardware. Several tests were performed on Morpheus in synchronous and self-synchronous encryption modes, i.e., when the generation of the key stream was both independent and dependent of the plaintext and cipher text.

Following the introduction, this paper is organized as follows. The related work section presents current efforts to the eSTREAM project with ciphers such as Phelix, LEX and Salsa20 suitable for hardware and/or software applications. The overview and definition sections analyse in detail the design of the Morpheus algorithm. The analysis section discusses security, implementation, and cryptanalysis issues of the algorithm. This paper concludes with remarks and comments on the proposed algorithm.

Related Work

Several stream cipher designs have been proposed that are efficient in either software or hardware or both. Here we present three relatively recent designs which introduce some interesting cryptographic techniques; some of which where adopted in the design of Morpheus. All of them were submitted to the eSTREAM Project as being both hardware and/or software efficient and have successfully passed the first round of evaluation.

Whiting et al. [7] proposed the Phelix algorithm, which has successfully passed the first evaluation phase, and is implemented together with a Message Authentication Code (MAC). According to the authors, encryption and authentication should be combined, otherwise significant vulnerabilities may result.

The Phelix design consists of a network of simple bitwise operations with an initial state of eight 32-bit words; four "active" words that participate in the block update function and four "old" words which are used in the key stream output function. The operations used in the network are bitwise exclusive-or, addition modulo 232 and fixed left cyclic shifts, or rotations. The generation of the MAC is conducted after the encryption of the plaintext, which consists of 12 Phelix rounds with specific parameters. The key streams generated by the last 4 of these rounds represent the MAC tag.

Like all stream ciphers, Phelix leads itself to a very common danger; the potential reducibility of its key stream. To overcome such a problem, Phelix is restricted to use a unique key and initialization vector (key, IV) for each plaintext. After each encryption the IV must change, or else Phelix loses most of its security properties. Some weaknesses have also been published by Wu and Preneel introducing some differential attacks against Phelix [9, 10].

Biryukov [3] proposed LEX stream cipher for software applications only and has successfully passed the first verification phase of the eSTREAM project. LEX introduces the notion of a leak extraction from the Advanced Encryption Standard (AES), which is used in a chain-like design. The key stream is generated by the intermediate rounds of AES; on each round, a certain part of the 16-byte state is leaked, depending on whether the round is odd or even.

Although LEX is introduced with a 128-bit key, it can also take keys with longer key lengths since AES can also be used with keys of 192 and 256 bits length. According to the author, this cipher is 2.5 times faster than AES in the 128-bit key version, 3 times faster in the 192-bit version and 3.5 times in 256-bit versions. However, based on an attack in [11], the

LEX design was slightly modified in order to qualify for the second phase of the eSTREAM project.

Salsa20, another stream cipher for software applications, was proposed by Bernstein [2] and has entered the second phase of eSTREAM in the software category. In fact, Salsa20 is a hash function with 64-byte input and 64-byte output and is used in counter mode as a stream cipher. The hash function is implemented by four mixing functions and an invertible function that transforms a 4-byte sequence into a 32-bit word in a little-endian manner.

The first of the mixing functions, called *quarterround*, mixes four 32-bit words, by using XORs, additions modulo 2^{32} and left rotations, and produces four new 32-bit words. The next two functions, *rowround* and *columnround*, are very similar to each other. They both mix sixteen 32-bit words, by applying four times the quarterround function, and return sixteen new 32-bit words. Their difference is that, if the sixteen words where seen as a 4x4 matrix, then the rowround function modifies the rows and the columnround function modifies the columns of this matrix. The last mixing function, named *doubleround*, mixes sixteen 32-bit words by applying the rowround first and next the columnround function.

The hash function first uses the little-endian function to transform the 64-byte input into sixteen 32-bit words. Then, it applies the doubleround function ten times and at the end uses the inverse little-endian function to transform the sixteen 32-bit words back to a 64-byte output.

As described above, Salsa20 encrypts 64-bytes of plaintext during each round. The hash function is used to hash the key, the nonce and the block number, in order to produce the 64-byte key stream, which is XORed with the plaintext. Although several attacks on Salsa20 were published, the cipher was left unchanged by its author.

Morpheus Stream Cipher, an Overview

Morpheus is a word-oriented stream cipher designed to use a 128, 256, and 512 bits key and a 128-bit initialization vector (IV). The key is secret, and the IV is typically public knowledge. Based on the key size, Morpheus is optimized for multiples of 32-bit platforms; all operations are multiple of 32-bit words. The only operations used are addition modulo 2^w, exclusive-or, and fixed left rotations. For a 128-bit key, Morpheus can process data in less than 7 clock cycles per byte to a Pentium M CPU, more than twice as fast as the best known AES implementation.

Morpheus is key flexible as mentioned above and it consists of four words of 32 or 64 or 128 bits each that form an initial state. The state is broken up into groups: 4 "new" state words, which participate in the block update function, and 4 "old" state words, which are only used in the key stream output function. As shown in Figure 2a, a single round of Morpheus consists of adding (modulo 2) one new state word with a key material, adding (modulo 2^w) a second new state into the first and rotating the second word. The first word is an input to a lookup table, or substitution box (S-Box).

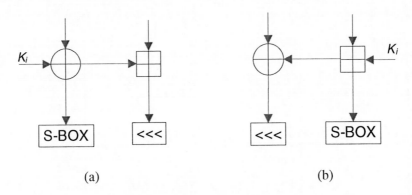

Figure 2. Single round on Morpheus.

However, Morpheus changes its form in the round as illustrated in Figure 2b. Morpheus now consists of adding (modulo 2^w) one new state with a key material, adding (modulo 2) a second state into the first and rotating the second word. The first word is also an input to an S-Box. The new states are shown as vertical lines in Figure 2. Two rounds are applied in a diagonal pattern to the new state and create one block (see Figure 3).

During the block i, one word of key stream (S_i) is generated and four words of key material are added ($K_{i,0}$, $K_{i,1}$, $K_{i,2}$, and $K_{i,3}$). The new state words Z_{i-1} are used as an input to the next one Z_i and as with any stream cipher the cipher text is created by XORing the plaintext with the key stream.

Morpheus, a Definition

The Morpheus encryption function takes as input a variable-length key K of up to 512-bits (64 bytes) and a 128-bit (16-byte) Initialization Vector (IV). It produces a key stream, which is XORed with the plaintext (P) to produce the cipher text (C). The decryption function takes the key and IV and produces the plaintext after XORing the cipher text with the key stream.

To demonstrate, let $\ell(x)$ denote the length of a string of bytes x. The input key K consists of a sequence of bytes k_0, k_1,..., $k_{\ell(K)-1}$ with $0 \leq \ell(k) \leq 128$. The IV consists of 16 bytes, interpreted as 4 words IV_0, ..., IV_3. Applications which use shorter IVs should zero-pad their IV to the full 16-byte length.

The plaintext P and cipher text C are both sequence of bytes of the same length with the restriction that $0 \leq \ell(P) \leq 2^{64}$. Both are manipulated as a sequence of words, P_i and C_i, respectively. The last word of the plaintext and cipher text might be only partially used. The padding bytes in the last word are taken to be zero and are never used.

The encryption is performed by using sequentially the block function illustrated in figure and each block is represented by a unique number i. For the i-th block, the input state is denoted by $Z_0^{(i)}$, $Z_1^{(i)}$, $Z_2^{(i)}$, $Z_3^{(i)}$ and the output state by $Z_0^{(i+1)}$, $Z_1^{(i+1)}$, $Z_2^{(i+1)}$, $Z_3^{(i+1)}$, which forms the input to the next block with number $i+1$.

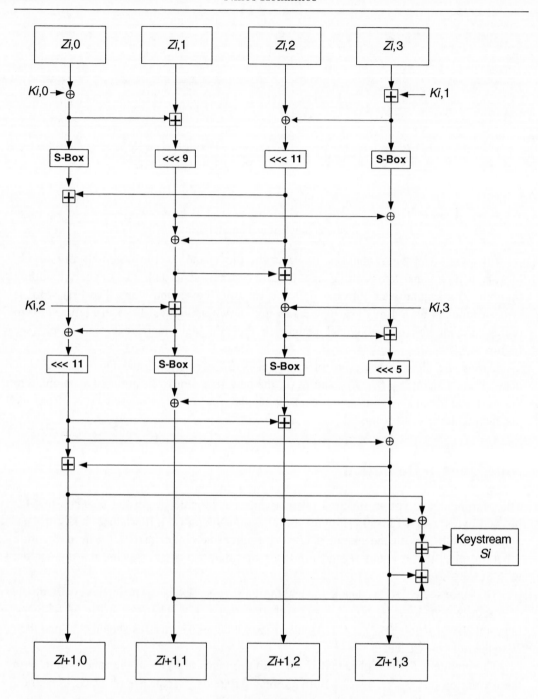

Figure 3. one block of Morpheus encryption.

All states can be 32-bit or 64-bit or 128-bit words according to the key length and for the clarity of this paper we will consider 128-bit key that results to 32-bit words. In Morpheus, exclusive-or is denoted by $\oplus$, addition modulo 2^w is denoted by $\boxplus$, left rotation is denoted by $<<<$, and lookup table is denoted by S-Box. The cipher block function F is defined as:

Function $F(Z_0^{(i)}, Z_1^{(i)}, Z_2^{(i)}, Z_3^{(i)}, K_{i,0}, K_{i,1}, K_{i,2}, K_{i,3})$

Begin

$$Z_0^{(i+1)} := Z_0^{(i)} \oplus Ki_{,0}; \qquad Z_0^{(i+1)} := \text{S-Box}(Z_0^{(i+1)});$$
$$Z_3^{(i+1)} := Z_3^{(i)} \boxplus K_{i,1}; \qquad Z_3^{(i+1)} := \text{S-Box}(Z_3^{(i+1)});$$
$$Z_1^{(i+1)} := Z_1^{(i)} \boxplus Z_0^{(i+1)}; \qquad Z_1^{(i+1)} := Z_1^{(i+1)} <<< 9;$$
$$Z_2^{(i+1)} := Z_2^{(i)} \oplus Z_3^{(i+1)}; \qquad Z_2^{(i+1)} := Z_2^{(i+1)} <<< 11;$$

$$Z_0^{(i+1)} := Z_0^{(i+1)} \boxplus Z_2^{(i+1)}; \qquad Z_2^{(i+1)} := Z_2^{(i+1)} \oplus K_{i,3};$$
$$Z_3^{(i+1)} := Z_3^{(i+1)} \oplus Z_1^{(i+1)}; \qquad Z_1^{(i+1)} := Z_1^{(i+1)} \boxplus K_{i,2};$$
$$Z_1^{(i+1)} := Z_1^{(i+1)} \oplus Z_2^{(i+1)}; \qquad Z_3^{(i+1)} := Z_3^{(i+1)} \boxplus Z_2^{(i+1)};$$
$$Z_2^{(i+1)} := Z_2^{(i+1)} \boxplus Z_1^{(i+1)}; \qquad Z_0^{(i+1)} := Z_0^{(i+1)} \oplus Z_1^{(i+1)};$$

$$Z_2^{(i+1)} := \text{S-Box}(Z_2^{(i+1)}); \qquad Z_2^{(i+1)} := Z_2^{(i+1)} \boxplus Z_0^{(i+1)};$$
$$Z_1^{(i+1)} := \text{S-Box}(Z_1^{(i+1)}); \qquad Z_1^{(i+1)} := Z_1^{(i+1)} \oplus X_3;$$
$$Z_3^{(i+1)} := Z_3^{(i+1)} <<< 5; \qquad Z_3^{(i+1)} := Z_3^{(i+1)} \oplus Z_0^{(i+1)};$$
$$Z_0^{(i+1)} := Z_0^{(i+1)} <<< 11; \qquad Z_0^{(i+1)} := Z_0^{(i+1)} \boxplus Z_3^{(i+1)};$$

Return $(Z_0^{(i+1)}, Z_1^{(i+1)}, Z_2^{(i+1)}, Z_3^{(i+1)})$;

End.

Given the function F, one round of encryption is computed as follows:

$$(Z_0^{(i+1)}, Z_1^{(i+1)}, Z_2^{(i+1)}, Z_3^{(i+1)}) := F(Z_0^{(i)}, Z_1^{(i)}, Z_2^{(i)}, Z_3^{(i)}, \quad K_{i,0}, K_{i,1}, K_{i,2}, K_{i,3})$$

Each round produces one word of key stream $S_i := [(Z_0^{(i+1)} \oplus Z_2^{(i+1)}) \boxplus (Z_1^{(i+1)} \boxplus Z_3^{(i+1)})]$. The cipher text words are defined by $C_i := P_i \oplus S_i$.

Initialization & Encryption-Decryption

Morpheus takes two parameters as input values; a secret key of 128-bits and a publicly known 128-bits IV. The IV value is considered as a four word input $IV = (IV_3, IV_2, IV_1, IV_0)$ where IV_0 is the least significant word. Likewise, the key is considered as a four word input $K = (k_3, k_2, k_1, k_0)$, where k_0 is the least significant word. States $Z_0^{(i)}, Z_1^{(i)}, Z_2^{(i)}, Z_3^{(i)}$ are initialized with K and IV according to function H.

Function $H(k_0, k_1, k_2, k_3, IV_0, IV_1, IV_2, IV_3)$

Begin

$$Z_0 := k_0 \oplus IV_3; \qquad Z_1 := k_1 \boxplus IV_2;$$
$$Z_2 := k_2 \oplus IV_1; \qquad Z_3 := k_3 \boxplus IV_0;$$

$$\textbf{Return } (Z_0, Z_1, Z_2, Z_3);$$

End.

The resulting 32-bit values Z_0, Z_1, Z_2 and Z_3 are used as an initial input to Morpheus block function F. F is executed for three times without producing any output bits. On the first time, the round- keys $K_{0,j}$ are equal to constant values (see section round key scheduling), but on the next two times the round-keys $K_{1,j}$ and $K_{2,j}$ are generated by the key scheduling function, described in the next section. The final four 32-bit words are used as the initial state of the encryption rounds.

After the initialization, the plaintext is encrypted. Each block generates one word of key stream, which is used to encrypt one word of plaintext. Decryption is almost identical to encryption. The key stream S_i generated after the first application of the F function in each block is used to decrypt the cipher text, producing the plaintext word. The implementation must insure that any unused bytes of the final plaintext word are taken as zero for purposes of computing the block function, regardless of the value of the extra key stream bytes.

Round Key Scheduling

The output states $Z_0^{(i+1)}$, $Z_1^{(i+1)}$, $Z_2^{(i+1)}$, and $Z_3^{(i+1)}$ of the initialization phase are used to generate the round keys $K_{i,j}$ according to function S.

Function $S(Z_0^{(i+1)}, Z_1^{(i+1)}, Z_2^{(i+1)}, Z_3^{(i+1)}, K_{i,0}, K_{i,1}, K_{i,2}, K_{i,3})$
Begin

$K_{0,0} := 0\text{xf35A};$ $K_{0,1} := 0\text{xB718};$
$K_{0,2} := 0\text{xC59A};$ $K_{0,3} := 0\text{xE46D};$
For $i \geq 1$ and $0 \leq j \leq 3$ do
$$K_{i,j} := \{[(Z_j^{(i+1)} <<< 3) \oplus ((i \bullet (j+1) <<< 10)] \boxplus K_{i-1,j}\};$$
Return $(K_{i,0}, K_{i,1}, K_{i,2}, K_{i,3});$

End.

Initially, $K_{0,0}$, $K_{0,1}$, $K_{0,2}$ and $K_{0,3}$ are randomly set to constant values 0xf32A, 0xB718, 0xC59A, 0xE46D, respectively. For the next 3 blocks, each round-key is calculated by XORing, adding modulo 2^{32} with variable values and rotating with fixed numbers.

S-box Design

Morpheus defines a 16×16 matrix of byte values (Table 1) that contains a permutation of all possible 8-bit values (i.e. 2^8 possible combinations = 256 values). Each individual byte's input is mapped into a new byte in the following way: The leftmost 4 bits of the byte are used as a row value and the rightmost 4 bits are used as a column value. These row and column values serve as indexes into the S-Box to select a unique 8-bit output value. For example, the hexadecimal value {67} references row 6, column 7 of the S-Box, which contains the value {C7}. Accordingly, the value {67} is mapped into the value {C7}.

Table 1. S-Box in Hexadecimal Values

		Y															
		0	**1**	**2**	**3**	**4**	**5**	**6**	**7**	**8**	**9**	**A**	**B**	**C**	**D**	**E**	**F**
	0	F1	93	A9	0B	6C	C9	AA	19	32	EF	03	8A	92	B6	49	35
	1	4A	4F	6B	3F	85	E6	B1	45	4E	94	CF	E3	0F	06	AB	78
	2	F5	6F	5F	53	C2	B7	9C	67	59	13	72	5C	8B	26	BF	B4
	3	62	83	E2	C6	86	9F	76	7A	AE	91	44	69	EB	FC	27	F2
	4	D5	3D	73	CB	71	81	25	31	98	0E	AF	9B	11	65	8D	1A
	5	1B	41	28	2F	02	88	C8	08	3E	1E	84	AD	D1	E7	39	D0
	6	B8	DA	A6	10	3A	80	A2	C7	04	C3	BC	0C	30	3C	FF	7F
x	**7**	87	96	4D	01	F7	A8	34	A3	DE	E5	A1	0A	D8	F3	48	16
	8	A4	BB	1C	D6	43	BD	FB	CD	9D	C1	F6	E0	7B	4C	3B	1D
	9	82	6E	C4	99	8F	24	29	8C	CC	FE	95	D7	A0	B2	50	14
	A	36	B3	1F	EA	D9	DF	55	66	58	38	47	4B	20	D4	05	5B
	B	DB	D2	23	33	57	F8	E9	ED	6D	68	89	54	A7	56	52	61
	C	21	CE	2B	90	74	F0	2A	5D	97	A5	EC	F9	75	63	E8	BE
	D	60	12	5A	D3	2D	6A	9A	64	9E	0D	46	07	F4	22	70	18
	E	79	09	B0	5E	7E	40	BA	DD	B5	7C	EE	15	7D	CA	8E	2C
	F	FA	42	E4	B9	51	77	AC	C0	00	17	E1	FD	C5	2E	DC	37

The S-Box is constructed as follows:

1. Initialize the S-Box with the byte values in ascending sequence row by row. The first row contains {00}, {01}, {02}, …, {0F}; the second row contains {10}, {11}, and so on. Thus the value of the byte in row x, column y is {xy}.
2. Use the Secure Hash Algorithm (SHA-256) to create 256-bit values for each byte in row and column, i.e., {00}, {01}, {02}, … etc. The MSB of the hash value is stored in the corresponding xy byte. When two MSBs are the same the next byte is chosen. The procedure carries on from the MSB to the LSB.
3. Statistically correct the columns and rows of the S-Box (i.e. balance with the frequency and block test the number of 0s' and 1s' in each row and column).

Modes of Operation

In Morpheus, two different modes of operation are specified. These are referred to as synchronous or **standard mode** and self-synchronous, or **IV mode**, respectively [6].

Standard mode: In standard mode Morpheus implements a fast cryptographic pseudo-random number generator. This means that for each seed, which in this case is a secret key, Morpheus outputs a pseudo-random number sequence. In this mode encryption and decryption of a plaintext is illustrated in Figure 4.

IV mode: In IV mode the generator is initialized using two variables, the secret key and a known IV. This means that for a given secret key the generator produces a set of pseudo-random number sequences, one for each IV vector. The length of the output sequence is usually larger than the IV length.

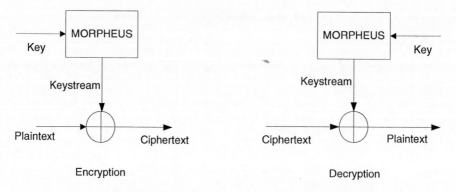

Figure 4. Standard Mode of Morpheus (Encryption/Decryption).

Applications requiring an IV value typically reinitialise the cipher frequently with a fixed key but the IV value is changed. This could be the case if two parties agreed on a common secret key but wish to communicate multiple messages, for example, in a frame based setting. Frequent re-initialisation could also be desirable from the resynchronisation perspective, for example, in a radio based environment (Figure 5).

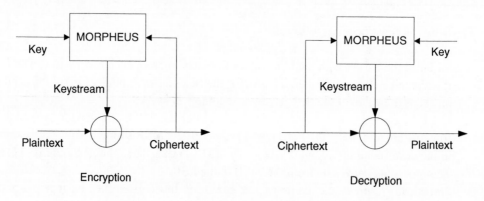

Figure 5. IV Mode of Morpheus (Encryption/Decryption).

Morpheus, an Analysis

Compared to many ciphers, Morpheus is relatively easy to implement in both software and hardware.

Implementation

If 32-bit addition, exclusive-or, and rotation functions are available, all the functions are easily implemented in software. A single round takes only one clock cycle to compute on most current Pentium CPUs because the superscalar architecture can perform an addition and/or XOR simultaneously with a 32-bit rotation [8]. A block of Morpheus takes 8 cycles plus some overhead for the handling of the plaintext, key stream and cipher text. The processing overhead of Morpheus is due to the initialization. The key scheduling only needs to be done once for each key value and thus do not require any processing.

Morpheus is also fast in hardware. The rotations incur no gate delays, only wiring delays although they do not consume routing resources in chip layouts. The key stream is generated after 8 additions, 9 XORs, 4 fixed rotations and 4 memory accesses to the S-Box. There are several techniques for high-speed implementation but a conservative estimate of a low-cost ASIC layout is 2.5ns per 32-bit adder, 0.5 ns per XOR and 1.5 ns per access [7], which adds up to 30.5 ns/output. This translates to more than 150 MByte per second, or just under 1.5 Gbit per second. We roughly estimate that such a design would consume fewer than 25,000 gates. Such a design would acquire about a 2 clock overhead per packet in order to process the initialization.

Security Issues

For flexibility, Morpheus allows several key sizes to be used as there are many situations in which larger than 128 bits of key material are available. The small set of elementary operations that Morpheus makes is efficient on a large number of software platforms. The absence of variable rotations and multiplications makes Morpheus small and efficient in hardware as well. The number of state words (i.e. 4) used for output was chosen so that the total amount of unknown internal state is always at least 128 bits, even after the key stream output.

Morpheus uses a lookup table (S-Box) to provide the necessary nonlinearity in conjunction with the mixing of XORs and additions. Neither of these operations can be approximated well within the group of the other.

The diffusion in Morpheus is fast and the attacker has very little control over the state it is not possible to limit the diffusion of differences. In those areas where dynamic attacks are possible, we use a sequence of 8 blocks instead of 3 to ensure thorough mixing of the state words with the round-keys.

The key initialization and round-key scheduling when combined is an unkeyed bijective function. The purpose is to spread the available entropy over all round key words. The round key scheduling ensures that all four key words depend on the key material. Using a bijective mixing function ensures that no two 128-bit input keys lead to the same working key values.

One of the dangers of a stream cipher is that the key stream will be re-used. To avoid this problem the sender must ensure that each (*Key*, *IV*) pair is unique for every encryption. A single sender must use a new and unique *IV* for each message. Multiple senders that want to use the same key must employ a scheme that divides the *IV* space into non-overlapping sets in order to ensure that the same *IV* is never used twice. If two different messages are ever encrypted with the same (*Key*, *IV*) pair, Morpheus loses most of its security properties.

Like any stream cipher, Morpheus is a cryptographically strong pseudorandom number generator (PRGN). For every input, it produces a stream of pseudorandom data. Using the full block function, we ran statistical tests on many candidate rotation count sets to see how these values would affect the ability of the block function to diffuse changes and mix together separate information within the internal state.

Statistical Tests

Morpheus is a strong cryptographic PRGN since the tests below were successfully passed. Among our tests, we considered different rotation numbers and tested the key stream and cipher text for:

1. the proportion of ones and zeros in the key stream;
2. the proportion of ones and zeros in the binary derivate of the key stream;
3. the difference between the proportion of ones up to and including the point and the proportion of ones after the point is noted;
4. the number of repetitions and the χ^2 value of sub blocks of the key stream;
5. the run in the key stream of all ones (block) and all zeros (gap);
6. the comparison between the actual sequence complexity and the sequence complexity threshold value for a bit stream of the same length;
7. the minimum number of bits required to re-create the whole key stream using a linear feedback shift register;
8. the probability of cipher text block change whenever any bit of the plaintext block changes;

Most rotation counts did pretty well but our carefully selected rotation count sets were slightly better than random ones.

Morpheus was tested in both standard and *IV* mode and passed statistics with frequent re-initializations of 160 and 256 bits of clipsheet.

Cryptanalysis

An attack is considered successful when an attacker can either predict a key stream bit he has not seen with a probability slightly higher than 50%. A number of attacking methods have been considered and analyzed in this section. We have not yet discovered any method of attacking Morpheus.

Static Analysis

A static analysis takes the key stream and tries to reconstruct the state and key. In Morpheus several properties make this type of attack difficult. Even if the whole state is known, any four consecutive key stream words are fully random. This is because each $K_{i,0}$ key value affects S_i in a bijective manner, so for any given state and any sequence of $K_{i,1}$ words, there is a bijective mapping from K_i to S_i. A similar argument applies when the block function is computed backwards. Any attempt to recover the key, even if the state is known at a single point, must span over at least 4 blocks.

Period Length

The Morpheus internal state is updated continuously by the round-keys $K_{i,j}$. The $K_{i,j}$ values depend on the "old" key words Z_j, the previous round-key $K_{i-1,j}$, the block number i, and the input key length. All 8 key words and all 4 *IV* words affect the state of every block.

The initialization and key scheduling also ensures that different (*Key, IV*) pairs produce different key sequences. To demonstrate this, we look at the sequence S_i of key words in the order they are used. Given just part of the sequence S_i, without the proper index values i, we cannot recover the key, *IV* and block number. This is due to the fact that the "old states" and the *IV* are different in the key scheduling and initialization phases. So long as the IV is not repeating, the key stream should have an arbitrarily long period, up to a maximum packet size of 2^{64} bytes. The non-repeating *IV* word values prevent the state from ever falling into a cycle.

State Collisions

To avoid internal collisions in less than 2^{128} words of chosen plaintext, Morpheus added 4 "old" state words, increasing the internal state significantly to 256 bits. Thus, the unknown state remains at 128 bits even after outputting the key stream word within a block, so consequently no collisions are reasonably expected within the security bounds.

Weak Keys

Morpheus makes constant use of the words of the working key. An all-zero working key effectively omits a few operations from the block function, but we have not discovered any possible attack based on it. Once again statistical tests were performed to the keystream when K and *IV* are set to zeros or pattern data were applied (i.e. 0s and 1s).

Chosen Input Differential Attacks

One powerful mode of attack is for the attacker to make small changes to the input values and look at how the changes propagate through the cipher.

In Morpheus, this can only be done only with the key or the *IV*. In each case, the block function is applied multiple times to the input. In Morpheus, areas where such attacks are possible have several consecutive blocks without any output. A change to the *IV*, such as is considered in [5], was thoroughly mixed into the state by the time the first key stream word was generated. A search found no useful differentials for 3 blocks of Morpheus, nor useful higher-order differentials.

Algebraic Attacks over GF(2)

Linearization and general algebraic techniques have been used to successfully analyze stream ciphers [1, 4]. The two round functions in Morpheus that combine integer addition, XOR, rotation and substitution yield to impractical algebraic attacks that require more than 2^{128} steps.

Conclusions

The design of Morpheus is based on various cipher design principles that have resulted from the intense research taken place in this area of cryptography. It combines the aspect of having a long chain of simple operations, rather than a small chain of complex ones for applications that work both in software and hardware. However, ciphers that are based on simple operations (i.e. addition, XORing and rotation) are susceptible to linear and algebraic attacks. The Morpheus design incorporates a lookup table and round keys to break such linearity.

Extensive statistical tests were performed to the key stream and to the cipher text with special and weak keys. Known cryptanalytic methods were also applied and to our knowledge we have not yet discovered any workable method of attacking Morpheus.

References

[1] Armknecht, F. A linearization attack on the Bluetooth key stream generator. Cryptology ePrint Archive, Report 2002/191, 2002. http://eprint.iacr.org/2002/191.

[2] Bernstein, D. J. Salsa20. eSTREAM, ECRYPT Stream Cipher Project Report 2005/025.

[3] Biryukov, A. A New 128-bit Key Stream Cipher: LEX, eSTREAM, ECRYPT Stream Cipher Project Report 2005/013. 2005

[4] Courtois, N. and Pieprzyk, J. Cryptanalysis of block ciphers with over defined systems of equations. In Yuliang Zheng, editor, *Advances in Cryptology ASIACRYPT2002*, volume 2501 of *Lecture Notes in Computer Science*, pages 267-287. Springer-Verlag, 2002.

[5] Daemen, J., Govaerts, R., and Vandewalle, J. Resynchronisation weaknesses in synchronous stream ciphers. In Tor Helleseth, editor, *Advances in Cryptology-EUROCRYPT '93*, volume 765 of *Lecture Notes in Computer Science*, pages 159-167. Springer-Verlag, 1993.

[6] Dj. Golic, J. Dj. Modes of operation of stream ciphers. In Douglas R. Stinson and Stafford Tavares, editors, *Selected Areas in Cryptography, 7th Annual International Workshop, SAC 2000*, volume 2012 of *Lecture Notes in Computer Science*, pages 233-247. Springer-Verlag, 2000.

[7] Whiting, D., Schneier, B., Lucks, S., and Muller F. Phelix: Fast encryption and authentication in a single cryptographic primitive. eSTREAM, ECRYPT Stream Cipher Project Report 2005/020. http://www.schneier.com/phelix.html.

[8] Lipmaa, H. and Moriai, S. Efficient algorithms for computing differential properties of addition. In Mitsuru Matsui, editor, *Fast Software Encryption 2001*, Lecture Notes in Computer Science. Springer-Verlag, To appear, 2001. Available from http://www.tcs.hut.fi/helger/papers/lm01/.

[9] Muller, F. Differential Attacks against the Helix Stream Cipher. In Bimal K. Roy and Willi Meier, editors, *Fast Software Encryption, 11th International Workshop, FSE'04*, volume 3017 of *Lecture Notes in Computer Science*, pages 94-108. Springer-Verlag, 2004.

[10] Wu, H. and Preneel, B. Differential Attacks against Phelix, eSTREAM, ECRYPT Stream Cipher Project Report 2006/056. http://www.ecrypt.eu.org/stream/.

[11] Wu, H. and Preneel, B. Attacking the IV Setup of Stream Cipher LEX, eSTREAM, ECRYPT Stream Cipher Project Report 2005/059. http://www.ecrypt.eu.org/stream/

In: Computer Security: Intrusion, Detention and Prevention   ISBN 978-1-60692-781-6
Editors: R. D. Hopkins and W. P. Tokere   © 2009 Nova Science Publishers, Inc.

Chapter 8

PRESERVING DATA AUTHENTICITY IN WIRELESS SENSOR NETWORKS: ATTACKS AND COUNTERMEASURES

Fan Ye[1],* Hao Yang[1],† Starsky H.Y. Wong[2],‡
Songwu Lu[2],§ Zhen Liu[1],¶
Lixia Zhang[2],‖ and Mani Srivastava[3],**
[1]IBM T. J. Watson Research, Hawthorne, NY 10532, USA
[2]UCLA Computer Science Department, Los Angeles, CA 90095, USA
[3]UCLA Electrical Engineering Department, Los Angeles, CA 90095, USA

Abstract

Preserving data authenticity in a hostile environment, where the sensor nodes may be compromised, is a critical security issue for wireless sensor networks. In such networks, once a real event is detected, nearby sensors generate data reports which are subsequently forwarded to the data collection point. However, the subverted sensors, which have access to the stored secret keys, can launch attacks to compromise data authenticity. They can act as sources for forged reports and inject an unlimited number of bogus reports that fabricate false events "happening" at arbitrary locations in the field. Such false reports may exhaust network energy and bandwidth resources, trigger false alarms and undesired reactions. In this chapter, we explain such attacks and critically examine more than a dozen state-of-the-art countermeasures proposed in the past several years. We look into both passive and proactive approaches for the defense mechanisms. For the passive defenses, we describe the basic en-route filtering framework and examine the cons and pros of both uniform and route-specific key sharing schemes. For the active defenses, we examine the merits and constraints of the group re-keying scheme and the log-based traceback scheme. Finally, we identify

*E-mail address: fanye@us.ibm.com
†E-mail address: haoyang@us.ibm.com
‡E-mail address: hywong1@cs.ucla.edu
§E-mail address: slu@cs.ucla.edu
¶E-mail address: zhenl@us.ibm.com
‖E-mail address: lixia@cs.ucla.edu
**E-mail address: mbs@ucla.edu

future research directions for comprehensive protection of data authenticity in sensor networks.

1. Introduction

Many sensor networks will be deployed in adverse or hostile environment. Due to their unattended nature, it is easy for an attacker to physically access and compromise sensor nodes. Once compromised, a sensor node exposes all the stored data, including secret keys, to the attacker. Subsequently, the attacker can use the secrets to launch attacks to compromise data authenticity. An important type of attacks is *false data injection*, where the compromised nodes pretend to be sources and forge bogus reports about non-existent events.

The false data injection attack can cause several serious damages. A large number of bogus reports can waste, or even deplete, the energy and network bandwidth along for-warding routes. As a result, l legitimate reports may not be delivered by the network, which is effectively a denial of service. The bogus reports may also contain wrong information about the physical phenomena being sensed. For example, in a fire monitoring system, the compromised nodes can report wrong locations for real fires, or report faked fire events that will trigger false alarms and waste response efforts.

In recent years, the research community has proposed many different countermeasures to address such attacks. The first, and foremost, one is to harden the network so that attacks become more difficult to launch and the damages become less severe. This is usually done by two means: securing the report generation process so that only multiple sensing nodes can collectively produce a valid report, and detecting/dropping bogus reports within the network so that less resources are wasted. This is a "passive" approach in that it makes the network more robust to endure attacks, but not punishing the perpetrators. An alternative approach is to proactively fight back. This can be done by either recovering damages, such as compromised keys, or identifying and isolating the compromised nodes.

In this chapter, we survey the state-of-art security proposals for both passive and active defense in sensor networks. We not only describe each specific design in detail but also, more importantly, compare them in a broader context and examine various tradeoffs in the design space. Specifically, we describe the network model and outline the general approaches to protecting data authenticity in Section 2.. We discuss various passive defense approaches in Section 3., in particular, various schemes in the general en-route filtering framework. In Section 4., we describe the existing proposals of proactive defense, including a group re-keying scheme and a logging-based traceback scheme. Finally, we conclude the chapter in Section 5. with future research directions for comprehensive protection of data authenticity in sensor networks.

2. Models and Approaches

2.1. System Model

The sensor network is usually considered static and nodes do not move once deployed. These nodes sense the nearby environment and produce reports about interested events, which usually contain the time, location and description (e.g., sensor readings) of the events. The reports are forwarded to a sink by intermediate nodes through multi-hop wireless channels. The sink can be a powerful machine with sufficient computing and energy resources.

Note that even in a static network, the network topology may change frequently due to power management schemes that alternate the nodes between active and sleep modes, or node/link failures that render some nodes unreachable. The routing protocols for sensor networks [6, 5, 14] can deal with such topology dynamics and ensure robust report delivery in normal cases.

Due to cost and size concerns, the sensor nodes are resource-constrained and have only limited computational power, storage capacity and energy supply. For example, the Mica2 motes [1] are battery powered and equipped with only a 4MHz processor and 256K memory. While public-key cryptography can be implemented in such low-end devices, it is prohibitively expensive in terms of energy consumption. Therefore, most existing solutions are solely based on efficient symmetric-key cryptographic techniques.

Sensor nodes usually have some secret keys and they may share keys among each other and with the sink. These keys can be used to authenticate the data. For example, a node can use its keys to generate Message Authentication Code (MAC) for the content of a report. Another node that share these keys can verify the correctness of the MAC, thus detecting whether the report is indeed produced by the claimed node. Various key management schemes can be used to establish key sharing among nodes.

2.2.   Threat Model

The adversary may compromise sensor nodes through physical capture or exploit software bugs, thus gaining full control of them. Once he compromises a node, he has access to all the stored information, including secret keys, and can re-program the node to behave in a malicious manner. These compromised nodes are used to inject bogus reports, either using their real identities and claiming events in their neighborhood, or pretending to be "forwarding" reports that originate in arbitrary locations (as illustrated in Figure 1). Multiple such compromised nodes may collude with each other and launch attacks in a coordinated manner, e.g., sharing their keys for more powerful attacks. The sink is usually well-protected and assumed secure in most existing work. However, it is not immune to attacks, and an adversary may possibly gain control of a sink, such as a PDA or mobile computer, through software bugs. Some work [17] has studied how to handle compromised sinks.

2.3.   Solution Approaches

There are different approaches to handle false data injection attacks. The first defense is to make forging more difficult, thus compromised nodes cannot successfully fake reports. Most work leverages the inherent sensing redundancy: one event is usually sensed by multiple surrounding nodes. Instead of allowing a single node to report an event, a report can be generated only through the collaborative efforts of multiple detecting nodes. Each detecting node will endorse the event by generating proofs (e.g., Message Authentication Code) using secret keys. The sink is able to verify such proofs and find out whether an event is observed by multiple nodes. This way, even though a single compromised node can still inject bogus

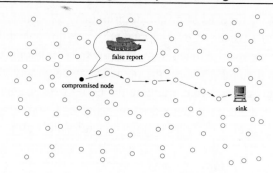

Figure 1. A compromised node injects false reports of non-existent "tanks" events. Such bogus reports can mislead reactions, delay or block legitimate reports by occupying the communication channel, and drain out network energy.

reports, they do not carry sufficient correct proofs and will be discarded by the sink. Thus false alarms can be avoided. Almost all passive approaches include this type of defense.

Eliminating false alarms is not yet sufficient. The delivery of bogus reports wastes energy and network bandwidth resources. The next line of defense is to detect and drop them en-route, before they reach the sink. Thus less energy and network bandwidth will be used in delivering bogus messages. The general method is to let reporting nodes and forwarding nodes share certain keys. Thus forwarding nodes are able to verify the proofs that are sent together with the message. Since compromised nodes do not have the required keys, they have to forge bogus proofs, which will be detected by forwarding nodes.

The majority of passive approaches have this en-route filtering capability. They differ mostly in ways they establish key sharing among nodes, thus presenting various tradeoffs. The simplest is uniform sharing: any two nodes may share keys, thus a node can potentially verify the reports claimed to originate from any location. This method is easy to implement on sensor hardware due to simplicity. It also makes the protection independent of topology and route changes. In other words, no matter on which path packets are delivered, forwarding nodes can always verify them.

Another way to achieve en-route filtering is to establish keys between reporting nodes and other nodes on the subsequent forwarding paths, but not arbitrary nodes. Since forwarding nodes are configured with keys specific to a small set of nodes (certain reporting nodes), as opposed to arbitrary nodes in the uniform sharing cases, they can store less keys and use less storage space. Because these keys are specific to certain reporting nodes, they have greater detecting and filtering power for bogus reports "produced" by those nodes. They can drop those bogus reports in less hops, saving more resources. The cost paid to gain this benefit is two-fold. Forwarding nodes have per-source keys and consumes more key storage when there are many sources. It also has higher complexity for establishing and maintaining route-specific key sharing. When routing changes happen, the set of forwarding nodes changes for a given reporting node. Thus certain control messages are needed to adapt to such routing changes and properly re-establish the shared keys.

The above two lines of defense are "passive" in that they enable the network to endure attacks. However, the compromised nodes are free to continue their attacks. Active fightback is needed to stop them from attacks. Rekeying ([16]) is one method for active defense.

After sensor nodes and their stored keys are compromised, these keys are periodically replaced by new keys. Thus compromised nodes can no longer use revoked keys to continue attacks. Monitoring ([9, 8] is a more active method. Sensor nodes overhear and record what messages have been forwarded by their neighbors. The sink may later query the network and find out which nodes have originated a bogus report.

3.   Passive Approaches

In this section, we describe a variety of security proposals for passive defense against false data injection. We start with a secure report generation protocol that can help the sink to detect bogus reports and avoid false alarms. Then we present multiple en-route filtering schemes that can provide stronger defense by dropping the bogus report en-route. Depending on how the keys are shared among the nodes, these schemes can be divided into three categories, namely uniform key sharing, route-specific key sharing and location-based key sharing, which will be described one by one.

3.1.   Secure Report Generation

Secure Event Reporting Protocol (SERP) [2] offers the first line of defense for data authenticity. It allows multiple sensing nodes to collaboratively produce a report. SERP uses two types of keys: a per-node key possessed by each node, and a pairwise key shared between each pair of neighboring nodes. All these keys are also known by the sink.

When an event is detected, each of the nearby sensor nodes broadcasts a message containing the event description, and multiple MACs, each of which is produced by a pairwise key shared with a neighbor. Each node maintains a table for MACs it has verified. Upon hearing such a message from node v, a node u adds all the MACs in the table. It verifies MAC_{uv} using the key shared with v, and marks it as valid if MAC_{uv} is correct. For other MACs, say MAC_{vw} between v and w, it waits for w to broadcast MAC_{wv}. If $MAC_{wv} = MAC_{vw}$, it marks MAC_{vw} as valid.

When a node has accumulated enough number of MACs, it is ready to send the final report. To avoid simultaneous reporting, it sets up a timer. Upon the expiration, it broadcasts a final report containing $\lceil T/2 \rceil$ MACs, where T is the minimum number of sensing nodes needed to endorse an event. A report is considered truthful only if at least T sensing nodes produce MACs for it. In SERP, every MAC presents the endorsement from two sensing nodes. If T is odd, one more MAC is needed for the last node.

When a node sends the final report, its neighbors will verify whether the included MACs are correct by examining their MAC tables. They cancel their timers only if all MACs are correct, and from T nodes. Finally the report is sent to the sink. The sink will use the pairwise keys to reproduce the MACs and verify whether the ones included in the report are correct.

SERP provides strict protection of data authenticity when less than $\lfloor T/2 \rfloor$ nodes are compromised, because the forged reports do not carry enough endorsement and will be rejected by the sink. However, it does not have filtering capability since forwarding nodes do not share keys with sensing ones.

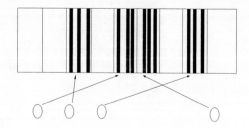

Figure 2. An example of a global key pool with $n = 9$ partitions and 4 nodes, each of which has $k = 3$ keys randomly selected from one partition. In a real system, k, n can be much larger.

3.2. Filtering with Uniform Key Sharing

Statistical En-route Filtering (SEF) [13] is among the first proposals for combating false data injection attacks. It provides the first and second lines of defense. In SEF, each report is endorsed by the MACs of multiple sensing nodes, and these MACs are verified by each forwarding node probabilistically. Bogus reports are dropped en-route once detected. Below we explain the SEF design in detail to illustrate the general framework of passive en-route filtering.

Key Sharing   SEF uses a global key pool and random key selection from the pool to achieve key sharing among nodes. There is a pre-generated global pool of N keys $\{K_i, 0 \leq i \leq N-1\}$, divided into n non-overlapping partitions $\{N_i, 0 \leq i \leq n-1\}$. Each partition has m keys (i.e., $N = n \times m$), and each key has a unique key index. A simple way to partition the global key pool is as follows:

$$N_i = \{K_j | im \leq j \leq (i+1)m - 1\}.$$

Before a sensor node is deployed, the user randomly selects one of the n partitions, and randomly chooses $k(k < m)$ keys from this partition to be loaded into the sensor node, together with the associated key indices (see Figure 2 for an example).

Such a key sharing scheme ensures that any two nodes have some probability of sharing keys. When two nodes draw keys from the same partition, they may choose some keys in common. These are the shared keys. The sharing is probabilistic in nature. Whether or not two nodes share any keys is purely decided by a probability, and independent of network conditions such as their locations.

Report Generation   When a set of sensing nodes detect an event, they work together to produce a report that contains multiple MACs. To this end, detecting node first elect a Center of Stimulus (CoS) node that generates the report using the mechanism in [14]. Each detecting node sets a random timer, upon the timer expiration it broadcasts the content of event $\{L_E, t, E\}$ (location, time and event type). Other nodes will compare whether they observe the same event. They cancel their timers if they do, otherwise they will broadcast their observation upon timer expiration. The node whose observation are accepted by others become the CoS node.

After the election process finishes, a detecting node A randomly selects K_i, one of its

k keys, and generates a MAC to endorse the event.

$$M_i = \overline{MAC}(K_i, L_E||t||E), \tag{1}$$

where $||$ denotes concatenation and $\overline{MAC}(a, b)$ computes the MAC M_i of message b using key a. The node then sends $\{i, M_i\}$, the key index and the MAC, to the CoS. The CoS collects all the $\{i, M_i\}$'s from detecting nodes and classify MACs based on the key partitions. MACs generated by keys of the same partition are in one *category*. Suppose CoS collects T categories ($T \leq n$). From each category, the CoS randomly chooses one $\{i, M_i\}$ tuple and attaches it to the report. The final report sent out by the CoS to the sink has a MAC in T different categories:

$$\{L_E, t, E, i_1, M_{i1}, i_2, M_{i2}, \cdots, i_T, M_{i_T}\}.$$

These MACs serve as the proof that T distinct nodes have independently detected the event. Note that they must be from different categories to prevent a compromised node from forging reports with multiple valid MACs. Since one node has keys in only one partition, the compromised node is allowed at most one valid "vote" in endorsing a forged report. It has to forge $T - 1$ MACs to make the report looks legitimate.

En-route Filtering   Due to the randomized key assignment, each forwarding node has certain probability to possess one of the keys that were used to generate the MACs in the report. This occurs if and only if the forwarding node happens to have loaded keys from the same partition as one of the sensing nodes, and chosen a key selected by that sensing node as well.

When a forwarding node receives a report, it first examines whether there are T key indices in distinct partitions and T MACs in the packet. Packets with less than T key indices, or less than T MACs, or more than one key index in the same partition are dropped. Moreover, if the node has any of the T keys indicated by the key indices, it re-produces the MAC using its own key and compares the result with the corresponding MAC attached in the packet. The packet is dropped if the attached one differs from the reproduced. it indicates that the report was not generated with the correct key. Such a MAC is considered forged, and the packet is dropped. Only if the MACs match exactly, or this node does not possess any of the T keys, the node passes the packet to the next hop.

Note that a forwarding node sends the report downstream if it does not have any of the T keys, because in such cases, the forwarding node is unable to verify whether the report is legitimate or not. As such, a forged report may escape the screening of certain forwarding nodes. However, it will be detected and dropped with higher and higher probabilities as it travels more and more hops. The detection power of a single sensor is constrained, but the collective detection power grows as more nodes deliver the report.

Summary   SEF leverages the scale of the network: every forwarding node has some probability of detecting bogus reports. A bogus report has less and less chance to escape the detection as it travels more hops. SEF is shown to drop up to 70% bogus traffic within 5 hops.

In terms of its resiliency, SEF can resist the compromise of up to T nodes, each of which has keys from a distinct partition. It has a threshold behavior shared by many other proposals: When more than T nodes (each with a distinct key partition) are compromised, they can inject bogus reports without being detected. Some of the later work [12] solves this threshold problem.

SEF is an exemplary design that consists of the three typical components in all filtering schemes: key sharing, report generation, and en-route filtering. Other schemes follow the same framework, but differs in exact ways they achieve key sharing, thus report generation and en-route filtering.

3.3. Filtering with Route-specific Key Sharing

En-route filtering can also be done with route-specific key sharing, in which the keys are shared only between the reporting nodes and their respective forwarding nodes. That is, a forwarding node stores only the keys used by its upstream reporting nodes. This can be more efficient than uniform key sharing because a node is likely to forward packets from some, but not all, reporting nodes. The tradeoff is that such schemes must incur extra complexity to decide which nodes forward packets from which reporting nodes.

There are two ways to establish shared keys along the forwarding paths. The first one is an explicit approach, in which the en-route filtering scheme explicitly maintains the routes and distribute the keys accordingly. This is suitable when the forwarding paths are unknown beforehand and decided by the routing protocol in situ. Thus, explicit control messages are needed to set up shared keys along the active forwarding paths. When such paths change due to topology dynamics, which can be frequent in sensor networks, the key sharing has to be re-established using similar control messages. The proposals in [18, 15, 3, 11] all fall into this category.

Another approach to route-specific key sharing is implicit sharing by leveraging the inherent property of routing protocols. For example, in geographical routing [5], a forwarding node is usually closer to the sink than reporting nodes. Based on the location, one can estimate which upstream nodes' reports are likely to traverse through a forwarding node. The forwarding node can share keys of those nodes beforehand, without explicit control messages to establish key sharing. Such location-based schemes will be described shortly in Section 3.4..

3.3.1. Interleaved Hop-by-hop Authentication

Interleaved Hop-by-hop Authentication (IHA) [18] is a representative design of explicit route-specific key sharing. It allows sensing and forwarding nodes along a path to form interleaved associations, where a node shares a key with an upstream (towards the sink) node t hops away and a downstream (toward the source) node t hops away.

Key Sharing   Each node shares a unique key (called individual key) with the sink. The set up of key sharing along routing paths is initiated by the sink. The sink floods a HELLO message in the network. A node attaches its own ID to the HELLO message before re-broadcasting it. A maximum of $t+1$ IDs are allowed in one HELLO packet. If the message already contains $t + 1$ IDs, a node removes the first ID and attaches its own. In this way, every node knows which are its downstream $t + 1$ neighbors on the forwarding path.

When a cluster head in a sensing cluster receives such a message, it assigns the IDs to each of the $t + 1$ nodes in the cluster (including itself). Thus every sensing node is associated with a forwarding node on the path, and every forwarding node is associated with a downstream one $t + 1$ hops away. Since the sharing is mutual, the cluster head sends back an ACK, going back to the same path but reverse direction, towards the sink. The ACK includes the cluster ID, and $t + 1$ IDs of sensing nodes in the cluster. Upon receiving an ACK, a forwarding node removes the last ID, and inserts its own ID at the beginning of the ID list. This way, a node learns which are $t + 1$ upstream neighbors on the routing path.

IHA assumes that by using an ID-based pairwise key establish scheme, two nodes that are $t + 1$ hops away can readily compute a shared key. This key is used for the en-route filtering purpose.

Report Generation   The report generation in IHA is similar to that of SEF. The difference is that each sensing node sends two MACs to the cluster head, one using its individual key, the other using its pairwise key shared with a forwarding node. The event and the two MACs are authenticated using the key shared with the cluster head. The cluster head verifies the message from each sensing node, it then XOR all individual MACs into a single, combined MAC. The final report it sends out includes the event, the combined individual MAC, and $t + 1$ pairwise MACs.

En-route Filtering   When a forwarding node receives a report, it checks the number of distinct pairwise MACs. If it is s ($s < t + 1$) hops away from the sink, it should see s such MACs; otherwise there should be $t + 1$ of them. It verifies the MAC from its upstream associated node. The report is dropped if the MAC is incorrect. To allow its downstream associated node to verify the report, it replaces the MAC using the key shared with the downstream associated node. This way, a report always carries $t + 1$ MACs produced by the most recent $t + 1$ nodes on the routing path, and these MACs are to be verified and replaced by the next $t + 1$ downstream nodes.

Summary   IHA relies on the HELLO and ACK propagation to discover and establish the key sharing between associated nodes. Whenever topology or wireless channel changes lead to different routing paths, the association must be re-established. IHA has two mechanisms, base station initiated repair when there are significant variations in routing paths, and local repair initiated by a forwarding node detecting a broken path.

Compared with SEF, IHA has the same threshold security behavior: compromise more than $t + 1$ nodes breaks the protection. The filtering has deterministic performance: It can drop reports containing forged MACs within $t + 1$ hops, because $t + 1$ forwarding nodes will verify all the MACs. Depending on the parameter settings, it can drop bogus reports earlier than SEF, whose filtering is probabilistic and requires enough hops (can be still a small number) to drop them.

IHA achieves this deterministic performance by paying the complexity of maintaining the association of nodes. This ties IHA to the underlying routing changes. When the routing path changes, explicit HELLO or local repairing is needed. It is not trivial to ensure the consistency of association in adverse environment, where routing changes frequently. On the other hand, SEF is immune to such routing dynamics, because the uniform key sharing in SEF is independent of the actual routing paths.

3.3.2.　Other Solutions with Route-specific Key Sharing

Source Authentication Protocol　SAF [3] is a protocol that authenticates the source to every forwarding node. It is designed to work together with DSR and leverages DSR's Route Discovery message to set up key sharing. ID-based key derivation is needed. When a source sends a Route Discovery message, a forwarding node can derive a key based on the IDs of itself and the source. When the source receives a Route Reply message, it can drive the same key of each forwarding node.

When the source sends out data packets, the packet includes one MAC for each of the forwarding nodes. These nodes will verify the MACs and drop packets if incorrect MACs are found. Thus SAF prevents a node from impersonating another: to successfully inject packets, one has to use its real identity. SAF does not have secure report generation, though. Compromising one single node is all that is needed to inject bogus packets.

Similar to IHA, SAF needs to maintain the key sharing relation when routes change. It uses a technique similar to the local repairing in IHA. The node that detects the broken route will switch to a new route. It computes a MAC for each forwarding node on the new route, and attaches these MACs to the message as if it is a source. The MACs will be verified by nodes on the new route.

Dynamic En-route Filtering　DEF [15] addresses the route changes in another way. Instead of establishing key sharing between reporting nodes and their forwarding nodes, the key sharing is also with *potential* forwarding nodes. Each forwarding node propagates key sharing messages not just its next hop, but q potential next hop nodes. When route changes among the q nodes at a hop, there is no need to re-establish the key sharing.

DEF uses a hash chain of authentication keys [10] to authenticate reports. Each node is preloaded with a seed key, from which a hash chain of keys can be derived. A node uses these keys to produce MACs. The last key on the chain is used first, and the node moves up the chain for different reports.

Before sending reports, sensing nodes need to let forwarding nodes know which authentication keys they use. A global key pool containing Key-Encryption-Keys (KEK) is used for this purpose. Each node selects l KEKs from this key pool and sensing, forwarding nodes may share some keys. Each sensing node encrypts its current authentication key using l KEKs and send l encrypted keys to the cluster head. The cluster head combines such messages, and propagates a $K(n)$ message containing these encrypted keys along a path. Since a forwarding node has picked some KEKs from the same key pool, it may have the same KEKs used to encrypt authentication keys. It decrypts and stores those authentication keys for future filtering, then sends $K(n)$ to q neighbors which are potential next hop. Finally, at each hop, q nodes have obtained the authentication keys.

When an event is detected, each node sends a report containing the event, the position of the current authentication key in the hash chain, and a MAC produced by the authentication key, to the cluster head. The cluster head combines t such messages and sends a report to the next hop u. The next hop forwards the report to its next hop v, which will wait for u to instruct whether it should continue forwarding.

To authenticate the report to forwarding nodes, each sensing node also encrypts its current authentication key using its l KEKs, and send them to the cluster head. The cluster head then sends a $K(t)$ message, containing encrypted keys from t sensing nodes, to node u. u verifies the integrity of $K(t)$ and decrypts the authentication keys similar as it does for $K(n)$. u can verify whether the authentication keys are correct by hashing them multiple times, see whether it is consistent with the claimed position in the hash chain. u finally verifies that whether MACs are correct. The message is considered legitimate if all checks succeed, and u sends an OK message to v. The same process then repeats between v and its next hop.

DEF avoids re-establishing key sharing by distributing keys to more potential forwarding nodes. Although more nodes store keys, the control message overhead is a one-time investment: small route changes can be handled immediately by using another forwarding node storing authentication keys. On the other hand, it incurs high message delivery delay due to the use of hash chain: each hop needs to wait for the OK message from previous hop to continue forwarding. The disclosure messages for authentication keys also increase the per-hop control message overhead.

Commutative Cipher Based Filtering   While the above protocols all use MACs, based on symmetric ciphers, to authenticate the packets to the intermediate forwarding nodes, CCEF [11] uses a different cryptographic primitive called the commutative cipher. A cipher CE is commutative if and only if it satisfies the following property: for any message M and any two keys K_1 and K_2,

$$CE(CE(M, K1), K2) = CE(CE(M, K2), K1) \qquad (2)$$

In other words, with commutative ciphers, the order of encryption operations does not change the final result. Clearly, most of the known ciphers, including all those symmetric-key-based ones, are not commutative. However, several public-key cryptography based implementation of commutative ciphers are available, e.g., the Pohlig-Hellman algorithm based on ECC and the Shamir-Omura algorithm based on RSA.

The use of public-key cryptography, in the form of commutative cipher, fundamentally changes the key sharing relationship that is needed to achieve en-route filtering. In CCEF, the credentials are generated and verified using two separate keys. Specifically, the source node possesses a signing key K_s, which is never released, and uses it to generate credentials for its packets. On the other hand, the intermediate forwarding nodes share another witness key, K_w, and uses it to verify the credentials carried in the packets. These two keys, K_s and K_w, satisfy the following constraint:

$$CE(M, K_w) = CE^{-1}(M, K_s) \qquad (3)$$

where CE and CE^{-1} are the encryption and decryption algorithms of a commutative cipher respectively, and M is an arbitrary message.

In CCEF, a unique signing/witness key pair is generated for each task that the base station deploys, and disseminated to the sensor nodes during the session setup phase. Specifically, the signing key is sent to the local cluster head (CH) node in an encrypted form, while the witness key is carried in the task as plain text and stored by all forwarding nodes. To authenticate its reports, the CH node generates a MAC for each report as

$MAC_R = CE(R, K_s)$, where R is the report content. Thanks to the commutative cipher, a forwarding node can readily verify this MAC using K_w, because a correct MAC should satisfy $CE(MAC_R, K_w) = R$.

Note that if a forwarding node always verify all reports passing through it, the fabricated reports can be dropped one hop after it is injected. However, the commutative cipher involved in report verification is computationally intensive. Thus, the energy spent on verifying legitimate reports at every hop may outweigh the savings due to such aggressive filtering of forged reports. To address this issue, probabilistic verification is used in which each forwarding node verifies a report with a small probability. As such, a forged report may traverse a few hops until a forwarding node decides to verify the MAC, after which the report is dropped. On the other hand, a legitimate report is verified en-route for only a small number of times.

3.4.   Filtering with Location-based Key Sharing

While the previous en-route filtering schemes each has its own merits, they all suffer from a threshold behavior: The design is secure against when the number of compromised nodes is below a threshold, but completely breaks down when the threshold is reached. In practice, however, graceful security degradation is desirable when the attacker compromises more and more sensor nodes. To achieve this goal, there are a few proposals that exploit additional location information in designing resilient en-route filtering schemes. In what follows, we briefly summarize two representative location-based schemes.

3.4.1.   Location-Based Resilient Security

The primary goal of Location-Based Resilient Security (LBRS) design is to avoid threshold security and achieve graceful performance degradation as the number of compromised nodes increases. It follows the general en-route filtering framework as previously used by SEF and IHA. However, it fundamentally differs from the existing designs in terms of the security keys in use, and the way that these keys are assigned to the nodes.

In LBRS, the secret keys are bound to geographic locations, rather than individual node identities. This is achieved by dividing the terrain into a geographic grid and binding multiple keys to each cell on the grid. Specifically, there are L network-wide master secret K_s^I ($1 \leq s \leq L$). Each cell is denoted by the location of its center, (X_i, Y_j), and bound to L cell keys as follows:

$$K_s^C = H_{K_s^I}(X_i || Y_j) \tag{4}$$

where s is an index between 1 and L, and K_s^I is the s-th master secret. As such, these keys are logically associated with geographic cells and independent of the actual network topology.

However, to perform en-route filtering, the nodes currently in the network must have access to some of these cell keys. This is done by pre-loading the master secrets in each node and exploiting a short bootstrapping phase for the node to derive the cell keys. Specifically, after a node is deployed, it first obtains its own location by certain localization methods [4], and then derives the keys for a few carefully chosen cells from the master secrets. At the end, the node permanently erases the master secrets, so that the attacker cannot access such critical information even if he compromises the node in the future.

Clearly, the performance of LBRS highly depends on which cell keys a node possesses. In general, there is a fundamental tradeoff between the filtering power and the resiliency that LBRS can achieve: The more keys a node stores, the more forged reports it can potentially filter, but the more damage it incurs when it is compromised. LBRS balances the conflicting goals of effective filtering and high degree of resiliency through a location-guided key selection scheme. In this scheme, a node stores one key for each sensing cell (i.e., those cells within the node's sensing range), so that it can properly endorse its own reports on events happening in these cells. In addition, the node estimates its upstream cells, whose reports may potentially traverse through it, and stores one key for each upstream cell with a probability proportional to the node's distance to the sink. As such, the node knows the keys of a few upstream cells, hence are able to verify reports that claim to originate from these cells. It has been shown that this particular random strategy in choosing upstream cells can lead to both strong filtering power and moderate key storage overhead.

With the location-binding cell keys and the location-guided key selection scheme in place, the en-route filtering in LBRS is performed as follows. When an event occurs, the nodes that have sensed the event collectively endorse a report with multiple MACs, each generated by one key bound to the event cell. On the other hand, each forwarding node checks the event location in the report, and verify the MACs if it has stored one key for the event cell. The report is dropped whenever an incorrect MAC is found; otherwise, the report is forwarded as usual.

The key insight of LBRS is that a resilient security design must constrain the usage of each key as well as the set of keys exposed to each node, so that the damage inflicted by a group of compromised can be minimized. For example, each cell key in LBRS can only be used to endorse a report originated from a particular cell. This greatly improves the system resiliency as compared to a node-based key that can be used to endorse reports from any locations. Moreover, each node in LBRS stores only a few remote cell keys, chosen from its entire upstream region in a uniformly random manner. As a result, the attacker can hardly combine the keys stored at different compromised nodes, because it is useless to combine two keys bound to two different cells.

3.4.2. Location-aware End-to-End Data Security

The security goals of Location-aware End-to-End Data Security (LEDS) include not only defending against false data injection attacks, but also ensuring data confidentiality and high availability. To achieve the latter goal, all nodes in the same cell share a key, which is used to encrypt the message originated from this cell. Furthermore, it uses a (t, T)-threshold secret sharing scheme to allow each node generate a share of the encrypted message, and the sink can recover a legitimate report from any t out of T shares. However, to stay focused, we do not elaborate further on these confidentiality and robust delivery techniques in LEDS.

From the en-route filtering perspective, LEDS adopts the same location-based approach as used by LBRS. Similarly, it binds secret keys to each cell on a geographic grid, and lets each node derive these cell keys from the pre-loaded master secrets during the bootstrapping phase. However, the key sharing relationship in LEDS is very different from LBRS. This is partially due to the special forwarding rule in LEDS: A report is always forwarded on a cell-by-cell basis along the line connecting the source cell center and the sink. As such, a source node can predict which cells its report will traverse. With such route knowledge in place, the keys are shared among remote nodes in the following manner. For any two given cells C_1 and C_2, in which C_2 is on C_1's route to the sink. If C_1 and C_2 are no more than $T + 1$ cells away, then all nodes in C_2 share a key with at least one node in C_1. However, if C_1 and C_2 are exactly $T + 1$ cells away, then all nodes in C_1 and C_2 share the same key.

In spirit, the key sharing in LEDS resembles that in the previously described IHA scheme. Not surprisingly, the en-route filtering is also done in a similar interleaved cell-by-cell manner. Specifically, each report is collectively endorsed by $T + 1$ nodes, and each nodes generates two MACs, using keys shared with two downstream cells (at most $T + 1$ cells away) respectively. A forwarding node verifies the MAC in a report, for which it happens to possess the corresponding key. If the MAC is invalid, then the node deletes it from the report. The report is finally dropped when it carries less than $t + 1$ MACs. As such, unless the attacker has compromised more than t nodes in a cell, he cannot forge any reports on events in that cell.

4. Proactive Approaches

In this section, we present three security designs that ensure data authenticity in a proactive manner. We first describe a group re-keying approach which allows sensors to change their keys periodically. Thus a compromised node cannot continue to use a revoked key to attack the network. Then we examine a coordinated packet traceback scheme where nodes use bloom filters to log previous packet transmission and answer queries for the route that a specific packet has traversed. Finally we present how to detect false data by correlation analysis at individual sensors.

4.1. Group Re-keying

Group re-keying means a wireless sensor network will keep changing its keys over time, which can prevent a compromised sensor node to continue to damage the network. PCGR [16] proposes a set of group re-keying schemes based on pre-distribution of key information and local collaboration. In PCGR, each sensor node belongs to a group and is preloaded with a polynomial $g(x)$, called group key polynomial, of that group. The group key is updated periodically and at period j, the group key is $g(j)$. Future group keys are derived base on this $g(x)$ and the collaboration with neighboring sensors.

In order to protect this important $g(x)$ from node compromise, it is not stored on any single node after the initial deployment. Another polynomial $e(x)$, called encryption polynomial, is used to encrypt the $g(x)$. After $g(x)$ is encrypted, both $g(x)$ and $e(x)$ are removed from the sensor node. Only through the collaboration with neighbors can a node re-construct $g(x)$ and derive future keys.

Pre-load Initial Keys   Initially, the sensor network is divided into i groups and a setup server will randomly assign each sensor into a group. Each group is associated with a t-degree polynomial, $g_i(x)$. The initial group key for group i is $g_i(0)$. Assuming a node N_u, where u is its ID, is assigned into group i and has been deployed. N_u will randomly pick a bivariate polynomial

$$e_u(x, y) = \sum_{0 \leq i \leq t, 0 \leq j \leq \mu} A_{i,j} x^i y^j$$

where t and μ are system parameters that determine the the security strength. N_u then encrypts $g(x)$ to $g'(x)$ by

$$g'(x) = g(x) + e_u(x, u)$$

After N_u obtain $g'(x)$, N_u will distribute the share of $e_u(x, y)$ to its neighbors. Each neighbor N_{v_i} receives a share of $e_u(x, v_i)$; these shares allow the original bivariate polynomial be reconstructed. Once N_u's neighbors receive the shares, N_u will delete both $g(x)$ and $e_u(x, y)$, and keeping $g'(x)$ for future use.

Derive Future Keys   PCGR assumes nodes are synchronized. A re-keying timer is used in each node to notify the node to rekey periodically. During the cth update period, each node will return the share of e-polynomials to its neighbors and receive its shares from neighbors. After N_u receive $\mu + 1$ shares $e_u(c, v_i)$ from neighbors, it can construct a unique μ-degree polynomial, $e_u(c, y)$. Finally a new group key is derived by

$$g(c) = g'(c) - e_u(c, u) \tag{5}$$

The authors have proved that in order to comprise a group key $g(x)$, a node N_u belonging to this group has to be compromised , and either 1) at least $\mu + 1$ neighbors of N_u are compromised or 2) at least $t + 1$ past keys of the group are compromised. To address the $\mu + 1$ neighbor and $t + 1$ key limits, the authors have proposed further enhancements that can tolerate the compromise of more neighbors or past keys.

Summary   Compared to passive approaches, group re-keying actively change group keys periodically. A compromised node cannot use past keys to continue its attacks. PCGR leverages local collaboration to distribute the shares of keying polynomials to multiple neighbors. One or a few compromised nodes cannot successfully reconstruct the keys without knowing a sufficiently number of shares. It can be combined with passive filtering approaches and enable them to revoke compromised keys.

Future directions for PCGR may include mechanisms to handle node isolation and node membership management, as currently each node needs at least $\mu+1$ neighbors to store the secret shares.

4.2. Packet Traceback

Packet traceback in the Internet has been studied for a long time. In [8], Sy and Bao point out that techniques for Internet packet traceback may not work well in sensor network domain due to factors such as the open wireless medium and in-network data processing. They propose CPATRA, a logging based technique to trace back the origin of packets. CAPTRA utilizes the broadcast nature of wireless communication, where neighboring nodes can overhear packet transmissions, and log which packets they have heard. Also, in order to save the memory storage and processing power, CAPTRA uses multi-dimensional

Bloom filters to log packet transmission events.

Logging a packet   Each sensor nodes in CAPTRA use a Bloom filter with k hash functions. When a sensor node i overhears a packet, it hashes this transmission event by

$$\bigcup_{j=1}^{k} Hash_j(pkt.id||pkt.tx||i||j)$$

Where j is the hash function ID, k is the number of hash function, $pkt.tx$ is the node ID who forwards the packet, and $pkt.id$ is the packet identification information, which can be a digest from certain fields such as the header and some payload of the packet.

A packet is hashed by a node if the node forwards the packet, or the node overhears the packet. Over time, the Bloom filter will fill up with packets, as more packets have been tracked. CAPTRA suggests to refresh the Bloom filters by "50% Golden Rule", which means if the saturation ratio of the Bloom filter reaches 50%, a node will reset every bit in the Bloom filter to 0.

Tracing a packet   To trace a packet, the sink will start a traceback query. This traceback query can be initialized by an alert from an intrusion detection system. A traceback query is a query with $pkt.id$ as payload. This query is sent to the direct upstream node of the forwarding path, but can also overhear by the neighboring nodes.

Assuming a packet comes from the path $src \rightarrow n_1 \rightarrow ... \rightarrow n_i \rightarrow sink$. When the sink sends the query, both node n_i and some of its neighbors will hear the query due to the broadcast nature. These nodes will examine their Bloom filters and find which node has forwarded the packet. The neighbors should have overheard n_i transmitting the packet in the past and they will send a verdict $TRAC_{Verd}$ message to n_i. These $TRAC_{Verd}$ messages confirm the overhearing of the transmission. The neighboring sensors can verdict a transmission if and only if they find a positive hit of the transmission in their Bloom filters. Once n_i collects enough verdicts, it can send back a $TRAC_{Conf}$ packet to the sink, to indicate that n_i is one of the forwarder of the packet with $pkt.id$. This process will continue recursively, from n_i to n_{i-1}, until a node has no other one-hop suspect that transmitted the packet, or a node cannot collect enough $TRAC_{Verd}$ messages.

Summary   CAPTRA provides packet traceback through logging and local collaboration. Every node logs all transmissions it overhears and produces verdict messages upon queries asking for the route. Due to the use of Bloom filters and periodic resetting, nodes can use less storage space in logging messages.

CAPTRA's security strength, however, might be limited. There is not mechanism to protect the various control messages such as query and verdicts against many potential abuses. A compromised node may attack such control messages, such as forging queries or verdicts, or suppressing verdict from neighbors, all of which can lead to incorrect traceback to innocent nodes. When multiple compromised nodes collaborate, they can pose more threats by helping each other to cover up the traces, such as dropping queries destined to another compromised node. Without concrete solutions on these issues, CAPTRA can only provide protection against limited types of attacks.

4.3.   Correlation among Data Content

Abnormal Relationship Test [9] (ART) presents another approach where a reporting node will quantify the correlation among data samples from other reporting nodes. When a compromised node injects bogus data, other nodes do not observe that false event and their data will have little correlation to it.

ART proposes two statistical tests to determine the correlation among the data from different reporting nodes. Assuming an event is detected by multiple sensing nodes, the forwarding node will gather the reading from all of them. After all the readings are gathered, it will conduct two tests, namely correlation coefficient and t^*-value. Correlation coefficient indicates linear relationships between data sets and t^*-value stands for the difference in the means between small sample sets. They both represent how similar or different data reports are.

If one neighbor does not pass the test, data from that neighbor is considered abnormal. The reporting node suspects the outlier neighbor might be compromised. It will verify the neighbor's identity. If the neighbor cannot prove its identity, or the neighbor can prove its identity but keep failing the tests, the node will report the suspect neighbor to the sink and the sink may conduct further investigation if needed.

4.3.1.   Correlation Analysis and Modified t-test

In ART protocol, a reporting node needs to calculate the correlation coefficient and t^*-value for each neighbor based on the data sets received from these neighbors. The correlation coefficient between two nodes X and Y, $r_{X,Y}$, is calculated by

$$r_{X,Y} = \frac{Cov(X,Y)}{S_X * S_Y}$$

where $Cov(X,Y)$ is the covariance between data set X and Y, and S_X and S_Y are sample variances of data set X and Y. The value range of $r_{X,Y}$ is between -1 and 1, while a higher value indicates close correlation. On the other hand, the t^*-value is calculated from a small set of sample readings.

$$t^* = \frac{X_i - (\mu_R \pm \delta)}{S_R/W}$$

where X_i is the reading from reporting node i, μ is the sample mean of forwarding node, S_R is sample standard deviation, and W is sample size. The thresholds for both correlation and t^*-value tests are system parameters.

When an outlier exists, its data will have little resemblance to that from others. The authors claim that either normal or interest events with abnormal value can pass through these two tests, while compromised and faulty sensors with error readings cannot pass through either one of these testes.

Summary   ART stands for a content aware approach where the exact content, or semantics, of the data is used to detect attacks. This is quite different from other approaches where only the syntax of data is used (e.g., to produce MAC code). The correlation among data set is explored to discover outliers, be it faulty or compromised node. ART demonstrates its effectiveness through an evaluation carried out at Great Duck Island.

ART has several limitations as well. First, the proposed correlation analysis applies only to continuous numeric samples. They do not work if the data is higher level events such as the location, type of fire occurrence. Second, it only detects a compromised node that reports false data "happening" in its own neighborhood. If the node pretends to be "forwarding" data originated from remote locations, there is no way for its neighbors to correlate because remote events are out of their sensing range. It is this kind of data injection that causes greater damage and requires more protection. Finally, similar to all approaches that introduce extra control messages, there is little protection on how it can avoid the forging of readings that contaminate correlation calculation. It introduces new mechanisms to solve one attack, without explaining how holes on these mechanisms are plugged.

5.   Conclusion

Many wireless sensor networks are expected to work in a hostile environment where nodes can be physically captured and compromised. Such compromised nodes can launch various attacks that corrupt data authenticity. To this end, we have described the state-of-the-art proposals for both passive and proactive approaches in fighting against such false data injection attacks.

In the passive approach, we examine the tradeoffs of various filtering mechanisms that detect and drop bogus packets en-route. This is achieved by exploiting sensing redundancy and different forms of key sharing schemes, which impact the tradeoff among the filtering power, the resiliency to node compromises and the capability of adapting to route changes. In the proactive approach, we investigate the pros and cons of rekeying, logging, and correlation based proposals. They present initial steps toward active defense that can fight back the compromised nodes. We have also pointed out that the current logging or correlation based proposals are not yet sufficient for accurately locating the attacking nodes due to limited storage and lack of protection on control messages.

An ideal proactive mechanism should identify compromised nodes while introducing *as few extra control messages* as possible. The reason is simply because every control message can be abused and forged as attacking ones. Shifting the problem to protecting control messages is not solving the problem. One possibility is to use packet marking based traceback [7]. Marks are piggybacked on packets and no extra control message is needed. But the large number of packets needed in Internet based marking schemes make them infeasible to sensor networks. They need to be adapted to the constrained environment in sensor networks. A complete solution needs to combine both passive and proactive approaches. The ultimate is to stop the attack traffic at its origin as quickly as possible, and isolate/remove the compromised nodes from the rest of the network. Only in such ways can the root cause of the false data injection attacks be eradicated.

References

[1] *Xbow sensor networks.* http://www.xbow.com/.

[2] Saurabh ganeriwal, Ramkumar Rengaswamy, Chih-Chieh han, and Mani Srivastava, *Secure Event Reporting Protocol for Sense-Response Applications*, technical report, Networked Embedded Systems Lab, UCLA, 2005.

[3] Qijun Gu, Peng Liu, Sencun Zhu, and Chao-Chien Chu, *Defending against Packet Injection Attacks in Unreliable Ad Hoc Networks*, in IEEE Globecom, 2005.

[4] Lingxuan Hu and David Evans, *Localization for Mobile Sensor Networks*, in Tenth Annual International Conference on Mobile Computing and Networking, 2004.

[5] Brad Karp and H. T. Kung, *Gpsr: Greedy perimeter stateless routing for wireless networks*, in ACM MOBICOM, 2000.

[6] Samuel Madden, Michael Franklin, Joseph Hellerstein, and Wei Hong, *TinyDB: An Acquisitional Query Processing System for Sensor Networks*, TODS, (2005).

[7] Stefan Savage, David Wetherall, Anna Karlin, and Tom Anderson, *Practical network support for IP traceback*, in ACM SIGCOMM, 2000.

[8] D. Sy and L. Bao, *CAPTRA: CoordinAted Packet TRAceback*, in The Fifth International Conference on Information Processing in Sensor Networks (IPSN), April 2006.

[9] Sapon Tanachaiwiwat and Ahmed Helmy, *Correlation Analysis for Alleviating Effects of Inserted Data in Wireless Sensor Networks*, in IEEE/ACM Mobiquitous, 2005.

[10] Victor Wen, Adrian Perrig, and Robert Szewczyk, *SPINS: Security Suite for Sensor Networks*, in ACM MOIBCOM, 2001.

[11] Hao Yang and Songwu Lu, *Commutative Cipher Based En-Route Filtering in Wireless Sensor Networks*, IEEE VTC, (2004).

[12] Hao Yang, Fan Ye, Yuan Yuan, Songwu Lu, and William Arbaugh, *Toward Resilient Security in Wireless Sensor Networks*, in ACM Mobihoc, 2005.

[13] Fan Ye, Haiyun Luo, Songwu Lu, and Lixia Zhang, *Statistical En-Route Filtering of Injected False Data in Sensor Networks*, in IEEE Infocom, 2004.

[14] Fan Ye, Gary Zhong, Songwu Lu, and Lixia Zhang, *GRAdient Broadcast: A Robust Data Delivery Protocol for Large Scale Sens or Networks*, ACM Wireless Networks (WINET), 11 (2005).

[15] Zhen Yu and Yong Guan, *A Dynamic En-route Scheme for Filtering False Data*, in IEEE Infocom, 2006.

[16] Wensheng Zhang and Guohong Cao, *Group Rekeying for Filtering False Data in Sensor Networks: A Predistribution and Local Collaboration-Based Approach*, in IEEE Infocom, 2005.

[17] Li Zhou, Jinfeng Ni, and Chinya Ravishanka, *Supporting Secure Communication and Data Collection in Mobile Sensor Networks*, in IEEE Infocom, 2006.

[18] Sencun Zhu, Sanjeev Setia, Sushil Jajodia, and Peng Ning, *An Interleaved Hop-by-Hop Authentication Scheme for Filtering of Injected False Data in Sensor Networks*, in IEEE Symposium on Security and Privacy, 2004.

In: Computer Security: Intrusion, Detection and Prevention   ISBN: 978-1-60692-781-6
Editors: R. D. Hopkins and W. P. Tokere   © 2009 Nova Science Publishers, Inc.

Chapter 9

LONG-TERM SECURITY FOR SIGNED DOCUMENTS: SERVICES, PROTOCOLS, AND DATA STRUCTURES

Thomas Kunz,[*] Susanne Okunick[†] and Ursula Viebeg[‡]
Fraunhofer Gesellschaft (FhG),
Institute for Secure Information Technology (SIT),
Rheinstr. 75, 64295 Darmstadt, Germany

Abstract

Long-term retention of electronically signed documents brings with certain problems: Signed documents may loose their probative value over the years and changing of data formats breaks the original signature. In this paper, we analyze the state of the art to resolve these problems and describe requirements, existing and partially field-tested concepts, data structures and specifications of service protocols. Solutions for the aging problem are already in an advanced state, whereas in the area of secure transformation merely first requirements and solution concepts may be presented. Since many organizations, and, in particular, SMEs and individuals are confronted by the challenge how to technically and organizationally implement existing concepts we describe services caring about the long-term and law-abiding preservation of electronic documents. In this way users of a web service are not forced to deal with the complex process of securing their documents over long periods of time.

1. Introduction

Today, most of the business relevant documents, like invoices, are created, exchanged, and stored in electronic form. The legislation on European level has provided the legal framework for a barrier-free electronic communication and electronic commerce: In 1999 the EU Directive 1999/93/EC [10] was enacted, providing legal requirements for a common introduction of electronic signatures in Europe. The German Signature Law (in German: Signaturgesetz or SigG) transposes this Directive into German legislation. Thereby for certain types of signature, e. g. the so called "qualified" signature, the legal recognition is

---

[*]E-mail address: thomas.Kunz@sit.fraunhofer.de
[†]E-mail address: Susanne.Okunick@sit.fraunhofer.de
[‡]E-mail address: Ursula.Viebeg@sit.fraunhofer.de

enabled in a way that the legal status of electronic signatures is equivalent to that of hand-written signatures in paper documents. For electronically issued and tax relevant invoices the German Value Added Tax Act (in German: Umsatzsteuergesetz) requires qualified signatures according to the German Signature Law. The legal basis for the usage of electronic signatures is provided also for the public sector within national and community administration, for public health, banking, and the justice system.

Record retention bases on legal requirements for both electronic and paper based documents in the same way. The change to electronic processes increases the need for the secure storage of electronic documents. Long retention periods, e. g. more than 30 years, cause problems especially for electronically signed documents. Two problems regarding the preservation of the probative value of signed documents have to be resolved:

1. Electronic signatures are aging. The increasing computing power, the possibility of networking, and progress of cryptography contribute to the "weakening" of electronic signatures, i. e., electronically signed documents may loose their probative value over the years. This process may already be significant after six years.

2. Electronic signatures break when changing the document format. The technological development, harmonization attempts, and also new juridical guidelines cause changes of user data and signature formats over the years. With electronically signed documents format changes are problematical, since changing the format breaks the original signature. A similar problem arises during the digitalization of paper documents. If, for instance, a document signed by hand is digitized, the signature looses its validity. The legal authenticity of the transformed document is at least doubtful.

In this paper, we first give a state of the art overview of solution concepts for these basic problems. Some concepts concerning the weakening process of signature algorithms exist and there are already standardization efforts. First concepts dealing with secure format changing are developed as well.

Currently many organizations are confronted with the challenges how to lawcompliantly preserve electronic documents for a long period of time and how to technically and organizationally implement the existing concepts. In particular, SMEs (small and medium-sized enterprises) and individuals are often overwhelmed.

Appropriate services for archiving and transformation of documents could produce relief and are of particular interest. To establish such services, consistent service descriptions, standardized interfaces, and interoperable data structures are essential.

Therefore we design some selected services with their architecture and basic tasks, to realize parts of above named concepts e. g., an archiving service caring about signature renewals, a certification service (in German: Beglaubigungsdienst) or a transformation service for conversion of data formats with subsequent notarization. We identify missing solution concepts and gaps in standardization.

Our goal is to increase the applicability and dissemination in this field of activity. Several archiving problems, such as the long-term readability of storage media and the protection of the documents against deletion or manipulation during the archive period, are not addressed in this paper.

The paper is organized as follows. Section 2 attends the long-term conservation of the probative value of signed documents. In section 3 we deal with the legally secure transformation of signed documents. In section 4 we compare the essential concepts and draw some conclusions. Finally we give a summary.

2. Long-Term Conservation of Signed Documents

In this section, we address the problem of signature aging. The following analyzes the state of the art and provides an introduction to existing concepts and standardization efforts in this field of development. We describe different services realizing these concepts and briefly propose field-tested data structures as a subject for standardization.

2.1. State of the Art

All existing concepts are based on the timely renewal of signatures by means of time stamps. Timely means to renew before the currently used signature algorithms become insecure. A time stamp is issued by a time stamp service, which receives a hash value of data, adds the current time, and signs this generated construct by its own signature based on stronger algorithms or parameters. The time stamp itself is a signed date and thus also subject to an aging process. For this reason it is integrated in the archiving process and continually renewed. In this way chains of time stamps are generated.

In [15] the European Telecommunications Standards Institute (ETSI) specifies signature formats based on CMS and XML signatures and also takes into account longterm conservation of provability of signed documents. By this concept an electronic signature is first completed with verification information (e. g., certificates and certificate revocation lists) needed to verify the signature. The collected data is encapsulated in one object and secured by a time stamp. As we will see later this signature oriented method is only suitable for small numbers of documents.

The IETF (Internet Engineering Task Force) working group LTANS (Long-Term Archive and Notary Services) deals with the same topic and has already defined requirements, data structures and protocols for the secure usage of archive services. The working group is initiated as a result of the project ArchiSig, funded from 2001 to 2003 by the German Federal Ministry of Economics and Technology [4].

For long-term archive services (LTA) which are responsible for the preservation of data over long periods of time the "Long-Term Archive Service Requirements" have been defined [6]. They can be roughly divided into requirements for the access protocol to communicate with the LTA and functionality requirements. A protocol has to support the basic operations: Submit data objects for archiving, retrieve and delete archived data objects, specify, extend or shorten archiving periods, specify metadata associated with a data object, and specify an archive policy under which the submitted data should be handled. An archive service must provide evidence records containing sufficient information for a non-repudiation proof that a data object existed at a certain time. Hereby the evidence record must allow detection of any modifications to it and the appropriate data objects. The service has to operate on the basis of an archive service policy consisting of rules for operational aspects and authorization concepts. It also must be possible to transfer data objects and its evidence record from one service to another without losing evidence value. Furthermore data confidentiality must be ensured between the submitter and the LTA.

The structure of evidence data for an archived data object is closely coupled with the underlying concept [7]. This concept is in contrast to ETSI document oriented and independent of signature formats. First the electronic document as a whole with all its signatures is hashed and time stamped. To optimize the process lots of signed or unsigned documents are merged in a hash tree, first described by Merkle [8], whose root hash value represents all documents. A time stamp is requested only for the root hash of the tree. This procedure is more cost effective and mass-capable. The hash algorithm used for building the hash tree may also become weak, which requires the more complex hash tree renewal by using a current suitable hash algorithm.

The ERS (Evidence Record Syntax) proposed by the LTANS group [1] describes the data structure of an evidence record. It contains all time stamp chains and other verification data necessary for the complete proof of existence of an archived data object or a data object group at a certain time. The ERS takes into account the archive requirements and meets the requirements, in particular, for data structures. It handles huge numbers of data objects and data of any format. The work on ERS is well advanced by now and first supporting software solutions are in the market.

Based on the archive requirements the LTAP (Long-term Archive Protocol) [9] describes basic functions of a protocol for communication between clients and a LTA. These are functions for transferring data to the archive service, accessing to and deletion of archived data as well as verifying the integrity and authenticity of the archived data. The LTAP draft is in an early development stage until now, so it does not define sufficiently concrete data structures for practical use.

Both the ETSI and the LTANS concepts of signature renewal are accepted by ISIS-MTT [16].

2.2.   Long-Term Archive Services

As we have seen, requirements for long-term archive services as well as concepts for preserving the probative value of electronic signatures already exist. We have therefore accomplished the prerequisites for the definition of LTAs. Basically we distinguish two kinds of services.

The first type of service is intended for larger organizations or companies. They already run some kind of document management system (DMS) to file their documents. They only need to add an additional service for ensuring the preservation of the probative value of their signed documents. This kind of service is characterized by the integration in an environment with an already existing document repository. We assume, for pure document management users want to use their familiar and already existing DMS clients. The process of long-term securing the documents can be done fully automatically in the background. An interaction with the user is not necessary. If a new document is stored in the document management system, the DMS informs the LTA on this fact. The long-term archive service must have access to this document. Accessing the document means in this context that the service only fetches the document in order to compute the hash value of the document

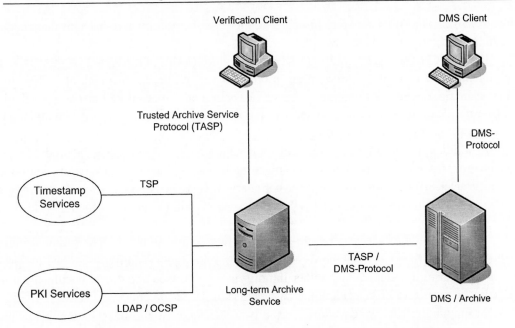

Figure 1. Long-term archive service in combination with a DMS.

and to obtain a time stamp. The document resides unchanged in the DMS. The LTA only holds the corresponding evidence record. Additionally the long-term archive service must offer methods to access the evidence records. Since accessing the evidence records is a rather infrequent task, we propagate a separate client for requesting and verifying evidence records. Thus, the whole process of securing the documents can completely be hidden from every day work. Figure 1 shows a possible architecture with a separate verification client and a DMS client.

The second type of long-term archive service is rather intended for SMEs and individuals who are often overwhelmed by the challenge of preserving the probative value of documents. The service can be imagined as a web service based on technologies like SOAP [12] and WSDL [13]. Alternatively the service can be accessed via a web browser interface. Privacy and confidentiality play a major role than in the other scenario. In general, users do not want to entrust their documents to the service. Hence the service is only used for performing the signature renewal and managing the evidence records i. e. it has no access to the user's documents. Instead the user only provides hash values of the documents to the service. In contrast, as pointed out in [11], the submission of encrypted documents is problematic since the evidence that encrypted data existed at a certain point of time is not necessarily an evidence for the existence of the appropriate unencrypted data. Just as the first service, also this service must offer the possibility to access the evidence records. Unlike the first type of service, here the user is more actively involved in the process. The user not only directly determines which documents have to be secured. It is supposable that the user can also make individual adjustments concerning supported cryptographic algorithms, used timestamp services and so on. That means, every user can force its own policy under which the service should act. Furthermore, the client has to care about the storage of the user's documents and must be able to hash documents. The service will inform the user if the used hash algorithm becomes insecure. In this case the user must re-hash his documents with the currently valid hash algorithm.

Both types of services require a PKI infrastructure (LDAP, OCSP etc.) as they collect certificates and revocation information in order to verify time stamps and, at least in the first scenario, document signatures. The services store all collected PKI artifacts to enable a later verification, even if the PKI services are no longer operating or at least do no longer provide the necessary information.

In addition, for both types of services we need the possibility to verify the produced evidence records. This can be done offline by a standalone application as well as by an online web service. Primarily in the web service scenario it is supposable that the rather complex process of verification is offered by the service as an additional functionality instead of burden the client with it.

The two kinds of services require a similar interaction protocol. The protocol must allow access to the evidence records and it must provide the possibility to initiate the process of securing the documents, either in notifying the service about new documents in a document repository or in sending the hash values of the documents.

At Fraunhofer SIT, we developed the software package ArchiSoft[1], which implements the above-mentioned concepts for the timely renewal of electronic signatures. In periodic intervals the validity of currently used algorithms is checked out. If an algorithm is threatened, the renewal process will automatically be launched. It offers an interface to integrate ArchiSoft in an arbitrary document management system. Furthermore ArchiSoft can act as a web service including the possibility for online verification of evidence records. Therefore, with ArchiSoft both kinds of long-term archive services can be realized.

Currently, neither proprietary protocols of document management systems nor standards for document management like the Open Document Management API (ODMA)[2] or the Open Archival Information System (OAIS) [14] support the handling with evidence records. The above mentioned LTAP aims at the interaction with long-term archive services but it is still in an early stage. For this reason, we specified the Trusted Archive Service Protocol (TASP), an archiving protocol that meets the requirements resulting from the two kinds of services. Besides operations for managing archived documents, the protocol supports access to and verification of evidence records as well as the initialization of the long-term security process for selected documents.

2.3. Security Suitability of Algorithms

Archiving services caring for the automatic signature renewal must be able to check the current security suitability of used signature algorithms. In Germany the Federal Network Agency (in German: Bundesnetzagentur) is the legally authorized institution for the valuation and annual publishing of the security suitability of signature algorithms. Since the publication is available in text form, it is not interpretable by machine or program.

Therefore a machine readable data structure has been defined holding the security suitability of algorithms and their parameters [3, 4, 17]. This structure is called a policy. It is already tried and field-tested both within the project ArchiSig and in the software ArchiSoft.

---

[1]http://www.sit.fraunhofer.de/archisoft
[2]http://www.infonuovo.com/odma/

A security suitability policy consists of policy name, different security suitabilities, validity period and the signature of the issuer. As seen in the following exemplary XML snip each security suitability is composed of the algorithm (algorithm identifiers, function, and parameters), validity start and end date.

```xml
<securitySuitability>
  <name>RSA</name>
  <algorithmType>asymmetric</algorithmType>
    <trustedAlgorithmOIDs>
      <OID>1.2.840.113549.1.1.5</OID>
      <OID>1.3.36.3.3.1.2</OID>
      <OID>1.2.840.113549.1.1.1</OID>
    </trustedAlgorithmOIDs>
  <trustedAlgorithmURIs>
    <URI>
      http://www.w3.org/2000/09/xmldsig#rsa-sha1
    </URI>
    <URI>
      http://www.w3.org/2001/04/xmldsig-more#rsa-ripemd160
    </URI>
  </trustedAlgorithmURIs>
  <function URI="http://www.archisig.de/id-RSAalgReq">
    <constraintValue>
      <RSAAlgConstraints modulusLen="768"/>
    </constraintValue>
  </function>
  <validityStart>1998-01-01</validityStart>
  <validityEnd>2000-12-31</validityEnd>
  <furtherInformation/>
</securitySuitability>
```

Up to now, the annually published security suitability policy has to be manually transformed from text document to this data structure by every user. This is an errorprone procedure. Additionally the administration and utilization of these policies expends effort.

For that reason a web service, which generates the machine readable policy and makes it available to the clients, could be an alternative. The created policy is electronically signed to protect it from manipulations and to enable authentication of the issuer.

Another web service may directly provide information about the security suitability of algorithms. Most important requests may be "Is an algorithm with explicit parameters currently suitable?", "Has an algorithm with explicit parameters been suitable at a specific time in the past?", "When is the validity of an algorithm with explicit parameters going to end?", "Until which date an algorithm with explicit parameters has being suitable?", "Which algorithms are suitable now?" and "Which algorithms will expire next?" The web service implements functions to perform such requests on the base of the policy and sends a response. In the process the web service has to care about the actuality of the security suitability policy. This alternative would relocate the preparation, updating and evaluation of the data structure from users to one trustful web service.

3. Legally Secure Transformation of Signed Documents

Solutions for the aging problem of electronic signatures are already in an advanced state, whereas the situation in the area of a secure transformation of signed documents is far from standard. First considerations concerning notary and certification services have been made in [18]. For the moment it's too early to speak of a state of the art technology in this field.

The German legislator has already passed respective laws that allow a certification in an electronic form. In particular these are the Administrative Procedures Law (in German: Verwaltungsverfahrensgesetz) and law concerning certifications by notaries (in German: Beurkundungsgesetz). Means combining organizational measures with technical solutions for legally secure transformations of signed documents are needed.

3.1. First Solution Concepts

The German Federal Ministry of Economics and Technology has funded the ongoing project TransiDoc[3] with the aim to develop concepts and solutions for the preservation of the probative value of transformed documents. TransiDoc has already delivered several results [2, 5], which are described in the following.

The primary concern of TransiDoc is that the probative value of the target document, i. e. the result of a transformation, is comparable to that of the source document. This is a prerequisite that the transformed document can be used in a later forensic argumentation instead of the source document. The presentation of the source must not be necessary.

The following ten principles defined by the project TransiDoc have to be met in order to achieve the abovementioned objectives of a secure transformation of signed documents. These requirements do not only address transformations between electronic documents (E→E), but also those involving paper documents as source or target (P→E and E→P):

1. Technical solutions are preferable; i. e., standardized technical proceedings should be used to mitigate human error and to increase (economic) efficiency.

2. Agreement of contents must be assured. The context of the respective use-case will determine the necessary degree of agreement resp. correlation between source and target contents. It may be required, for example, that errors and deficiencies of the source document, like invalid signatures, have to be recorded. In some transformation cases purposeful changes of the source contents are necessary, e. g., in order to make the contents anonymous.

3. Authentication of the authorship, i. e., the signers of the source documents must be authenticated. The authentication results including all used verification data, like certificates and revocation information, must be recorded. Handwritten signatures must be scanned in a careful way. If necessary, further information of the authorship has to be collected.

---

[3]http://www.transidoc.de

4. Data integrity of the source and target documents and of all protocols and verification results generated during the transformation has to be assured.

5. Attributability of the transformation, i. e., it must be verifiable who was responsible for the transformation. An electronic signature of an adequate security level will reach attributability of the transformation, if the result of the transformation is an electronic document. Otherwise a paper document will be hand signed, if required.

6. Authorization of the responsible persons, i. e., transformations should only be performed by authorized persons. It must be possible to verify the identity, role and authorization of the responsible persons later on. The respective use-case determines proper credentials, e. g., attribute certificates for an electronic signature. For a paper document the handwritten signature may be completed with an official seal. Institutions where transformations take place must develop own authorization concepts based on legal regulations.

7. Data protection and secrecy must be guaranteed, i. e., only authorized persons are allowed to access data used or generated during the transformation process. The personal data collected in order to verify an electronic signature must be restricted to the absolutely necessary amount.

8. Long-term usability of the target document, i. e., the source document should be converted in a long-term preservation format, which is unambiguously interpretable and standardized. This is the precondition for both the usability of the document over a long period of time and protection of the probative value of its content. Besides the converted content the target document contains protocols and verification results. These data must be structured in a way that it can be presented in various levels from giving an overview to going into the smallest detail. The presentation of the target document shall be adaptable to different purposes and users who may be specialists in this field or persons with less previous knowledge.

9. Traceability of the transformation, i. e., the complete workflow of a transformation, including information about the used systems and acting persons must be recorded to enable forensic evaluation. Evaluation must be possible independently of the transformation system.

10. Reliability of the transforming system, i. e., only certified and / or well audited systems should be used during the transformation process.

Considering the principles presented above it is obvious that it is not enough to just convert the content of a document to fulfill these principles. Even in the case of simple format conversions, additional process steps, like assay steps, and organizational measures are required to ensure security. To identify these requirements, a procedural analysis of a generic transformation process is helpful. In the following, a secure document transformation is presented as a sequence of high-level transformation phases. This phase model is generic, i. e., it is independent of the kind of transformation (E→E, P→E, or E→P) and it can be applied to a wide range of applications. Use-cases determine which phases are

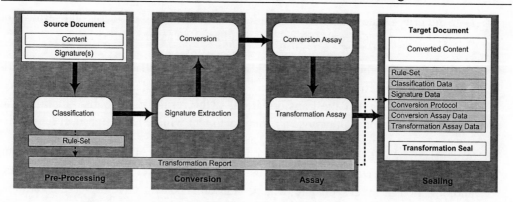

Figure 2. Procedural view on secure document transformations.

necessary, which one may be subsumed under or combined with another, or which may be parallelized if they become logically independent.

Figure 2 shows a secure transformation process starting from the source document consisting of its content and one or more signatures and resulting in the target document.

The intended purpose of a transformation influences especially the initial transformation phase called *classification*. The purpose may be to create a replacement, where the target shall be usable in the same way as the source document, such that, ideally, the source can be dispensed with. Another purpose may be to get a partial copy of the source usually containing only parts of the source content and accordingly limiting the possible usages of the target. In the classification phase the source document is inspected and those properties are determined which shall be recovered in the target document in order to fulfill the purpose of the transformation. That means, the classification does not only determine the relevant properties of the source but also those of the target and the complete transformation process, which have to be satisfied to achieve the desired reliability. From this classification follow the rules that govern the transformation process. The *rule-set* depends on every special application case, comprising organizational provisions, technical measures, attributions of responsibility, rules for signature verification and generation, etc. In general, the rule-set consists of a combination of machine-processable instructions, with normative prescriptions understandable only by humans. The *transformation report* is a data container which carries the information compiled during the transformation, such as protocols and assay results performed in later phases.

The real conversion is divided in two phases: *signature extraction* and *conversion*. During signature extraction, all relevant information of the source's signatures are gathered and added to the transformation report. The rule-set determines whether electronic signatures must be verified or the signers of the handwritten ones must be authenticated. The rule-set prescribes verification policies and decides the signature data to be carried to the report (e. g. time stamps, attributes etc.), and the result of the validation is also added to the report. In the conversion phase the proper conversion of source to target contents takes place according to the rules of the rule-set. Apart from the target contents, a conversion protocol and an error log are filed in the report. In the next phase the *conversion assay* follows, i. e., the correctness of the conversion is verified, e. g. by inspecting logs in the report and / or explicit comparisons of source and target contents. The final phase *transformation assay* serves two purposes; at first a consistency check on all preceding phases takes place, after that the result of the transformation with all data generated during transformation is secured. For this, a *transformation seal* is attached to the transformed document and signed by the transforming entity. The result of a transformation needs to be secure even if the source is not available for later comparison. This is the main reason why relevant data produced in the transformation process must be persistently and trustworthy bound to the target to enable a thorough forensic inspection. This possibility to assess the quality of a transformation is an important building block for the probative value of the target. It is embodied in three subordinate goals, which describe the essential purpose of the transformation seal:

1. Securing the integrity of the transformed document and other recorded data.

2. Attestation of the correctness of the transformation according to the specified rule-set.

3. Attribution of the transformation to the transforming entity and non-repudiation of that fact.

The result of a secure document transformation is the target document consisting of the converted content, the rule-set, the transformation report and the transformation seal. The project TransiDoc has developed data structures in XML notation for all parts of the target document. The data structures are as far as possible generic, i. e. application independent. They are flexible and extendable to support diverse certification services, architectures and different security levels. They enable the later verification of the transformation and provide means to prove the authorization of attesting authority.

The data structure of the rule-set is designed like a workflow definition, which determines how the transformation process shall be performed. The workflow definition consists of a sequence of activities. Each activity is either a manual or an automatic activity. A manual activity has to be executed by a human, whereas an automated activity shall be performed by a software or hardware component. The correspondent part of the workflow definition is the transformation report which provides what has actually been done during the transformation. For example the rule-set may require that a signature creation device conforming to the German Signature Law shall be used for creation of the transformation seal. The task of the transformation report is to provide the information about the actually used device, inclusive name, version and manufacturer. In detail, the transformation report consists of data processing protocols, documentation of the operations over the data, used software and hardware components and intermediate results, like signature verification results. It provides both traceability of data processing and authentication of the signer(s) of the source document. The transformation seal consists of an annotation and a signature. The annotation contains e. g. names of signers of the source document, including the authentication results, credentials of the certification service and its operators, time of certification and the attestation, e. g. of the correctness of transformation. Signatures contain the signature itself and e. g. certificates and attribute certificates. Hence the transformation seal provides the meaning and the trustworthiness of the assertion and data integrity and authenticity of the target document.

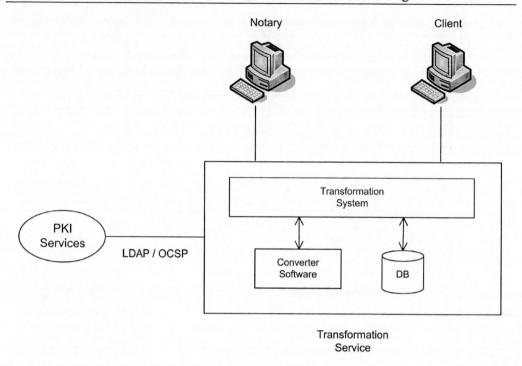

Figure 3. Transformation Service.

3.2. Transformation Services

Based on the introduced concepts and data structures, we propose a service for legally secure transformation of signed documents (see Figure 3). Examples are certification and
notary services acting as a trusted third party who may attest that two documents contain
the same information as well as the validity of the contained electronic signatures. Users
can submit signed documents in order to let them transformed by the service into another
data format without loss of their probative value. Note that different from paper-based documents, attestations of literal copies of digital documents only make little sense. In many
cases the transformation process cannot be performed completely automatically. Only individuals can in general determine that the contents of two documents are equivalent. Another
reason is that at least according to German law an attestation must be signed by means of
a qualified signature, i. e. the signature of the resulting target document must be authorized by an individual. That means the service must allow the possibility of interventions
by individuals. As a consequence, the service must support asynchronous communication
since the user does not get the target document as an immediate response. After receiving
a signed document from a user, the service performs the transformation according to the
above mentioned transformation phases. After that, the service notifies the notary (e. g.
via e-mail) so that he can perform the final transformation phase by verifying the correctness of the transformation and signing the target document. When the target document is
completed, the user will be notified by the service so that he can fetch the target document.

     Besides services for transforming documents, we need the possibility to verify target
documents. This can be realized as a stand-alone application as well as an online service.

Verification of a target document means verifying the transformation seal and presenting the components of the target document (converted content, result of signature extraction etc.) in a comprehensible and retraceable manner.

To use this service, we need a rather simple protocol which allows the client to order a transformation, to query the status of the transformation, and to fetch the result of the transformation.

Both the transformation service as well as the verification service are currently developed by Fraunhofer SIT within the project TransiDoc.

4. Conclusions

We presented concepts and services for both main topics regarding long-term security: aging of signatures and changing of data formats. For both topics we have data structures which represent the performed processes and we have protocols for the interaction with the respective service. In principle the protocols could be combined to one protocol which covers all kinds of services introduced in this paper. But there is a difference in these concepts concerning the probative value. The probative value which can be obtained when using the concepts for the renewal of signatures is of another quality than the probative value achieved when transforming a signed document according to the introduced concepts.

The renewal of signatures by building hash trees and time stamping leads to a probative value that is based on cryptography. By means of the evidence record, the whole renewal process can be verified at any time. But the precondition of the security of this concept is that the signatures have always been renewed before the respective algorithms became insecure.

In contrast the probative value achieved when performing a legally secure transformation is primarily based on trust in the attestor or the service who transformed the document. Since in general, the source document is no longer available after the transformation, we cannot compare the original with the transformed document, and thus we cannot verify if the transformation is done correctly. We can only comprehend which steps were accomplished during the transformation process and – most important – we can verify whether the transformation seal was created by an authorized individual. For this reason, meeting the principles for legally secure transformations is essential to guarantee a correct transformation process. Furthermore, organizational instructions, e. g. concerning the security of the working environment, the choice of adequate technical security devices, or the individual who is allowed to perform the transformation, are of greater importance as with the process of signature renewal.

With this conclusion and the results presented in the sections before, we can now describe a service which cares for the timely renewal of signatures as well as for the transformation of documents. Because in general, document formats will change over the years, the service can automatically convert documents into subsequent data formats. It is noticeable that after a transformation, the existing evidence record cannot longer be verified since the hash value of the transformed document does not match to the one contained in the evidence record. Therefore, before transforming a document we must verify the evidence record together with the source document. The verification result must be recorded in the target document which is created when transforming the document. After that, we can delete the source document as well as the old evidence record. The target document will now be filed as a new data object and it will be time stamped and so, a new evidence record is generated. When we verify the new evidence record at a certain point of time in the future, we must also verify the target document, which means that we present the verification result concerning the old evidence record. As pointed out before, at this point of time, we can only trust in the correct transformation. If sometime in the future another transformation will be necessary, we will not only have to preserve the verification result of the last evidence record but also the verification results of all previous evidence records.

In order to automatically choose an appropriate data format, we can imagine a catalogue of data formats and their suitability for transformations. For example, some data formats should be avoided because of active contents they are not transformation-secure. Therefore requirements for data formats like long-term stability or platform independence must be established.

5. Summary

As we have shown, mature concepts for both the renewal of electronic signatures and the secure transformation of signed documents exist. Based on these concepts, we introduced different kinds of services which may help organizations to long-term and law-compliantly preserve electronic documents. In particular by the definition of web services SMEs and individuals gain the possibility to easily secure their documents over long periods of time without to be forced to deal with complex processes. This can contribute to encourage the application of electronic signatures.

Nevertheless, there are still some open issues. A prerequisite for the establishment of the evaluation of cryptographic algorithms and for their usage by national agencies (e. g. the Federal Network Agency) is that the proposed data structures will be standardized. Furthermore, it would be desirable to push on the standardization efforts for secure transformations.

References

[1] Brandner, R.; Pordesch, U.; Gondrom, T.: *Evidence Record Syntax (ERS), RFC* **4998**, August 2007.

[2] Fischer-Dieskau, S.; Kunz, T.; Schmidt, A. U.; Viebeg, U.: *Grundkonzepte rechtssicherer Transformationen signierter Dokumente*, Sicherheit 2005, GI-Edition, *Lecture Notes in Informatics* (LNI), Vol. P-62, pp. 401-412, 2005.

[3] Kunz, T.; Okunick, S.; Pordesch, U.: *Data Structure for Security Suitabilities of Cryptographic Algorithms (DSS)*, Internet-Draft <draft-ietf-ltans-dssc-00.txt>, June 2007.

[4] Roßnagel, A.; Schmücker, P.: *Beweiskräftige elektronische Archivierung – Bieten elektronische Signaturen Rechtssicherheit?*, Economica Verlagsgruppe Hüthig Jehle Rehm GmbH Heidelberg, 2006.

[5] Schmidt, A. U.; Loebl, Z.: Legal Security for Transformations of Signed Documents: Fundamental Concepts, EuroPKI 2005, *Lecture Notes in Computer Science,* Vol. 3545, pp. 255-270, Springer-Verlag, 2005.

[6] Wallace, C.; Pordesch, U.; Brandner, R.: *Long-Term Archive Service Requirements,* RFC 4810, March 2007.

[7] Brandner, R.; Pordesch, U.: *Long-term conservation of provability of electronically signed documents,* ISSE Paris, October 2002.

[8] Merkle, R. C.: Protocols for Public Key Cryptosystems, *IEEE Symposium on Security and Privacy,* Oakland, CA, U.S.A., 1980.

[9] Jerman Blazic, A.; Sylvester P.; Wallace, C.: *Long-term Archive Protocol (LTAP),* Internet-Draft <draft-ietf-ltans-ltap-05.txt>, July 2007.

[10] Directive 1999/93/EC of the European Parliament and of the Council December 1999 on a Community framework for electronic signatures, *Official Journal of the European Communities,* 19 January 2000, L13/12.

[11] Fischlin, M.; Pordesch, U.: *Nichtabstreitbarkeit trotz Verschlüsselung,* Datenschutz und Datensicherheit (DuD), Vol. 3/2004, pp. 163-168, Vieweg Verlag, 2004.

[12] Gudgin, M.; Hadley, M.; Mendelsohn, N.; Moreau, J.-J.; Nielsen, H. F.: *SOAP Version 1.2 Part 1: Messaging Framework,* W3C Recommendation, 24 June 2003.

[13] Chinnici, R.; Moreau, J.-J.; Ryman, A.; Weerawarana, S.: *Web Services Description Language (WSDL) Version 2.0 Part 1: Core Language,* W3C Candidate Recommendation, 27 March 2006.

[14] Consultative Committee for Space Data Systems: *Space data and information transfer systems – Reference Model for an Open Archival Information System (OAIS),* Blue Book, Issue 1, CCSD, S2002, ISO 14721.

[15] European Telecommunications Standards Insitute: *ETSI TS 101 733 v1.5.1. – Electronic signature formats,* 2003.

[16] ISIS-MTT Specification, Preliminary Specification: *Long-term conservation of electronic signatures,* final draft, June 2004.

[17] Frye, F.; Pordesch, U.: *Berücksichtigung der Sicherheitseignung von Algorithmen qualifizierter Signaturen,* Datenschutz und Datensicherheit (DuD), Vol. 2/2003, pp. 73-78, Vieweg Verlag, 2003.

[18] Schmidt, A. U.; Gondrom, T.; Masinter, L.: *Requirements for Data Validation and Certification Services,* Internet Draft <draft-ietf-ltans-notareqs-03.txt>, December 2005.

n: Computer Security: Intrusion, Detection and Prevention ISBN: 978-1-60692-781-6
Editors: R. D. Hopkins and W. P. Tokere © 2009 Nova Science Publishers, Inc.

Short Communication

ACCESS CONTROL IN HEALTHCARE INFORMATION SYSTEMS – CONTEXT AWARE ATTRIBUTE BASED APPROACH

Snezana Sucurovic[1] and Dejan Simic[2]

[1]Institute Mihailo Pupin,Volgina 15, Belgrade, Serbia
[2]Faculty of Organisational Sciences, Belgrade, Serbia

Abstract

Role based access control has been in use for years. However, when the Internet based distributed large scale information systems come in use a need for context aware access control becomes evident. This approach has been implemented using attributes of subject of access control, resource of access control environment and the action used while the resource is accessed. Implementing this approach doesn't exclude RBAC. A role becomes a subject's attribute. EXtensible Access Control Markup Language is standardized language for writing access control policies, access control requests and access control responses using attributes. XACML can provide decentralized administration and credentials distribution. In the 2002 version of CEN ENV 13 606 attributes have been attached to EHCR components, and in such a system context aware or Attribute Based Access Control and XACML have been easy to implement. In 2008 CEN ENV 13 606 has been revised and becomes ISO 13 606 while access control in a healthcare information system has been standardized in ISO 22 600. This paper presents writing XACML policies in the case when attributes are in hierarchical structure and examines performances.

Keywords:computer security, access control, eXtensible Access Control Markup Language

1. Introduction

Access control is the process of mediating every request to data and services maintained by a system and determining whether the request should be granted or denied. A typical access control and authorization scenario includes three main entities -- a subject, a resource, and an action -- and their attributes. A subject makes a request for permission to perform an action on a resource. For example, in the access request, "Allow the finance manager to create files in the invoice folder on the finance server", the subject is the "finance manager," the target resource is the "invoice folder on the finance server," and the action is "create files." In such a context "It is allowed to the finance manager to create files in the invoice folder on the finance server" is the part of a security policy.

In a healthcare information system, for example, access control to a medical record can be limited only to users with an appropriate role and belonging to a provider and the access can be allowed only during an episode of care. According to Comitee European de Normalisation (CEN) ENV 13606 access control model "Role", "Healthcare agent" and "Episode of care" are to be attributes of medical record. It is supposed that security policy is "If a user presents the same attributes as they are connected to a medical record, access will be allowed." That is, a user has to present his attributes: role, provider and episode of care. The problem which is considered in this paper is related to CEN (ISO) 13606 based access control in large scale healthcare information systems such as national and regional electronic healthcare record. The main problem in such an information system is that there are large numbers of attributes. Control of them can be simplified if they are hierarchically organised (Joshi, Sucurovic).

XACML is an OASIS (Anderson) standard that describes both a policy language and an access control decision request/response language (both written in XML). The typical setup is that someone wants to take some action on a resource, so the elements of request are user'stributes, action and resource to be accessed. The request/response language lets you form a query to ask whether or not a given action should be allowed and interpret the result. The response always includes an answer about whether the request should be allowed using one of four values: Permit, Deny, Indetreminate or Not Applicable.

The currency that XACML deals in is attributes. Attributes are named values of known types. Specifically, attributes are characteristics of the subject, Resource, Action or Environment in which the access request is made. A user's name, their security clearance, the file they want to access, and the time of day are all attribute values. When a request is sent to a Policy Decision Point (PDP) (which makes decision), that request is formed almost exclusively of attributes, and they will be compared to attribute values in a policy to make the access decision.

2. CEN ENV 13606 Access Control Model

The main item in the CEN healthcare information system architecture (CEN, 2002) standard is an Architectural Component. The Architectural Components are organised in a hierarchical structure. Each Architectural Component has a reference to access control list for that component defined as Distribution Rules (Table 1). A Distribution Rule comprises classes Who, Where, When, Why and How which define who, where, when, why and how is allowed to access the component (Table 1). To access the system a user presents his attributes that correspond to attributes of class Who, When, Where, Why and How. Classes Who, When, Where, Why and How are processed with operator AND. There can be one or more DR attached to AC and they are processed with operator OR.

Table 1. Distribution Rules attributes

Class	Attribute	Type
Who	Profession	String
	Specialisation	String
	Engaged in care	Boolean
	Healthcare agent	Class
When	Episode of care	String
	Episode reference	String
Where	Country	String
	Legal requirement	Boolean
Why	Healthcare process code	String
	Healthcare process text	
	Sensitivity class	String
	Purpose of use	
	Healthcare party role	String
		Class
		Class
How	Access method	String
	Consent required	Class
	Signed	Boolean
	Encrypted	Boolean
	Operating system security rating	String
	Hardware security rating	
	Software security rating	String
		String

3. ISO 22 600 Access Control in Healthcare Information Systems

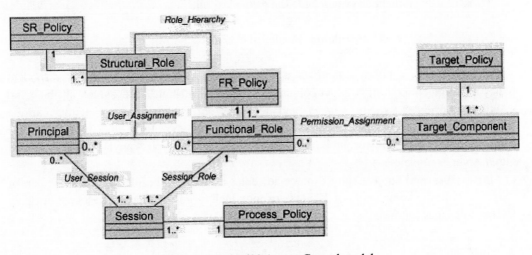

Figure 1. ISO 22 600 Access Control model.

ISO 22 600 Access Control in healthcare information systems has been presented at figure 1. Target Policy Functional Role Policy Structural Role Policy and Process Policy can be combined as a Policy Set in XACML. There are much work on policy combining (Bertino, 2007). There can be digital signature also, and therefore a verification is needed.

4. SUN'S XACML

This paper presents work with Sun's version of XACML (Sun). Sun's XACML has supported only XACML 1.0 and not XACML 2.0 yet. XACML 2.0 supports Security Access Control Markup Language (SAML) protocol which is enveloping protocol and provides standardized protocol for encryption and decryption of attributes and policies on the net.

Since Sun XACML is in developing phase (toward version XACML 2.0) in order to work with it, it is necessary to download form Code Version System (CVS) (from sourceforge.net) the last version of java classes and then compile them using given build.xml file. Finnally it is necessary to build jar archive using Apache's Ant tool. In that way, we can obtain the most stable version of Sun's XACML, since code for version 2.0 is added in this phase of development.

5. Writting XACML Policies

A policy is a Policy Set which comprises one or more policies, where a policy comprises one or more rules. There are also combining algorithms for policies and rules. For example if the combining algorithm is "ordered-permit-overrides" the firstly rules that permit access have advantage. In that case the last rule is

<Rule RuleId="FinaleRule" Effect="Deny"/>

that means that if there is not previously written permit rule access is forbbiden.

There is also another case when we write as the last rule

<Rule RuleId="FinaleRule" Effect="Permit"/>

Besides Rules, a Policy comprises a Target which is necessary to find correspodent policy to the given request. A target comprises <Subject> attribute, <Resource> attribute and <Action> Attributes, where subject and resource are mandatory and action can be <AnyAction/>. Subject attribute has to be of datatype RFC 822 (for example users.example.com), and resource attribute has to be of type <anyURI>(for example http://server.example.com).

It can be several Subject and Resource attributes in Request (besides ones that are part of Target in Policy). An example of XML segment which represents Target Resource attribute has been given as follows:

<Resource>
 <Resource Match MatchId=anyURI-equal>

```
   <AttributeValue
DataType=anyURI>http://server.example.com<AttributeValue/>
   <ResourceAttributeDesignator
DataType=anyURI
AttributeID=resource_id>
 <ResourceMatch>
<Resource>
```

It means that matching evaluation operator is anyURI-equal, that attribute is of type anyURI and that its value is http://server.example.com . Also, name of the attribute is resource_id, that is how it is compared with attributes from Request.

In a Policy a Target is followed by one or several Rules. While a target is simplified condition for access decision, the heart of most Rules is a Condition which is mostly boolean or set function. If the Condition evaluates to true, then the Rule's effect (a value of Permit or Deny that is associated with successful evaluation of the Rule) is returned. A Condition can be quite complex, built from an arbitrary nesting of non-boolean functions and attributes. The following XML segment presents a complex Condition:

```
<Condition FunctionId=string-at-least-one-member-of>
 <SubjectAttributeDesignator
  DataType=string
  AttributeId=group />
 <Apply FunctionId=string-bag>
  <AttributeValue
   DataType=string>GP<AttributeValue/>
  <AttributeValue
   DataType=string>SCP<AttributeValue/>
 </Apply>
</Condition>
```

It means that this is attribute of subject with name *group* and type *string*. Set function string-at-least-one-member-of means «at least one member of set whose elements are of type string». This segment means that attribute of subject with name group has to have at least one of given values (GP, SCP) in oder to access decision evaluates to Permit.

6. Working with Hierarchical Attributes

XACML has no explicit built-in support for hierarchical attributes. It is necessary to define Conditions for attributes. There are two possibilities to implement that as follows:

Lets subject's attributes hierarchy is presented on the figure 1.

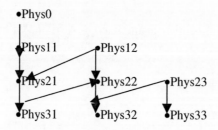

Figure 2. Attributes hierarchy (phys – physician in hierarchy).

First way to write Condition is as follows:

```
<Condition FunctionId=and>
<Apply FunctionId=string-equal>
 <SubjectAttributeDesignator
  DataType=string
  AttributeId=group />
  <AttributeValue
    DataType=string>Phys00<AttributeValue/>
 </Apply>
<Apply FunctionId=string-equal>
 <ResourceAttributeDesignator
  DataType=string
  AttributeId=groupr />
  <AttributeValue
    DataType=string>Phys21<AttributeValue/>
 </Apply>
</Condition>
```

It means if in Request Resource attribute with name *groupr* is *Phys21* and Subject Attribute with name *group* is *Phys00* access decision will be Permit.

To complete the Policy it is needed to write such Rules for all permited values and Policy will be (for this example) very large – 22 pages TimesNewRoman 12 pt font. It is clear that that performances will be poor, which is indeed problem with dealing with ABAC policies in standardized languge such as XACML. Because taht it is necessary to write more compact policy with better performances.

The second way to write the Policy for our example (fig. 1.) is:

```
<Condition FunctionId=and>
<Apply FunctionId=string-at-least-one-member-of>
 <SubjectAttributeDesignator
  DataType=string
  AttributeId=group />
  <AttributeValue
```

```
        DataType=string>Phys00<AttributeValue/>
     </Apply>
     </Apply>
<Apply FunctionId=string-at-least-one-member-of>
  <ResourceAttributeDesignator
   DataType=string
   AttributeId=groupr />
   <Apply FunctionId=string-bag>
    <AttributeValue
     DataType=string>Phys11<AttributeValue/>
    <AttributeValue
     DataType=string>Phys21<AttributeValue/>
    <AttributeValue
     DataType=string>Phys31<AttributeValue/>
    <AttributeValue
     DataType=string>Phys22<AttributeValue/>
    <AttributeValue
     DataType=string>Phys32<AttributeValue/>
   </Apply>
   </Apply>
</Condition>
```

On this way written Policy has half in size and performances are 10% better. It has been written in such a way that for a subject in hierarchy for all resources down in hierarchy access is allowed.

7. Performance Examination

All performance examinations which follows are obtained on 256 M RAM and 800 MHZ PC. If access control policy from figure 2. is to be written as follows and XML parser is SAX parser, using simple non-XACML application:

```
<?xml version="1.0"?>
<Physicians>
  <Roles>00,11</Roles>
  <Roles>00,21</Roles>
  <Roles>00,31</Roles>
  <Roles>00,22</Roles>
  <Roles>00,32</Roles>
  <Roles>11,21</Roles>
  <Roles>11,31</Roles>
  <Roles>11,22</Roles>
  <Roles>11,32</Roles>
  <Roles>21,31</Roles>
  <Roles>21,22</Roles>
```

```
<Roles>21,32</Roles>
<Roles>12,21</Roles>
<Roles>12,31</Roles>
<Roles>12,22</Roles>
<Roles>12,32</Roles>
<Roles>31,22</Roles>
<Roles>31,32</Roles>
<Roles>22,32</Roles>
<Roles>23,32</Roles>
<Roles>23,33</Roles>
</Physicians>
```

Policy1.xml

then access control time is:

Table 2. Access time according to Fig 2. and Policy1.xml using SAX parser and simple non-XACML application

Node 1	Node 2	Access time (ms)	Access decision
00	11	221	True (Permit)
00	21	261	True
00	31	251	True
00	12	311	False (Deny)
00	22	341	True
00	23	381	False
00	33	320	False
00	32	361	True
11	21	391	True
11	31	351	True
11	12	191	False
11	22	371	True
11	32	350	True
11	23	271	False
11	33	331	False
21	31	311	True
21	12	311	False
21	22	281	True
21	32	290	True
21	23	300	False
21	33	300	False
31	12	300	False
31	22	380	True

Table 2. Continued

Node 1	Node 2	Access time (ms)	Access decision
31	32	311	True
31	23	361	False
31	33	381	False
12	22	290	True
12	32	301	True
12	23	290	False
12	33	380	False
22	32	330	True
22	23	190	False
22	33	360	False
32	23	310	False
32	33	390	False
23	33	320	True
		Taverage =11390 /36=316,39	

If access control policy from figure 1. is to be written as follows and XML parser is SAX parser, using simple non-XACML application:

```
<?xml version="1.0"?>
<Physicians>
  <Roles>00,11,21,31,22,32</Roles>
  <Roles>23,33</Roles>
  <Roles>23,32</Roles>
</Physicians>
```
Policy2.xml

Table 3. Access time according to Fig 2. and Policy2.xml using SAX parser and simple non-XACML application

Node 1	Node 2	Access time (ms)	Access decision
00	11	190	True (Permit)
00	21	170	True
00	31	190	True
00	12	201	False (Deny)
00	22	190	True
00	23	220	False
00	33	160	False
00	32	200	True
11	21	200	True
11	31	141	True

Table 3. Continued

Node 1	Node 2	Access time (ms)	Access decision
11	12	191	False
11	22	220	True
11	32	201	True
11	23	230	False
11	33	200	False
21	31	180	True
21	12	211	False
21	22	190	True
21	32	221	True
21	23	241	False
21	33	260	False
31	12	190	False
31	22	200	True
31	32	261	True
31	23	231	False
31	33	251	False
12	22	260	True
12	32	231	True
12	23	200	False
12	33	200	False
22	32	180	True
22	23	250	False
22	33	160	False
32	23	240	False
32	33	211	False
23	33	140	True
		Taverage=7412 /36=205.9	

If access control policy from figure 2. is to be written using XACML (as it has been explained in previous chapter) access control time is:

Table 4. Access time according to Fig 2. using Sun's XACML and Policy1.xml (T1) and Policy2.xml (T2)

Node1	Node2	T1 (ms)	T2(ms)	Access Decision True=Permit False=Deny
00	11	2012	1942	True
00	21	1952	1843	True
00	31	1963	1642	True
00	12	1873	1682	False
00	22	1893	1622	True

Table 4. Continued

Node1	Node2	T1 (ms)	T2(ms)	Access Decision True=Permit False=Deny
00	23	1853	1662	False
00	33	1853	1692	False
00	32	1853	1622	True
11	21	1913	1683	True
11	31	2033	1682	True
11	12	1943	1792	False
11	22	1913	1642	True
11	32	1943	1632	True
11	23	1913	1652	False
11	33	1973	1692	False
21	31	1833	1672	True
21	12	1863	1752	False
21	22	1802	1763	True
21	32	1843	1642	True
21	23	1912	1633	False
21	33	1833	1672	False
31	12	1863	1633	False
31	22	1913	1673	True
31	32	1862	1753	True
31	23	1823	1762	False
31	33	1872	1663	False
12	22	1852	1852	True
12	32	1812	1742	True
12	23	1963	1753	False
12	33	2013	1662	False
22	32	1833	1622	True
22	23	1903	1663	False
22	33	1853	1723	false
32	23	1953	1653	False
32	33	1843	1682	False
23	33	1872	2113	True
		Taverage=1894ms	Taverage=1698ms	

Graph from Fig 2. has been denoted as "forest". If we exclude elements of forest and examine performances in such a case the results are as follows.

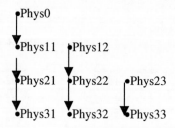

Figure 3. Elements of a forest are excluded.

Table 5. Access time according to Fig 3. and Policy1.xml using SAX parser and simple non-XACML application

Node 1	Node 2	Access time (ms)	Access decision
00	11	141	True (Permit)
00	21	130	True
00	31	130	True
00	12	230	False (Deny)
00	22	181	False
00	23	250	False
00	33	411	False
00	32	191	False
11	21	200	True
11	31	120	True
11	12	180	False
11	22	370	False
11	32	431	False
11	23	391	False
11	33	371	False
21	31	170	True
21	12	200	False
21	22	230	False
21	32	220	False
21	23	200	False
21	33	330	False
31	12	231	False
31	22	130	False
31	32	200	False
31	23	371	False
31	33	260	False
12	22	140	True
12	32	301	True
12	23	231	False

Table 5. Continued

Node 1	Node 2	Access time (ms)	Access decision
12	33	200	False
22	32	361	True
22	23	200	False
22	33	210	False
32	23	180	False
32	33	180	False
23	33	230	True
		Taverage =8542 /36=237.27	

Table 6. Access time according to Fig 3. and Policy2.xml using SAX parser and simple non-XACML application

Node 1	Node 2	Access time (ms)	Access decision
00	11	130	True (Permit)
00	21	120	True
00	31	130	True
00	12	130	False (Deny)
00	22	161	False
00	23	120	False
00	33	130	False
00	32	160	False
11	21	130	True
11	31	130	True
11	12	130	False
11	22	130	False
11	32	130	False
11	23	120	False
11	33	210	False
21	31	120	True
21	12	120	False
21	22	190	False
21	32	201	False
21	23	130	False
21	33	120	False
31	12	120	False
31	22	150	False
31	32	180	False
31	23	161	False
31	33	141	False
12	22	160	True
12	32	110	True
12	23	150	False

Table 6. Continued

Node 1	Node 2	Access time (ms)	Access decision
12	33	120	False
22	32	121	True
22	23	190	False
22	33	180	False
32	23	150	False
32	33	140	False
23	33	120	True
		Taverage =5135 /36=142.63	

Table 7. Access time according to Fig 3. using Sun's XACML and Policy1.xml

Node1	Node2	T1 (ms)	Access Decision True=Permit False=Deny
00	11	2153	True
00	21	1672	True
00	31	1742	True
00	12	1873	False
00	22	1683	True
00	23	1682	False
00	33	1703	False
00	32	1673	True
11	21	1702	True
11	31	1663	True
11	12	1692	False
11	22	1722	True
11	32	1722	True
11	23	1702	False
11	33	1753	False
21	31	1712	True
21	12	1732	False
21	22	1702	True
21	32	1773	True
21	23	1733	False
21	33	1722	False
31	12	1712	False
31	22	1713	True
31	32	1753	True
31	23	1762	False
31	33	1792	False
12	22	1763	True

Table 7. Continued

Node1	Node2	T1 (ms)	Access Decision True=Permit False=Deny
12	32	1813	True
12	23	1832	False
12	33	1782	False
22	32	1713	True
22	23	1672	False
22	33	1783	False
32	23	1672	False
32	33	1703	False
23	33	1812	True
		Taverage=1744ms	

Table 8. Access time according to Fig 3. using Sun's XACML and Policy2.xml

Node1	Node2	T2(ms)	Access Decision True=Permit False=Deny
00	11	1722	True
00	21	1723	True
00	31	1703	True
00	12	1672	False
00	22	1692	False
00	23	1713	False
00	33	1673	False
00	32	1673	False
11	21	1783	True
11	31	1773	True
11	12	1682	False
11	22	1643	False
11	32	1642	False
11	23	1733	False
11	33	1652	False
21	31	1742	True
21	12	1652	False
21	22	1703	False
21	32	1682	False
21	23	1712	False
21	33	1752	False
31	12	1632	False
31	22	1722	False

Table 8. Continued

Node1	Node2	T2(ms)	Access Decision True=Permit False=Deny
31	32	1652	False
31	23	1673	False
31	33	1703	False
12	22	1713	True
12	32	1672	True
12	23	1742	False
12	33	1762	False
22	32	1673	True
22	23	1723	False
22	33	1732	False
32	23	1743	False
32	33	1733	False
23	33	1682	True
		Taverage=1702ms	

In conclusion, we can see that for non-XACML simple aplication performances are 30% better for using hierarchically structured policy2.xml compared to policy1.xml in forest-like graph, while in the same comparasition for Sun's XACML performances are 10 % better. If we look at non-forest structure of attributes non-XACML performances are 40% better if hierarchically organised policy is used. In XACML used case results for access time are almost the same. In every case XACML has overhead and performances are 10 times worse compared to properitary non-XACML application that doesn't have such a XACML structure overhead. In conclusion, if we don't plan to multi domain connections properitary access control application may be better solution.

8. Conclusion

This paper presents how standardized language for writting context aware Attribute Based Access Control policies, requests and resonses can be used in EHCR based on year 2002 CEN and ISO 2008 standards. The contribution is presentation of writting policies for hierarchical attributes. It has been presented how using set functions can improve compactness of policy and performances in the same time. The paper presents and discuss performances in such structures.

References

Anderson A., A comparasion of Two Privacy Policy Languages: EPAL and XACML, http://research.sun.com/techrep/2005/smli_tr2005-147.pdf
Bertino E., Rao P., Lin D., XACML Functional Annotations, In Proc. of IEEE POLICY 2007

CEN ENV 13606 Extended Architecture, http://www.centc251.org , accessed March 2002.

ISO 22 600 Access Control In Healthcare Information Systems, 2008

Joshi, J. , Bhatti, R., Bertino, E., Ghafoor, A., 2004., Access Control Language for Multidomain Environments, IEEE Internet Computing, IEEE Computer Society.

Sucurovic, S., MEDIS – A Web Based Health Information System, In Proceedings of ICEIS 2006.

Sun's XACML Implementation. http://sunxacml.sourceforge.net/

INDEX

A

academic, 85
acceleration, 70, 87
accelerator, 78
access, 108, 109, 119, 121, 122
accounting, 80
accuracy, 13, 17, 54, 113
ACM, 24, 25, 27, 30, 48, 60, 61, 66, 87, 90, 105, 123, 156
ACR, 150
ACS, 89
activation, 6
adaptability, 41
adaptation, 3, 5
adjustment, 5, 120
administration, x, 24, 163, 173
administrators, 13, 14, 15
agent, 174, 175
agents, 10, 16, 61
agility, 71
aging, x, 157, 158, 159, 164
aging process, 159
aid, vii, 1, 6, 16, 67
algorithm, vii, ix, 1, 2, 3, 4, 5, 6, 7, 8, 9, 10, 11, 12, 13, 14, 15, 16, 17, 18, 19, 20, 21, 22, 26, 27, 60, 61, 64, 67, 71, 73, 74, 75, 76, 77, 79, 81, 82, 83, 85, 86, 87, 88, 89, 91, 92, 93, 94, 95, 96, 97, 108, 111, 112, 113, 115, 126, 127, 149, 160, 162, 163, 176
Altera, viii, 63, 66, 70, 75, 76, 79, 80, 81, 84
alternative, 53, 58, 71, 78, 95, 97, 140, 163
alternatives, 77
annealing, 6
annotation, 167
anomalous, 8, 12, 23, 28
API, 162

application, viii, ix, x, 7, 14, 15, 17, 18, 20, 22, 27, 34, 35, 37, 42, 53, 63, 64, 67, 68, 82, 86, 88, 89, 91, 94, 96, 101, 108, 109, 112, 119, 120, 123, 125, 132, 162, 166, 167, 168, 170, 179, 180, 181, 184, 185, 188
argument, 136, 164
arithmetic, 81, 96
ART, 7, 9, 13, 155, 156
artificial intelligence, 20
ash, 83, 93
Asia, 84, 89
ASIC, viii, 63, 64, 71, 72, 78, 89, 90, 135
assessment, 59, 61
assets, 2
assignment, 145
asynchronous, 84, 168
asynchronous communication, 168
Athens, 49, 125
attacker, 135, 136, 137, 140, 150, 151, 152
attacks, x, 9, 10, 11, 14, 15, 16, 18, 22, 23, 26, 27, 28, 52, 53, 57, 59, 72, 88, 93, 105, 125, 127, 128, 135, 137, 138, 139, 140, 141, 142, 143, 144, 151, 153, 154, 156
authentication, ix, 17, 32, 36, 46, 71, 73, 77, 86, 93, 106, 107, 108, 126, 127, 138, 148, 149, 163, 164, 167
authenticity, x, 93, 139, 140, 143, 152, 156, 158, 160, 167
authority, 167
automata, 65
availability, vii, 151

B

back, ix, 10, 65, 76, 94, 108, 128, 140, 142, 147, 153, 154, 156
bandwidth, x, 48, 139, 140, 142
bandwidth resources, x, 139, 142

banking, 158
barrier, 157
base rate, 53, 54, 55, 57, 58
battery, 141
Bayesian, 11, 13, 16, 55
BDI, 61
behavior, 29, 72, 145, 147, 150
behaviours, 14
benchmark, 25, 84
benchmarking, 60
benchmarks, 53, 70
benefits, 67, 68, 76, 92, 95, 103
binding, 150, 151
biometric, 17, 121
biometrics, 17
blocks, 67, 69, 70, 72, 76, 78, 94, 97, 98, 99, 100,
     132, 135, 136, 137
Bluetooth, 18, 77, 86, 138
Boston, 28
bots, 20
bottom-up, 77
bounds, 137
brain, vii, 1, 3, 20
breaches, 79
browser, 161
buffer, 7, 9, 12, 15, 16
buses, 69, 70
buttons, 112

C

C++, 70, 84
cache, 68
Canada, 85, 89
candidates, 73
case study, 82
cast, 106
catalyst, 84
cell, 13, 65, 69, 119, 150, 151, 152
cellular phone, 93
cellular phones, 93
certificate, 159
certification, 158, 164, 167, 168
certifications, 164
changing environment, 52
cipher, x, 71, 73, 74, 75, 78, 79, 82, 85, 86, 87, 88,
     89, 125, 126, 127, 128, 129, 130, 131, 132, 134,
     135, 136, 137, 138, 149, 150
ciphers, 72, 80, 83, 92, 93, 125, 126, 127, 134, 137,
     138, 149
classes, 11, 15, 112, 113, 115, 174, 176
classification, 2, 6, 7, 10, 11, 12, 14, 15, 17, 20, 21,
     22, 23, 25, 28, 29, 57, 67, 122, 123, 166
clients, 32, 33, 39, 41, 44, 94, 160, 163

clustering, ix, 2, 3, 5, 6, 9, 11, 12, 15, 17, 19, 20, 21,
     22, 25, 27, 29, 108, 111, 112, 115
clusters, 6, 10, 16
codes, 77, 86, 106
coding, ix, 64, 79, 91
collaboration, 152, 153, 154, 156
collisions, 137
commerce, 157
communication, 32, 33, 34, 35, 37, 39, 40, 41, 42,
     44, 45, 46, 47, 48, 49, 68, 85, 92, 93, 94, 126,
     142, 153, 157, 160, 168
communication overhead, 68
community, vii, 1, 2, 73, 110, 140, 158
compatibility, 70
compilation, 70
compiler, 70, 84
complex systems, 2
complexity, 11, 21, 73, 76, 77, 95, 136, 142, 146,
     147
components, viii, ix, xi, 63, 72, 73, 74, 77, 80, 92,
     94, 95, 96, 107, 110, 113, 122, 146, 167, 169, 173
comprehension, 45
computation, 4, 20, 24, 28, 64, 65, 66, 67, 68, 69, 73,
     84, 95, 96, 97, 100, 101, 102, 103
computer architecture, vii, 1
computer graphics, 64
computer science, vii, 1, 2, 17
computer virus, 14, 48
computing, viii, 2, 10, 21, 22, 25, 63, 64, 65, 66, 69,
     70, 76, 77, 81, 82, 83, 84, 86, 101, 132, 138, 141,
     158
concrete, 33, 48, 114, 115, 119, 154, 160
confidence, 93
confidentiality, x, 53, 71, 77, 90, 125, 151, 160, 161
configuration, 33, 42, 45, 48, 54, 66, 68, 69, 70, 75,
     84
conflict, 39, 40, 151
consensus, 52
conservation, 159, 171
constraints, vii, x, 69, 77, 139
consumer electronics, 86
consumption, 18, 19, 72, 78, 80, 83, 90, 141
contingency, 54, 57
control, x, 17, 29, 32, 33, 34, 35, 39, 40, 41, 42, 43,
     44, 45, 48, 49, 59, 69, 70, 108, 109, 110, 135,
     141, 142, 146, 149, 154, 156, 173, 174, 179, 180,
     181, 182, 188
convergence, 66
conversion, 53, 158, 166
coping, 44, 46
correlation, 7, 13, 14, 18, 29, 152, 155, 156, 164
correlation analysis, 156
correlation coefficient, 155

corruption, vii
cost-effective, 92, 93, 98
costs, 17, 55, 56, 57, 58
countermeasures, x, 139, 140
coupling, 67, 68
CPU, 10, 21, 72, 128
CRC, 85, 105
credentials, xi, 149, 165, 167, 173
credit, 19, 28
credit card, 19, 28
credit card fraud, 19, 28
crimes, 19
criticism, 12
cryptanalysis, 28, 127
cryptographic, ix, 71, 72, 73, 77, 79, 80, 82, 85, 87,
    89, 91, 92, 93, 94, 95, 96, 104, 126, 127, 133,
    136, 138, 141, 149, 161, 170
cryptography, ix, 7, 63, 72, 82, 85, 91, 92, 93, 105,
    137, 141, 149, 158, 169
Cryptosystems, 171
cues, 123
currency, 174
Cybernetics, 22, 26, 29, 30, 123
cycles, 76, 82, 98, 128, 134
Cyprus, 89

D

danger, 127
DARPA, 8, 60
data analysis, 6, 19, 29
data collection, x, 139
data communication, 71
data mining, 6, 19, 20, 27, 28, 30
data processing, 2, 153, 167
data set, 4, 155
data structure, x, 157, 158, 159, 160, 162, 163, 164,
    167, 168, 169, 170
data transfer, 67
database, ix, 7, 15, 34, 47, 59, 108, 109, 110, 111,
    112, 119, 120, 121
dating, 65
death, 65
decision support tool, 19
decisions, 72
decoding, ix, 69, 91
decomposition, 82
decryption, 73, 74, 75, 76, 77, 78, 79, 85, 87, 129,
    133, 149, 176
defense, x, 139, 140, 141, 142, 143, 144, 156
defense mechanisms, x, 139
defenses, x, 139
definition, 7, 127, 160, 167, 170
degradation, 150

delivery, 34, 71, 141, 142, 149, 151
denial, 9, 27, 140
denial of service attack, 27
density, viii, 63, 66
designers, 64, 80, 92
detection, vii, viii, ix, 1, 6, 7, 8, 9, 10, 11, 12, 13, 14,
    15, 16, 17, 18, 19, 20, 21, 22, 23, 24, 25, 26, 27,
    28, 29, 30, 47, 51, 52, 53, 54, 55, 56, 58, 59, 60,
    61, 72, 73, 77, 78, 80, 85, 107, 108, 109, 110,
    111, 112, 113, 114, 115, 117, 118, 119, 121, 122,
    123, 145, 154, 159
detection techniques, 78
deviation, 155
diffusion, 135
dimensionality, 5
disabled, 116
disclosure, 149
Discovery, 8, 24, 148
discrimination, 14, 115, 118
distortions, 118
distribution, xi, 32, 35, 53, 84, 152, 173
diversity, 88
division, 5, 97
DNA, ix, 14, 107
download, 176
draft, 160, 170, 171
duration, 6

E

education, 49, 122
election, 53, 58, 65, 144
electric field, 18
email, 16
encapsulated, 159
encapsulation, 78
encoding, ix, 69, 91
encouragement, 12
encryption, x, 70, 71, 73, 74, 75, 76, 77, 78, 79, 80,
    85, 86, 87, 88, 89, 109, 125, 126, 127, 129, 130,
    131, 132, 133, 135, 138, 149, 152, 176
energy, x, 78, 139, 140, 141, 142, 150
energy consumption, 78, 141
energy supply, 141
entitlement programs, 108
entropy, 135
environment, x, 10, 36, 52, 53, 57, 59, 67, 71, 122,
    134, 139, 140, 147, 156, 160, 169, 173
Europe, 66, 85, 157
European Parliament, 171
evolution, 14, 24, 65, 77, 80
examinations, 179
execution, ix, 4, 5, 6, 18, 68, 69, 70, 76, 81, 84, 91,
    92, 94, 96, 113

Expert System, 23, 28
explicit knowledge, 10
exploitation, 67
extraction, ix, 16, 107, 108, 110, 111, 115, 119, 120, 122, 123, 127, 166, 169
eye, 17, 24, 25, 115, 117, 118, 119
eyes, ix, 107, 109, 113, 114, 115, 116, 117, 118

F

fabricate, x, 139
face recognition, ix, 17, 107, 108, 109, 110, 111, 112, 113, 114, 115, 116, 117, 118, 119, 120, 121, 122, 123, 124
facial expression, 17, 27, 121
false alarms, x, 139, 140, 142, 143
false positive, 10, 13, 15, 17, 18, 52
family, 15, 66, 90, 103, 104
feature selection, 11, 60
federal government, 93
feedback, 74, 75, 78, 136
FFT, 70
Field Programmable Gate Arrays (FPGAs), viii, 63, 64, 66, 67, 70, 71, 72, 73, 74, 75, 76, 77, 78, 79, 80, 81, 82, 83, 84, 85, 86, 87, 88, 89, 90, 94, 103, 104, 105, 106
filters, 69, 152, 154
financial support, 65
FIR filters, 69
fire, 30, 140, 156
fire event, 140
fires, 140
first generation, 84
flexibility, viii, 63, 64, 71, 72, 126, 135
flooding, 9
flow, 38, 53, 66, 96
focusing, ix, 9, 91
forensic, 19, 22, 23, 27, 53, 164, 165, 167
Fox, 23
France, 60, 88, 89
fraud, 18, 19, 22, 24, 28, 108
functional programming, 82
funds, 93
fusion, 3
fuzzy logic, 10, 11

G

games, 126
Games-On-Demand, x, 125
gas, 23
Gaussian, 5
GCC, 30
general purpose processor (GPP), viii, 20, 63, 64

generation, vii, 4, 16, 18, 19, 20, 31, 84, 127, 140, 143, 146, 147, 148, 166
genetic algorithms, 11, 61
genetics, 61
Georgia, 61
Germany, 157, 162
gestures, 2
goals, 52, 77, 151, 167
government, iv, 93
grain, viii, 63, 67, 69
graph, 188
graphics processors, viii, 63, 64
Great Lakes, 85
Greece, 49, 61, 91, 125
grounding, 56
groups, 11, 14, 16, 25, 52, 66, 128, 152
guidelines, viii, 51, 158

H

handheld devices, 79
handling, viii, 31, 32, 41, 134, 162
handwriting, 108
haptic, 17
hardware accelerator, 78
harmonization, 158
Hawaii, 83
hazards, 80
HDL, 80, 94
health, 158
healthcare, xi, 173, 174, 176
hearing, 45, 143
heart, 177
height, 117, 118
helix, 127
Helix, 138
heuristic, 10
high-level, 67, 69, 82
high-speed, ix, 74, 91, 96, 135
hip, 18, 65, 77
Homeland Security, 24, 86
Hong Kong, 90
host, 7, 8, 9, 10, 14, 24, 33, 42, 44, 67, 68, 70, 72
hostile environment, x, 139, 140, 156
House, 104
human, vii, ix, 1, 3, 11, 13, 17, 20, 24, 25, 107, 108, 109, 116, 123, 164, 167
human brain, vii, 1, 3, 20
humans, 166
hybrid, 8, 10, 11, 12, 26, 28, 29, 66, 72, 122

I

IDEA, 71, 73, 82, 85, 87

identification, ix, 10, 19, 20, 21, 107, 108, 109, 110, 111, 112, 115, 116, 119, 120, 121, 122, 154
identification problem, ix, 108
identity, ix, 108, 120, 148, 155, 165
IDS, viii, 7, 8, 10, 12, 13, 15, 16, 18, 20, 47, 51, 52, 53, 54, 55, 56, 57, 58, 59
IETF, 32, 33, 105, 159
illumination, 123, 124
images, 19, 109, 110, 111, 113, 121, 123
immune system, 13, 26, 28
implementation, viii, ix, 48, 63, 64, 65, 69, 70, 71, 73, 74, 75, 76, 77, 78, 79, 80, 81, 82, 83, 84, 85, 86, 87, 88, 89, 90, 91, 92, 93, 94, 95, 97, 101, 103, 104, 105, 127, 128, 132, 135, 149
in situ, 125, 146
incentive, 126
inclusion, 21, 65, 73, 93
independence, 68, 170
India, 86
indication, 34, 37, 94
indicators, 9, 10, 18, 19
indices, 144, 145
individual character, 126
industrial, 70
industry, viii, 51, 66, 104, 108
infection, 14, 44, 46, 47, 48
information exchange, 105
information retrieval, 22
Information System, vi, 28, 162, 171, 173, 175, 189
information systems, x, 173, 174, 176
information technology, 79
Information Technology, 27, 49, 90, 125, 157
infrastructure, viii, 31, 32, 85, 162
inherited, 52
initial state, 127, 128, 132
injection, 140, 141, 143, 144, 151, 156
inspection, 15, 16, 54, 57, 167
inspiration, 2, 3
instruction, 69, 78, 84
integrated circuits, 64
integration, 11, 25, 65, 66, 68, 72, 104, 160
integrity, 71, 90, 93, 149, 160, 165, 167
Intel, 65, 70, 84
intelligence, 6, 7, 20, 21, 22, 28, 72, 80
intentions, 11
interaction, 160, 162, 169
interface, 18, 36, 47, 67, 68, 69, 111, 161, 162
internet, x, 16, 21, 32, 48, 49, 60, 71, 94, 105, 109, 110, 121, 153, 156, 159, 170, 171, 173, 189
Internet Engineering Task Force, 32, 105, 159
interoperability, 3
interval, 38
intrinsic, 64

Intrusion Detection Systems, v, viii, 51
intrusions, viii, 7, 9, 10, 14, 20, 25, 51, 53
intuition, 56
investment, 149
IP, 34, 35, 36, 37, 39, 40, 41, 42, 44, 46, 47, 103, 156
IP address, 36, 37, 39, 40, 41, 44, 46, 47
iris, ix, 107, 108, 115
ISC, viii, 63, 89, 90, 105
ISO, xi, 171, 173, 174, 175, 176, 188, 189
isolation, 153
ISPA, 61
ITC, 25, 86

J

Java, 48
judgment, 33, 39
Jun, 28, 30, 86, 123
Jung, 86
justice, 158

K

kernel, 4, 5
Kohonen maps, 12

L

language, x, 70, 80, 82, 94, 173, 174, 188
latency, 75, 84
law, x, 2, 157, 164, 168, 170
laws, 164
learning, 3, 5, 6, 10, 12, 13, 14, 20, 21, 25, 26, 28, 29, 52, 53, 54, 59, 60, 61
learning process, 5
leg, 3
legislation, 157
lice, 27
likelihood, 55
limitations, 13, 21, 156
linear, 5, 25, 26, 69, 98, 102, 103, 136, 138, 155
linear function, 98, 102, 103
literature, 122, 123
loading, 68, 70, 79, 150
local area network (LAN), 32, 77, 79, 86, 105
localization, 123, 150
location, 5, 141, 142, 143, 144, 146, 150, 151, 156
location information, 150
logging, 34, 40, 41, 140, 153, 154, 156
London, 24, 89
long period, x, 68, 137, 157, 158, 159, 165, 170
Los Angeles, 65
low power, 78, 79
low-level, 75
LSI, 87

LTA, 159, 160, 161

M

machine learning, 20, 21, 25, 29, 52, 53, 54, 59
machines, 25, 93
MACs, 143, 144, 145, 147, 148, 149, 151, 152
mainstream, 2
Malaysia, 87
malicious, 2, 7, 8, 14, 16, 18, 19, 141
malware, 20
mammalian brain, 20
management, viii, 29, 31, 32, 33, 44, 45, 47, 48, 93,
    95, 141, 153, 160, 162
manipulation, 158
manufacturer, 167
manufacturing, 64, 66
map unit, 5
mapping, 64, 69, 75, 80, 136
market, ix, 65, 66, 67, 91, 95, 160
market share, 66
Markov, 7, 11
mask, 15, 76
masking, 76
mathematics, 93
matrix, 54, 57, 70, 128, 132
MATRIX, viii, 63, 69
Mauritius, 49
measurement, 60
measures, iv, 48, 54, 56, 164, 165, 166
media, 66, 158
mediation, 3
Mediterranean, 87
membership, 153
memory, 6, 9, 67, 69, 70, 72, 73, 74, 75, 76, 95, 96,
    104, 135, 153
men, 115, 121
mentor, 104
messages, 16, 92, 134, 135, 142, 143, 146, 148, 149,
    154, 156
metric, 52, 54, 55, 56, 57, 58, 59
metropolitan area, 105
Mexico, 9
microcontrollers, viii, 63, 64, 65
microprocessors, 64, 65
Microsoft, 93, 105
military, 2, 71
mines, 167
mining, 6, 19, 20, 27, 28, 30, 60
Ministry of Education, 122
misconceptions, 52, 59
misleading, 56
MIT, 23, 53, 57
mixing, 128, 135

mobile communication, 85
mobile phone, 18, 19, 22, 93
mobile telecommunication, 19
mobile telephony, 18, 19, 24
models, 26, 52, 111
modules, 93, 95
Moon, 11, 29
MorphoSys, viii, 63, 64, 69, 70, 84
motion, 69
motivation, viii, 31, 32
mouth, ix, 107, 109, 118
movement, 42, 70
MUA, 35
multidimensional, 3, 14
multidimensional scaling, 3
multimedia, x, 69, 84, 125
multiple nodes, 141
multiples, 128
multiplication, 69, 71, 79, 95, 96
multiplier, 69, 79, 87

N

naming, 15
National Institute of Standards and Technology
    (NIST), 59, 61, 88, 105
NCS, 24
negative selection, 24, 26
nesting, 177
network, vii, viii, x, 1, 7, 8, 9, 10, 11, 12, 13, 14, 15,
    18, 19, 21, 22, 23, 24, 26, 28, 29, 31, 32, 33, 34,
    35, 36, 39, 40, 41, 42, 44, 45, 47, 48, 51, 53, 59,
    60, 61, 66, 69, 70, 73, 80, 85, 86, 127, 139, 140,
    141, 142, 143, 144, 145, 146, 150, 152, 153, 156
networking, 17, 158
neural network, 3, 7, 9, 10, 13, 15, 21, 22, 23, 24, 25,
    26, 27, 28, 61
neural networks, 3, 7, 21, 22, 24, 25, 27
neurons, 3, 4, 6
New Mexico, 9
New York, 24, 25, 30, 83, 85, 87, 88, 90
next generation, vii, 31
Ni, 26, 156
Nielsen, 171
NIST, 59, 73, 93, 104, 105
nodes, x, 4, 5, 6, 9, 10, 18, 20, 139, 140, 141, 142,
    143, 144, 145, 146, 147, 148, 149, 150, 151, 152,
    153, 154, 155, 156
non-repudiation, 71
normal, 7, 9, 11, 13, 16, 52, 53, 141, 155
nose, ix, 107, 109, 113, 114, 115, 116, 118
novelty, 6, 7

O

occlusion, 110, 121
off-the-shelf, 82
OID, 163
Oman, 63
online, 162, 168
operator, 174, 177
optimization, 75, 92
ores, 72
outliers, 156

P

Pacific, 84, 89
packets, 8, 9, 53, 142, 146, 148, 149, 153, 154, 156
parallel algorithm, 82
parallel computation, 20
parallelism, 21, 65, 67, 68, 70, 77, 83
parallelization, 73
parameter, 65, 147
Paris, 29, 66, 88, 89, 171
Parliament, 171
partition, 59, 144, 145, 146
passive, x, 139, 140, 142, 143, 144, 153, 156
pattern recognition, 111, 115
PCs, 93, 126
PDAs, 71
PDP, 33, 174
peer, 93
penalty, 78, 96
PEP, 33
performance, 110, 114
periodic, 154, 162
permit, 176
PGA, 78, 84
pH, 56
phase transformation, 166
phone, 18, 19, 22, 93
Physicians, 179, 180, 181
pipelining, 73, 74, 76, 81
platforms, 66, 77, 79, 86, 93, 95, 128, 135
play, 57, 126, 161
PLD, 94
point-to-point, 69
Poland, 60
police, 19
polynomial, 93, 152, 153
polynomials, 153
poor, 2, 178
portfolios, 20
ports, 9
Portugal, 85

posture, 17, 24
power, 64, 72, 77, 78, 79, 80, 83, 90, 95, 96, 119, 122, 141, 142, 145, 151, 153, 156, 158
preprocessing, 53
prevention, 18
prices, 72
primitives, ix, 91, 92, 94, 104, 126
principal component analysis (PCA), 11, 16, 17, 20, 26, 122, 123
printing, 49
prior knowledge, 22
PRISM, viii, 63, 69, 70
privacy, ix, 20, 53, 59, 91
private, 48, 53, 126
proactive, x, 139, 140, 152, 156
probability, 55, 136, 144, 145, 150, 151
production, viii, 63, 66
profit, 18
profitability, 67
program, 29, 34, 35, 40, 46, 67, 68, 69, 70, 141, 162
programmability, 67, 68
programming, 16, 66, 67, 70, 82, 94
programming languages, 67
propagation, 5, 9, 10, 81, 125, 147
property, iv, 9, 20, 146, 149
protection, vii, x, 140, 142, 143, 147, 154, 156, 165
protocol, 9, 12, 14, 35, 37, 42, 48, 86, 93, 143, 146, 148, 155, 159, 160, 162, 166, 169, 176
protocols, ix, x, 2, 12, 16, 18, 20, 71, 79, 89, 91, 93, 141, 146, 149, 157, 159, 162, 165, 166, 167, 169
prototype, 70, 78, 110, 121
prototyping, 67, 83
proxy, 16
pseudo, 81, 133
public, 52, 53, 59, 93, 128, 141, 149, 158
public health, 158
public sector, 158
public-key, 93
pupil, 116
pupils, ix, 107, 113, 115, 116, 117

Q

quantization, 26
quarantine, 32, 49
query, 143, 154, 169, 174

R

Radial Basis Function (RBF), 7, 11, 13, 15, 17
radio, 18, 20, 21, 134
Radio Frequency Identification (RFID), 18, 88, 93
random, 3, 4, 53, 81, 133, 136, 144, 151
range, 2, 64, 71, 104, 108, 151, 155, 156, 165

RaPiD, viii, 63, 69
rapid prototyping, 67, 82,
RAW, viii, 63, 69, 84
RC, viii, 63, 64, 67, 68, 69, 70, 71, 72, 73, 74, 82, 83
RC-systems, viii, 63, 64, 67, 68, 69, 70, 72, 83
reading, 155
real estate, 65
reasoning, 57, 82
recall, 55
recalling, 92
reception, 36
recognition, ix, 17, 23, 24, 26, 27, 28, 107, 108, 109,
    110, 111, 112, 113, 114, 115, 116, 117, 118, 119,
    120, 121, 122, 123, 124, 157
recognition algorithms, 111
redundancy, 92, 95, 141, 156
refining, 80
regional, 174
regular, 69, 76, 77
regulations, 165
reinforcement, 10
reinforcement learning, 10
rejection, 120, 121
relationship, 6, 52, 57, 58, 149, 151
relationships, 3, 54, 155
reliability, 82, 119, 122, 165, 166
REMARC, viii, 63, 69
repair, 147
repetitions, 136
reservation, 6
reserves, 20
resources, x, 66, 69, 73, 74, 75, 77, 79, 80, 81, 82,
    83, 95, 135, 139, 140, 141, 142, 179
retention, x, 157, 158
retina, 108
RISC, viii, 63, 64, 69
robustness, 59, 122
rotations, 126, 127, 128, 135
routing, 18, 66, 67, 69, 135, 141, 142, 146, 147, 148,
    156
RSA encryption, 79, 87

S

SAC, 138
safety, 85
sample, 155
sample mean, 155
saturation, 154
savings, 150
scalable, 21, 69, 76, 79, 87, 89
scaling, 3, 12
scheduling, 132, 135, 137
scientific community, vii, 1, 110

sclera, 17, 25
SCP, 177
SEA, 80, 89
search, 6, 22, 61, 94, 109, 114, 115, 137
searching, 19, 22
secret, x, 19, 76, 128, 131, 133, 134, 139, 140, 141,
    150, 151, 153
secrets, 2, 140, 150, 151
secure communication, 72
security, vii, viii, ix, x, 1, 2, 6, 7, 8, 14, 16, 17, 18,
    20, 21, 23, 24, 29, 30, 31, 32, 34, 39, 41, 42, 48,
    49, 51, 61, 63, 70, 71, 72, 73, 76, 77, 78, 79, 80,
    83, 84, 86, 87, 88, 91, 93, 94, 97, 105, 107, 108,
    109, 120, 122, 125, 127, 135, 137, 139, 140, 143,
    147, 150, 151, 152, 153, 154, 162, 163, 165, 167,
    169, 173, 174, 175
seed, 133, 148
segmentation, ix, 107, 108, 109, 110, 111, 112, 113,
    114, 115, 116, 117, 119, 121, 122, 123
selecting, 4, 43, 52
self, vii, 1, 2, 6, 13, 17, 21, 23, 25, 26, 29
self-organizing, 21, 22, 23, 24, 25, 26, 27, 28, 29, 30
semiconductor, 65, 66
sensing, 140, 141, 143, 144, 145, 146, 147, 148, 149,
    151, 155, 156
sensitive data, 92
sensitivity, 10, 12
sensor nodes, x, 139, 141, 143, 149, 150, 154
sensors, x, 80, 88, 139, 152, 154, 155
Serbia, 173
series, 5, 65, 66, 70, 74
services, vii, x, 31, 34, 42, 93, 94, 157, 158, 159,
    160, 161, 162, 164, 167, 168, 169, 170, 173
shape, 4
shares, 146, 151, 153
sharing, x, 75, 93, 139, 141, 142, 143, 144, 146, 147,
    148, 149, 151, 152, 156
sign, 41
signals, 3, 9, 14, 17, 80, 96
signs, 51, 159
silicon, 65, 66, 72
Silicon Valley, 49, 105
similarity, 10
simulation, 53, 59, 71
skin, 111, 113, 115, 123
sleep, 141
SMEs, x, 157, 158, 161, 170
software, viii, ix, x, 7, 16, 17, 20, 21, 33, 44, 51, 64,
    67, 71, 79, 85, 91, 92, 93, 94, 97, 105, 121, 125,
    126, 127, 128, 134, 135, 138, 141, 160, 162, 167
sorting, 70
South Pacific, 84
Spain, 51, 107, 122

spam, 16, 25, 27
spatial, 3, 95, 96, 100
species, 2
spectrum, 72, 77
speech, 79
speed, viii, ix, 6, 11, 13, 63, 64, 72, 74, 75, 77, 79,
    80, 81, 82, 86, 87, 91, 95, 96, 114, 135
Spyder, viii, 63, 69, 70
stability, 122, 170
stages, ix, 3, 76, 94, 97, 98, 101, 103, 104, 107, 109,
    110, 112, 114, 121, 122
standard deviation, 155
standardization, 158, 159, 170
standards, x, 79, 93, 125, 188
Standards, 59, 60, 61, 73, 88, 105, 159, 171
statistics, 136
steady state, 38
stimulus, 4
storage, 51, 69, 70, 92, 95, 141, 142, 151, 153, 154,
    156, 158, 161
storage media, 158
strategies, 82
Stratix-2, viii, 63
streams, 127
strength, 93, 153, 154
subnetworks, 47
subscribers, 126
substitution, 76, 128, 137
Sun, 29, 70, 92, 176, 182, 186, 187, 188, 189
supply, 141
surveillance, ix, 107, 108, 109
survival, 2
suspects, 155
switching, 65, 71, 75, 81
symmetry, 114
synchronous, x, 125, 127, 133, 138
syntax, 156
synthesis, 78, 79, 80, 82, 84, 87
systems, viii, ix, x, 2, 7, 8, 9, 11, 12, 13, 15, 17, 18,
    20, 23, 27, 51, 52, 60, 61, 63, 64, 67, 68, 69, 70,
    72, 74, 77, 80, 83, 85, 86, 93, 105, 107, 108, 109,
    110, 116, 122, 126, 138, 162, 165, 171, 173, 174,
    176

T

Taiwan, 89
tanks, 142
taxonomy, 57
TCP (Transmission Control Protocol), 9, 41, 42, 44,
    53
TCP/IP, 42
technology, viii, 32, 63, 64, 65, 66, 78, 79, 82, 86,
    104, 105, 108, 164

telecommunication, 18, 19
telecommunication networks, 18, 19
telecommunications, 125
telephone, 44
telephony, 18, 19, 24
temporal, 18, 19, 53, 95, 96, 102, 103
terminals, 109, 126
test data, 57, 59
testes, 155
Texas, 65
Thailand, 25, 89, 90
theft, vii
thinking, 110
third party, 168
threat, 20, 162
threats, 2, 154
threshold, 5, 6, 54, 55, 57, 110, 111, 120, 121, 122,
    136, 145, 146, 147, 150, 151
thresholds, 18, 155
tics, 156
time constraints, 69
timing, 34, 38
topological, 4, 6, 26
topology, 6, 53, 141, 142, 146, 147, 150
tracking, 17, 25, 109
trade, 88
trade-off, 88
trading, 109
traffic, 8, 9, 11, 14, 16, 18, 22, 28, 52, 53, 60, 145,
    156
training, 4, 5, 11, 52, 53, 59
trans, 135, 157, 163, 165, 169, 170
transfer, 2, 93, 159, 171
transformation, ix, x, 91, 94, 95, 96, 101, 126, 158,
    159, 164, 165, 166, 167, 168, 169, 170
transformations, 92, 95, 96, 164, 165, 166, 169, 170
transistors, 66
transition, 29, 38
transmission, 38, 39, 77, 125, 152, 154
transmits, 36, 47
transparent, 42
transport, 42, 53
trust, 169, 170
trustworthiness, 167
tunneling, 41, 43
two-dimensional, 69

U

uncertainty, 56
unfolded, 96
uniform, x, 53, 139, 142, 143, 146, 147
United Arab Emirates, 89
United Kingdom, 87

United States, 61
units of analysis, 53
updating, 163
upload, 71
user data, 158
Utah, 49

V

vacuum, 65
validation, vii, 1, 59, 166
validity, 158, 162, 163, 168
values, 4, 5, 54, 56, 58, 76, 95, 96, 98, 100, 101, 102,
    103, 113, 115, 119, 131, 132, 133, 135, 136, 137,
    161, 162, 174, 177, 178
variability, 53
variables, 96, 133
variation, 18, 117
vector, 4, 5, 25, 26, 111, 116, 117, 118, 119, 120,
    127, 128, 133
versatility, viii, 63, 64, 67, 72
video surveillance, 109
Virtex-2 Pro, viii, 63
virus, 7, 14, 15, 30, 44, 46, 47, 48
virus infection, 44, 46, 47, 48
viruses, 14, 15, 16, 21, 23, 30
vision, ix, 17, 107
voice, ix, 107, 108
voting, 93, 105
VPN, 32, 33, 93, 104
vulnerability, 7, 15, 29

W

W3C, 171
war, 2

Warsaw, 60
wastes, 142
weapons, 2
web, x, 16, 17, 22, 48, 93, 157, 161, 162, 163, 164,
    170
web browser, 161
web service, x, 157, 161, 162, 163, 164, 170
welfare, 108
windows, 14, 30, 105
winning, 4, 5
wireless, vii, x, 1, 17, 18, 22, 60, 71, 73, 76, 77, 78,
    79, 82, 83, 85, 86, 87, 93, 139, 141, 147, 152,
    153, 156
wireless devices, 78
Wireless LAN, 105
wireless networks, 86, 87
Wireless Sensor Network, v, 139, 141, 145, 149,
    151, 153, 155, 156
wireless systems, 77
wires, 70
WLAN, 77, 78, 79, 87
women, 115, 121
workflow, 165, 167
workstation, 126
worms, 16, 30
WPAN, 77, 78
writing, x, 173
WWW, 93

X

Xilinx, viii, 63, 66, 70, 73, 74, 75, 76, 77, 78, 79, 80,
    81, 83, 89
XML, 159, 163, 167, 174, 176, 177, 179, 181